Jean Galbraith

Jean Galbraith

Writer in a Valley

MEREDITH FLETCHER

MONASH University
Publishing

State Library
of Victoria

Monash University Publishing
Building 4, Monash University
Clayton, Victoria 3800, Australia
www.publishing.monash.edu

Monash University Publishing brings to the world publications which advance the best traditions of humane and enlightened thought.

Monash University Publishing titles pass through a rigorous process of independent peer review.

Published in association with the

State Library of Victoria
328 Swanston Street
Melbourne Victoria 3000 Australia
slv.vic.gov.au

http://www.publishing.monash.edu/books/jg-9781922235398.html

Series: Biography

Design: Les Thomas

Cover image reproduced courtesy of the Ian Hyndman Collection.

National Library of Australia Cataloguing-in-Publication entry:

Author:	Fletcher, Meredith, 1952- author.
Title:	Jean Galbraith : writer in a valley / Meredith Fletcher.
ISBN:	9781922235398 (paperback)
Notes:	Includes index.
Subjects:	Galbraith, Jean.
	Gardeners--Australia--Biography.
	Gardening--Australia.
	Naturalists--Australia--Biography.
	Authors--Australia--Biography.
Dewey Number:	635.0994

Printed in Singapore by Markono Print Media Pte Ltd.

To Jean Galbraith

Enveloped
By the scent
Of native mint
I stepped into fantasy's reality –
A garden of love and lingering
Where beauty and wildness tangle,
Through a gate where time bends
    Is it now or then?
… an hour or a year?
The air dripped with green and silver
But the blossoms burst over it all.

A mirror of the garden's sparkle
Were her eyes
Surrounded by fading walls and books
She, too, is growing worn
But warm!
Warm as the fire's welcome
With its black kettle steaming.

Julie Langford
(written after a visit to Jean Galbraith's garden)

JEAN GALBRA

1906~

TO WALHALLA

② ①

TYERS RIVER

④

TYERS

LATROBE

HAUNTED HILLS

YALLOURN

⑤

TRARALGON

MORWELL

⑦

TRARALGON CREEK

MORWELL RIVER

⑧

TARRA BULGA NATIONAL PARK

① *Grassy Forest :*
   Red Box, Yellow Box, Golden Wattle,
   Narrow~Leaf Peppermint.

② *Damp Forests and Gullies :*
   Messmate, Mountain Grey Gum, Tree Fern,
   Maidenhair, Wonga Vine, Mountain Clematis.

③ *Dry Ridges and Foothills :*
   Silver~top Ash, White Stringybark, Heath,
   Cassinia.

④ *Swamp Scrub :*
   Thickets of Swamp Paperbark and Tea Tree,
   Sedges, Common Reeds.

⑤ *Plains Grasslands, Grassy Woodlands :*
   Redgum, Kangaroo Grass, Native Daisies, Lilies.

⑥ *Heathy Woodlands :*
   Saw Banksia, Narrow~Leaf Peppermint,
   Grass Trees, Heath, Correa.

ITH'S VALLEY

1999

N

③

RIVER

ROSEDALE

⑥

HOLEY PLAINS STATE PARK

GORMANDALE

JEAN GALBRAITH'S VALLEY

MELBOURNE

⑦ *Shrubby Foothill Forest*:
Messmate, Correa, Peas, Orchids,
Purple Coral Pea, Daisy Bush, Narrow Leaf Wattle.

⑧ *Wet Forest and Cool Temperate Rainforest*:
Mountain Ash, Tree Fern, Ground Ferns,
Silver Wattle, Blackwood, Mint Bush
Myrtle Beech, Sassafras, Mountain Clematis.

CONTENTS

LIST OF ABBREVIATIONS

ABC: Australian Broadcasting Commission

ACT: Australian Capital Territory

ANZAAS: Australian and New Zealand Association for the Advancement of Science

APM: Australian Paper Manufacturers

FNCV: Field Naturalists' Club of Victoria

LCC: Land Conservation Council, Victoria

LVFNC: Latrobe Valley Field Naturalists' Club

NMA: National Museum of Australia

PROV: Public Record Office Victoria

SEC: State Electricity Commission of Victoria

SLV: State Library of Victoria

ACKNOWLEDGEMENTS

Throughout the research and writing of this biography, I have been extremely fortunate to have wonderful help and encouragement from members of Jean Galbraith's family. I am particularly grateful to Ian Hyndman, custodian of a large family history collection, for facilitating access to the collection, sharing his knowledge and for being so generous with his time, and to Jean Galbraith's niece, Marjory Burgess, for the regular meetings we shared and our discussions over lunch. Peter Galbraith sent an evocative memoir of living at 'Dunedin', laced with thoughtful reflections on his aunt's life, and other family members, including David, Joanna and Dena Galbraith, contributed their memories and perspectives. I am grateful to Judy Hyndman for her hospitality while I was researching in Beechworth.

There are many people who have contributed research material, insights and information that has greatly helped my research. They include Bon and Ollie Thompson, Helen Aston, Evan Chesterfield, Elizabeth Dexter, Carmel Mastwyk, Ollie Archbold, Sue Allen, Joan Good, David Langmore, Terri Allen, Susan Lendon and Lin Bullen. Peter Cuffley opened his archive to me with great kindness and generosity, and Esther Wettenhall passed on the material she had collected on Jean Galbraith in the early 1990s. Linden Gillbank answered many questions on botany and botanical history.

My friends and colleagues have been a great support and I have appreciated their advice and encouragement. I would particularly like to thank Bain Attwood, wonderful gardener Sue Hides, Paul Atkinson, Karen Barker, Sue Yell, Libby Robin, Alan and Eunice Harding, Sarah Mirams, Keith and Anne Wilson, Rebecca Jones and venerable gardener, Flo Pearce. Sue Adams and Jack Bramah provided ideal conditions for writing while I was living in New Zealand, and my sisters, Pam Crabtree and Jenny Blackson, have been unfailingly supportive.

Much of the initial research for this project was supported by a Creative Fellowship at the State Library of Victoria, where Jean Galbraith's papers are held. The fellowship provided access to the collection and the expertise of the staff, as well as an office off the famous domed reading room. I would like to thank former State Library staff Shane Carmody and Shelley Roberts for their early support and Lois McEvey for assistance with the Jean Galbraith Papers. I am extremely grateful to Margot Jones, publishing project manager at the State Library of Victoria, for her contribution to the publishing process and for all her advice. I greatly appreciate the assistance I have received from Jill Thurlow and Sally Stewart at the National Herbarium of Victoria where an extensive collection of Jean Galbraith letters is held, and I would also like to thank Michael Piggott for introducing me to the University of Melbourne Archives, where another large collection of Galbraith correspondence is housed. On a trip to Canberra to visit the National Museum of Australia, I had an enjoyable time as a visiting fellow at the NMA's Centre for Historical Research. I would also like to thank curator Anne Kelly for her help in accessing the Jean Galbraith Collection at the NMA's repository. I received assistance from staff at the Mitchell Library in Sydney, the National Library in Canberra, and also at the University of Melbourne's Burnley Campus Library where there is an extensive collection of Australian and international gardening magazines, including *My Garden*. I have not met reference librarian Marie Long at the LuEsther T Mertz Library, New York Botanical Garden, but I am particularly grateful for the copies she provided of Jean Galbraith's articles in the *Gardeners' Chronicle of America* published in the 1920s and 1930s. She couldn't locate any articles by Jean Galbraith, the name I had given her, but found numerous articles by 'Correa'.

I have also been helped by Gary Presland of the Field Naturalists' Club of Victoria; David Stickney, president of the Latrobe Valley Field Naturalists' Club; Thelma Mayze, secretary of the Traralgon and District Historical Society; and Anne Vale of the Australian Garden History Society. I would particularly like to thank Kylie Singleton of the Department of Environment and Primary Industries, Traralgon, for discussions on the vegetation of the

ACKNOWLEDGEMENTS

Latrobe Valley and for taking me to see the extremely rare *Prostanthera galbraithiae* at the Holey Plains State Park, a red letter day. I thank Ken Harris, photographer, botanist and member of the Latrobe Valley Field Naturalists' Club, for his epic journey with a camera through the Strzeleckis in search of the elusive 'red correa'. I am especially grateful to designer Sharon Harrup for her many contributions to the book – drawing the map of Jean Galbraith's valley, helping with design concepts and digitising images – as well as for her friendship and interest in the project. I am also grateful to the friends and colleagues who have read sections, or all, of the manuscript: Bain Attwood, Rebecca Jones, Linden Gillbank, Sue Hides, Marjory Burgess and Janice Chesters. Their comments have enhanced my writing and interpretation.

I would like to acknowledge individuals and organisations who have given me permission to reproduce images and creative works: Julie Langford for permission to reproduce her poem 'To Jean Galbraith'; Geoffrey Galbraith for permission to quote from a poem he wrote for his aunt's ninetieth birthday; the Literary Trustees of Walter de la Mare and the Society of Authors as their representative for permission to quote from 'The Scribe'; Peter Cuffley for permission to reproduce his painting of the 'garden in a valley'; Patricia McCubbin for permission to reproduce her husband Charles McCubbin's artwork on the cover of *Field Guide to the Wild Flowers of South-East Australia*; Barrie Turpin for his portrait of Jean Galbraith; Sherry Phillips for permission to reproduce her father Stan Kelly's painting of *Eucalyptus preissiana*; Noela Young for permission to reproduce an illustration in *Grandma Honeypot*; Bauer Media for permission to reproduce a photograph of Winifred Waddell originally published in *Woman's Day*; the Department of Environment and Primary Industries for permission to publish photographs of *Prostanthera galbraithiae* and *Boronia galbraithiae*; and the *Gippsland Times* for permission to reproduce a photograph of Jean Galbraith and Bill Cane.

The person I have most to thank is Janice Chesters for her continuous support and encouragement throughout the long process of research and writing. Janice has read the manuscript many times, discussed 'biography issues', offered valuable suggestions and shared many wildflower adventures.

INTRODUCTION

In October 1925, a young Jean Galbraith, well protected in a large black apron, was stationed at the classifying table of the Melbourne wildflower show in the St Kilda Town Hall, identifying and labelling flowers that were flooding in from around the state. Just like a certain horse race in November, the annual wildflower show, organised by the Field Naturalists' Club of Victoria, was a popular fixture of Melbourne's spring calendar. In the days leading up to the show, naturalists, farmers, school children and teachers from throughout Victoria had been out in the bush picking wildflowers to send by train to Melbourne. Wildflowers were also arriving from interstate, flowers that many Victorians had seen only in photographs, such as kangaroo paw from Western Australia and waratahs from New South Wales. But most spectacular was the Sturt's desert pea, making its first appearance at the show. Red and black and glistening, it had travelled from Broken Hill. The scent of the bush, buzz of the crowd and the array of intriguing and beautiful flowers – orchids resembling miniature flying ducks, striking eucalypt blossom, vibrant flowers from the Mallee, sprays of thryptomene from the Grampians – all contributed to the heady atmosphere. Organisers could sense that the show was a great success. Above all, it was spreading knowledge of Australian wildflowers, showcasing their beauty and also promoting their potential as garden plants.[1]

It was certainly a significant wildflower show for Jean Galbraith. In the crowds milling around the exhibits was Ralph Boardman, editor of the recently launched *Garden Lover*, a magazine full of helpful gardening information on topics such as rose growing, maintaining colourful flower beds and seasonal advice on vegetables. But Boardman was also keen to include information on growing native plants, a rare activity for most home gardeners in the 1920s. He was introduced to Jean Galbraith, well known among her field naturalist colleagues as a passionate grower of wildflowers in her country garden in Gippsland. Their fleeting conversation continued in letters, with Boardman soon discovering that Jean was an aspiring writer, as well as an emerging botanist and successful grower of wildflowers. Impressed by her writing, his initial plans for publishing occasional notes on growing native plants snowballed, and he asked her to start writing a series of articles instead. Jean was nineteen. This new series, 'Australian Native Flowers', was her first commissioned writing: the beginning of her writing career.[2]

In this book of a writer and her valley, I tell the story of a shy young woman with little formal education, and isolated from research libraries and herbaria, who became Australia's most influential writer on nature, plants and gardening. Because of the diversity of her writing, Jean Galbraith was known to many as a gardener or as a botanist, but she was, first and foremost, a writer. Her writing career began with the publication of her first article in the *Garden Lover* in 1926, and continued until failing eyesight forced her, reluctantly, to put down her pen. Her last article was published in 1995 when she was 89. During this long career, Galbraith wrote about plants and nature in many forms and for diverse readerships. For gardeners, she wrote nearly seventy years of articles, many of them inspired by her own garden and later collected and published as books. She wrote about growing both native and exotic plants, but it was her tireless promotion of Australian flora that set her apart from her contemporary garden writers. For naturalists, she was commissioned to write field guides to Australian wildflowers and she published numerous botanical articles. She wrote extensively for children: nature stories for monthly Education Department publications in New South Wales and Victoria, scripts for school broadcasts, books about the wonder of nature. Through her nature writing, she evoked the spirit of places that she knew and gave agency to the natural environment. Her writing reached multiple audiences, from breathless pre-schoolers listening to her stories read out on the ABC's 'Kindergarten of the Air' to readers of gardening magazines in Britain and America, intrigued by articles conveying the beauty of Australian plants.

As a writer, Galbraith developed new forms of garden and botanical writing in Australia. Her garden writing drew on story, autobiography, botany and reflection. Evocative and lyrical, her work has been compared with that of Reginald Farrer, who revolutionised English garden writing in the early twentieth century, and Gilbert White, the greatest of England's nature writers.[3] She could convey colour as 'few artists can manage to paint'.[4] Unlike renowned English garden writers such as Vita Sackville-West and Gertrude Jekyll, Jean Galbraith was not an arbiter of taste and shied away from telling gardeners what to do. She wrote about the plants she loved, fashionable or homely, native and exotic. Her readers were seduced by garden writing that they found so compelling and different.[5] Jean Galbraith also turned botanical writing into a literary art and used literary devices and a poet's sensibility to make botanical information accessible to lay readers. Her field guides to Australian wildflowers were considered so essential to naturalists that they were dubbed 'glovebox Bibles'. Through spreading knowledge and a love of native plants, they contributed to conservation and protection of Australian flora.

As the title reflects, this book is also the story of a writer and her place, and explores the relationship between an Australian writer and her landscapes. Jean Galbraith's place was a valley in Gippsland in south-eastern Australia, where she lived on land her family had selected in the 1870s, thirty years before she was born. She described it as 'the very fabric of my being' and she had no desire to live anywhere else.[6] Her valley was bounded by the foothills of the Great Dividing Range to the north and the Strzelecki Ranges to the south, with the Latrobe River flowing eastwards on its way to the Gippsland Lakes and Bass Strait. Born in 1906, Jean grew up among farming landscapes where sheep and dairy cows grazed on the river flats and lower slopes. But remnant bush was close by. Carpets of wildflowers grew along the roadsides: milkmaids, early Nancies, buttercups, bush peas, orchids, billy buttons. In spring, chocolate lilies formed 'waving tides of purple bloom'. In summer, bluebells made swathes of blue along roadsides and flat hilltops. Sweet bursaria filled riversides with creamy blossom and scent. In winter, red heath ran like fire under the trees and white heath covered hilltops with snow.[7] Across the Latrobe River to the south, high in the Strzeleckis, was a different wonderland for Jean to explore, temperate rainforest, fern gullies and towering mountain ash.

The valley was a lifelong source of inspiration for Jean and shaped her career as a writer. Discovering wildflowers in the bush with her parents led to botanical study and nature writing. Collecting seed from the hills and heath led to experiments with growing native plants and her first commissioned writing. Later, when she was an established writer but was also caring for relatives and unable to leave the house, she relied even more on her place and surroundings to provide material for her many writing commitments. Her garden became a living archive of plants, stories and people that she could fashion into articles. Her landscapes were imprinted with memories of beauty and botanical discovery that featured in nature writing or children's stories. Parochial in its origins, her writing became national in its significance and impact.

Landscapes are not static and this is also a story of one woman's response to a changing environment. Jean's valley lay over vast reserves of brown coal. In the postwar years, she saw the wide valley floor transformed into an industrial region. The wildflower haunts of her childhood were cleared for power stations, open cut mines, briquette factories and transmission lines. The Latrobe River became polluted with industrial waste that was carried eastwards and deposited in the Gippsland Lakes. Tributaries were diverted for expanding open cut mines and native forest was stripped for pine plantations. Observing this from her home on the northern slopes of the valley, Jean drew on her environmental memory and used her writing to document the destruction and its implications. Her writing in all its forms – from gardening articles to children's stories – became a platform for conservation that highlighted the vulnerability of Australian flora and alerted readers to its rapid disappearance.

Jean Galbraith's story also provides insights to what 'country' can mean for settler Australians. Her garden of exotic and native plants that she created with her parents in the 1920s, and was the subject of her first book, *Garden in a Valley* (1939), serves as a metaphor for her inheritance as a settler Australian. The exotics reflect her British heritage, a heritage reinforced by her education and the literature she read, while the native plants that she brought back from the bush to grow in the garden express her Australian heritage, a love of country and belonging expressed through botany. Australian garden historians have written of the significance of memory in the gardens planted by settlers. By filling their gardens with the familiar plants of the homes they had left, memories of Britain and 'home' were perpetuated.[8] But when Jean Galbraith first wrote of her 'garden of memories' in 1927, different associations and memories were perpetuated. She described a sheoak she had planted and remembered 'a stony hill netted with the regal loveliness of Purple Coral Pea circled with Bursaria, blossoming now above the stream it loves, and crowned with Sheoaks like dark spires of pines'. A silky hakea in the garden reminded her of a day spent scrambling down Hakea Hill to a golden carpet of guinea flower and a creek almost lost in ferns, pink bells and bush pea. A woolly pomaderris brought to the garden from a nearby river recalled the sound of the water, the fold of hills and the creamy golden cloud of the pomaderris growing there.[9] As a settler Australian who loved the remnant bush, she re-introduced to the garden some of the trees, shrubs and flowers that her family had cleared fifty years before. This story of botanical belonging reveals the connection between one Australian and her landscapes, a love of country expressed through a passion for native flora and devoid of nationalism.

When the Australian Historic Records Search began its bicentennial project of listing archival material held in private hands, Galbraith registered to have her records included in the national inventory. Later, she donated her papers to the State Library of Victoria. Now held in the Library's Australian Manuscripts Collection, her archive is an extraordinary trove of letters, manuscripts, photographs, diaries, field notes, plant lists and nature notes. Jean lived in the same house for almost eighty years and she didn't throw things out. Her papers document important themes in Australia's twentieth century history, including botanical and gardening history, attitudes to native flora and evolving environmental awareness. They contain new insights to how Australians have lived with their landscapes in the recent past, and how they have written about them. Jean Galbraith's archive is also a repository of environmental memory, where eighty years of letters, field notes, writing and publishing provide a record of one person's detailed observation of native flora, landscape and change in her region.

Jean speaks to us from her archive for, unusually, it contains many of her own letters, including both sides of the correspondence between Jean and her most important mentors, to whom she wrote some of her most passionate and joyful letters. It was also her practice to make longhand copies of the more important or difficult letters she had to write. Publishing the field guides was a particularly hair-raising experience at times and required firm responses from Jean to publishers in both Australia and London. She remained a devoted letter writer throughout her life, even after she had a telephone connected in the 1960s. Her archive contains detailed correspondence with Australia's most prominent writers, botanists and gardeners. From the archive, too, it is possible to gauge the impact of Jean Galbraith's writing as her articles, books and field guides elicited numerous responses from readers. They range from gratitude for learning about Australian flora to expressing the comfort received from her garden writing during times of loss – the death of parents, a son killed during the war. Her articles inspired younger readers to try gardening, and older readers to keep on gardening. There were readers who described themselves as fans, and sought out everything she wrote: her field guides and botanical articles, her nature writing, her gardening articles and books and, finally, her 'cuttings', short newspaper articles on plants and gardening that were her last publications.

As the recipient of a State Library of Victoria creative fellowship to begin researching Jean Galbraith's life, I had an office in the State Library, accessed from a secret passage off the library's magnificent domed reading room. It was a magical year of immersion in Galbraith's papers, reading years of correspondence, dipping into school exercise books and childhood field notes, leafing through Edna Walling photographs that the garden designer had sent to Jean for a collaborative project, or reading long runs of gardening magazines in the Library's collection. Here in Jean's archive is the compelling story of how a shy young woman becomes a gardener, a botanist, a promoter and defender of Australian flora and a writer of significance. Here is evidence of her strong faith that underpinned her writing and passion for nature. Here is her simple way of living, where sunrises and sunsets or an opening flower could fill her with joy. Above all, her archive reveals the life of a good person.

Sudden fame came to Jean Galbraith in her eighties when *Garden in a Valley*, the story of her garden at 'Dunedin', was re-issued in a handsome new edition in 1985. People from around Australia flocked to see the garden. They met the good person who emerges so strongly from her archive and her writing, a modest woman who lived simply and with great joy. 'The beautiful simplicity and charm of your writing is matched by your character and personality', venerable gardener Dame Elisabeth Murdoch wrote to Jean after a visit to 'Dunedin'.[10] Visitors remember feelings of timelessness, of slipping between fantasy and reality, or experiencing a sense of 'holiness with nature', when they came to 'Dunedin'.[11] Some described their visit as a pilgrimage.[12]

They pushed open an old picket gate – 'the gateway to a kind of paradise', as garden historian Peter Cuffley described it – and entered a place of wonder.[13] Mosquitoes aside, they found a garden out of a fairytale as they stooped under archways supporting waterfalls of flowers, wandered through drifts of petals or strolled in the orchard where wildflowers grew under gnarled trees and wild cyclamen was known to seed.[14] The magic of their visit continued when they were invited inside, for stepping into Jean Galbraith's dining room in the home where she had lived for over seventy years was like stepping into her life. 'Comfortably shabby and delightful' was how her friend and botanical colleague, Professor John Turner, described the room, knowing Jean was not interested in material possessions.[15] There was a large kettle simmering on the open fire, ready for Jean to dispense morning or afternoon tea. Bookshelves covering the walls were filled with literature, poetry, philosophy, religion, children's stories and an expanding collection of garden books. The room reflected her scholarship: an extensive botanical library with well-used references held together by sticky tape and index cards of botanical notes on Australian flora filed in boxes around the room. Vases on every flat surface contained specimens as well as flower arrangements. A track was worn on the carpet through to the bedroom where her herbarium was housed.[16] There was no television.

Through the window overlooking the east garden were flashes of wings and constant movement as birds came to visit the bird feeders outside. This was Jean Galbraith's view as she wrote, her large table pushed up against the window and covered with papers, journals and overflowing correspondence. It was here that she put her vision of nature into words and helped Australians of all ages to see their own landscapes in new ways and appreciate the beauty surrounding them.

While many biographies are memorable for exposing long-suppressed secrets or uncovering disconcerting information about their subjects, this biography contains no sensational or shocking revelations. Instead, it tells the story of a woman known for her compassion, selflessness and 'big-hearted capacity to see only the better side of everyone else's nature'.[17] My task has been to avoid sentimentalising her life as I write my interpretation of her story, explore her interaction with nature and consider how a modest person living simply in her valley could enrich so many lives. An appreciation written by a botanist soon after Jean Galbraith's death in 1999 provides some clues:

> Her simplicity of life, wanting for nothing, coveting nothing, in thorough appreciation and enjoyment of every moment, of every happening, her great first hand knowledge of her environment and philosophy of life has become greatly meaningful to me … [W]ith age, I am appreciating it more and more.[18]

Chapter 1

SETTLING IN THE VALLEY

In 1984, when Jean Galbraith drafted a new introduction to the story of her garden, *Garden in a Valley*, first published in 1939 and about to be reissued in an impressive new edition, she didn't begin with the garden but took readers to nineteenth century Edinburgh instead. 'I have never seen the small house at 38 Howe Street, Edinburgh, where Andrew Galbraith, my grandfather, lived', was her opening sentence. 'In 1856, when he was about 19 he sailed for Australia in the clipper ship *Lightning*, working his passage as a baker's mate'.[1] Her introduction to the garden began as a story of migration and life on the goldfields, and then continued as a pioneering epic, of moving to a selection in the foothills of the Great Dividing Range on timbered slopes that stretched down to the Latrobe River valley. Her family and the place where they settled were so integral to Jean's identity that she told the story of how they came to the valley many times, in different modes and for different audiences. She wrote about it for her readers in gardening articles, she wrote it for children to read in the *Victorian School Paper*, she began writing it as a children's story in 'The Boys of Mount Hope Farm'.[2] And she told it again, when she was nearing eighty, in her new introduction to *Garden in a Valley*. Her family stories usually started with her grandfather, Andrew Galbraith, who had worked as a confectioner in Edinburgh before leaving for Victoria, and were based on what she heard from her father and other family members. Combined with more recent family history research, these stories provide an insight to how the Galbraiths came to settle in the valley, the place that Jean described as 'the very fabric of my being'.[3]

When Andrew Galbraith left Scotland for Victoria, sailing with his two older cousins in 1856, he joined the great wave of migration to the colony that had begun five years before when gold was discovered. After arriving in Melbourne, the cousins left for Beechworth, the administrative centre of the Ovens goldfields in Victoria's mountainous north east. Andrew didn't intend to try his luck panning for gold, but worked as a baker instead. Substantial buildings of local granite had been built in Beechworth during the late 1850s, giving the young town an air of solidity. There was a court house, gold administration buildings, churches and a hospital. A post office with a clock tower was built on the main intersection and miners gathered there when the post arrived, hoping for letters from home.[4] The streets were lined with shops and hotels. Andrew rented a shop and residence in Ford Street where he operated a bakery.

Andrew met Sarah Ross in Beechworth. Sarah had arrived in Melbourne from England in 1853, and the family moved to Beechworth after her mother's sudden death. Sarah's father, John Ross, served as a deacon in the Congregational Church where Andrew Galbraith was also a member. Andrew and Sarah married in February 1859, in the shop residence above the bakery. Andrew was 21 and Sarah only 17 but she had become used to shouldering responsibilities after her mother's death. She was described by one family member as 'small and dainty as a Dresden china shepherdess'.[5]

The ties between Andrew and his father-in-law strengthened. John Ross had worked as a chemist and printer in England and as a carpenter and gold miner in Beechworth, and now he began working in Andrew's bakery. He bought land at Newtown, on the western entry to Beechworth, where Andrew built a house, 'Nithsdale', with sweeping views across to Mount Buffalo. It was a substantial nine-roomed home, and the expanding Galbraith family lived there with Sarah's father and brother. Andrew bought adjoining land and planted a large orchard and garden around the new house. He also built a bakery on the property, but continued to keep a shop front in Ford Street where his bread and pastries were sold.[6]

Sarah was soon caring for a family of two daughters and five sons. Matthew, Jean's father, was born in 1869, the fourth of Andrew and Sarah's children. When a handsome new primary school was built in the town, Matt, as he was known, began his education there, crossing the granite bridge over the gorge on his way into Beechworth. But a year later, in 1876, the Galbraith and Ross families decided to leave Beechworth and try farming in Gippsland. The decision is a puzzling one. Why did the Galbraiths decide to leave Beechworth where they had a profitable business, comfortable home, access to medical facilities and a new school that would provide their younger children with a good education, and move to an isolated forested selection in Gippsland?

According to stories Jean had heard from Matt, who was eight at the time the family left Beechworth, Andrew did not feel a goldmining town awash with hotels was the right place to bring up a family. She expressed this in a children's story she began in 1950, 'The Boys of Mt Hope Farm', writing an imagined account of the family conference at 'Nithsdale' when the decision to leave Beechworth and select land was discussed by Grandfather John, Father Andrew and Uncle James, Sarah's brother. The goldfields were 'no place for boys and girls to grow up … no openings for them – the danger of gold fever which may lead to riches or ruin but rarely to happiness were in his [Andrew's] mind', Jean wrote.

> "A farm is what you want", said Grandfather John, "plenty of room and a healthy life …"
>
> "That's what I thought", said Father Andrew, "but this is no place for farms. Now in Gippsland …"
>
> "That's what I thought", said Grandfather John. "There is evidently good land, low priced, near some of those Gippsland towns."
>
> "Along the Latrobe River", said Uncle James, "I've read of it – rich river flats and well-timbered hills."
>
> "We seem to have all thought the same thing", said Father Andrew.[7]

It was at this point in Jean's story that Andrew turned to Sarah for her opinion. In family stories, Sarah remained a shadowy figure and Jean portrayed her as a quiet, faithful, steadfast woman. As Jean imagined:

> "I'll go where you go", said Mother Sarah, and no-one knew, then or afterwards, whether she thought of her comfortable home – the gardens they had made for her – the orchard in full bearing – with regret – whether she sighed at the thought of a home on those wild timbered hills – a slab home with a bark roof and earth floor, she knew it must be.
>
> She looked at her blue-eyed husband and smiled a very little – "If it's best for the children", and that was all.

Although hotels proliferated in the Ovens district and goldmining continued after the initial rush, Beechworth in the 1870s was no longer the frontier gold town of the 1850s.[8] In the last twenty years, it had expanded as a regional centre when imposing new institutions such as a gaol and mental hospital were built there. But there was a perception among Beechworth residents that their town was declining. Its position as the main city of the north east had been threatened when the proposed route for a railway linking Melbourne and Sydney by-passed it. Also, there may have been the influence of *Zeitgeist*, with people in Victoria moving from mining to farming in the 1870s. The Victorian government had passed a series of selection acts making Crown land available for people with limited capital to 'select' and develop as farms, part of government policy to promote more intensive use of the land. Residents from goldmining communities around Victoria were leaving for Gippsland in south east Victoria, where land was being opened for selection. For Andrew Galbraith with seven children whose ages ranged from one to sixteen, farming may have seemed to provide opportunities for a large family.

The Galbraiths' pioneering epic began as Andrew set off on horseback to inspect land in Gippsland. With him was a neighbour, Robert Tucker, who had also decided to leave Beechworth and take up farming. They left in 1876, crossed the Great Dividing Range and rode down on the southern side of the mountains through Aberfeldy to the famed gold town of Walhalla, and then followed tracks leading down to the valley of the Latrobe River.[9]

The valley was bordered by foothills of the Great Dividing Range to the north and the Strzelecki Ranges to the south and had been settled thirty years before by squatters who brought sheep and cattle to the wide river flats along the Latrobe River and the creeks that drained into the river from the hills to the north and south. It had been the land of the Brataulong people. Jean's story, though, was not one of squatters or of the Brataulong people they had dispossessed in the 1840s; it was a story of government-sponsored settlement, a story of her family coming to find a home and make a farm in the vicinity of the Latrobe River. 'The river flats had been settled – they turned to the hills', she wrote in 'The Boys of Mount Hope Farm'.

Andrew Galbraith, the baker and pastry cook from Edinburgh and Beechworth, began inspecting the slopes and ridges around Tyers to the north of the river, where six families had already settled. There was a limit of 129 hectares that one person could select and Andrew pegged out two allotments, one in his name and the other in John Ross's name, altogether 218 hectares that they planned to work as one farm. The selection consisted of steeply forested land that sloped down to more undulating open country, and included a small section of river flats. Andrew was pleased with the land he chose, Jean wrote in her introduction to *Garden in a Valley*, 'not realising that the stringy tussock grasses under the trees made for poor cattle grazing'.[10] Their selections pegged, Andrew Galbraith and Robert Tucker returned to Beechworth via Melbourne where they lodged applications for the land. These would be considered by a land board in Sale, the closest administrative centre to Tyers.

The family prepared for the move to Tyers. John Ross, his son James and grandson Will Galbraith, who was twelve, formed an advance party and travelled to Gippsland to begin clearing the land and building a house. They set off in May with a dray specially built for the journey, loaded with equipment and supplies, and were on the road for three arduous weeks, travelling from Beechworth to Melbourne and then east along the rough coaching route into Gippsland. They battled fallen timber in the forests, lurched into potholes and became bogged in the notorious 'Gluepot' near present day Moe. 'We got up to our future abode with horse and dray and part goods feeling truly thankful that we had been directed by God to such a fine and beautiful place', John Ross wrote in his diary. 'We at once began to clear the ground of trees for a dwelling house'.[11] Winter was setting in. At 67, he was undaunted by a new beginning.

Back in Beechworth, just as they were selling the house and bakery, Sarah discovered she was pregnant. Ahead of her was the prospect of giving birth in a hut on an isolated selection. They set off for Gippsland in September on a journey that combined coach, boat and train travel and was a great adventure for the children. They caught the coach to Melbourne and then boarded the boat for Gippsland at Queen's Wharf, sailing out through the Port Philip heads and east into Bass Strait. When they reached the entrance to the Gippsland Lakes, they had to transfer to a smaller boat that could take them over the bar, through the network of lakes and into the Latrobe River near Sale. The next section of their journey was by train. Work on a railway line connecting Sale with Melbourne was in progress, and the most easterly section, from Sale to Morwell, had just been opened. The Galbraiths piled into one of the two little carriages and the train steamed west through the red gum plains. John Ross met them at Loy Yang, a small stop near Traralgon. The last part of their journey was by dray, with a steep climb up the Walhalla Road to the new farm. Waiting for them was a slab hut built from red box trees, with a bark roof and earth floor. There was also a wattle and daub dairy, a woolshed and an orchard that John and James Ross and young Will Galbraith had just finished planting. 'On first of October I had the pleasure of seeing and welcoming my dear children to their mountain home', John Ross wrote in his diary.[12] They called the farm 'Mt Hope' and the new house 'The Pines'. Three months later, Sarah gave birth to her last child, Jessie.

Ever the botanist, the account Jean wrote in *Garden in a Valley* of the pioneering move from Beechworth to Gippsland was also a story of moving between two environments. Beechworth, north of the Divide, was dry granite country with rocky outcrops 'silvered by lichen', the crevices filled with heath myrtle, orchids and lilies, and where groves of pointed cypress pines grew.[13] In their new environment, the foothills of the Great Dividing Range were like 'fingers' stretching down to the Latrobe River. Deep gullies sheltered mountain grey gum, tree ferns, wonga vines and clematis, while growing on the dryer slopes and ridge tops was more open forest of silvertop-ash and stringybark. Behind the new house was the blue haze of Mount Erica, and below it slopes of peppermint and box led down to swampy river flats covered with thickets of tea tree and paperbark. South of the river was a blue line of hills, the eastern Strzelecki Ranges, where towering forests of mountain ash and cool temperate rainforest of myrtle beech and sassafras grew on the higher slopes. Selectors had not penetrated far into the eastern Strzeleckis yet and the forests had not been subjected to the clearing that resulted in failed farms, erosion, rabbit plagues and a new name, 'the Heartbreak Hills'.

To help finance the farm, Andrew opened a bakery in Traralgon, the nearest town to Tyers, and fast developing as a regional centre with the opening of the railway line. He worked there with his two eldest sons, John and Will, and only came home to Tyers on Sundays. Sarah remained on the farm with five of the children: her eldest daughter Alice, the new baby and the three younger children, as well as her father and brother who were developing the farm. Jean's father Matt also lived in Traralgon, as there was no school in Tyers. He helped out by delivering the bread before breakfast. On Fridays after school, he set off alone on horseback for the farm. It was ten kilometres from Traralgon to Tyers as the crow flies, but Matt was faced with a twenty-seven kilometre ride as there was only one bridge over the Latrobe River, and it lay further to the east. His description of his solitary ride through darkening bush was one Jean always remembered. 'I said to myself, "I only have to think about getting to the next corner. And then to the next corner … "'[14]

Although he was based in Traralgon, Andrew Galbraith became a leader in the new community of Tyers. Educating the children was an early priority and he joined other parents in petitioning the Education Department for a school which was eventually built on a southern portion of the family's selection. When the school opened in 1879, Matt moved to the farm and was among the first pupils to enrol.[15] Andrew cut a track from the house on the ridge for his children to walk to school, and Jean wrote several times of the number of snakes they killed along the way. Andrew was also active in establishing the mechanics' institute, which consisted of a hall and a library and was built next to the school in a stand of red box.[16] His campaign for a new bridge to be built over the Latrobe River was successful. The bridge more than halved the journey between Tyers and Traralgon and provided easier access to the railway station, saleyards and businesses in the growing town. John Ross also made his mark in the community and conducted church services at Tyers, first in the new school and then in the hall.

With the Tyers settlement developing around the nucleus of the school and hall, the Galbraiths built a new home closer to the hub, moving from their slab hut. Called 'Mt Hope', the house was built on a lower ridge overlooking the river flats, and the younger children now had an easy walk to school. With its sawn timber walls and iron roof, the new home represented progress and permanency that came with an increasingly productive farm. Another orchard and a garden were planted around the new house.

As Jean listened to Matt's stories of the pioneering days, she learnt not only of the family's early experiences at Tyers but also about the vegetation of the hills and flats when the family arrived. When he started at the Tyers school, Matt told her, there were no fences between the school and the river, a distance of nearly five kilometres. Instead, there was swamp scrub: thick tea tree with small sunny glades filled with wildflowers. One of the teachers – possibly the one who had been dismissed for 'intemperance' before he was re-instated and sent to Tyers – liked a good drink with his lunch and then fell into a deep sleep every afternoon. This was the signal for the children to slip out of the schoolroom and head for the river to play, careful to return by three o'clock. 'He always woke at three', Matt said. Jean felt her father's love of nature was nurtured in that playground stretching from school to river, where day after day he observed birds in the tea tree and discovered pink bells, parrot pea and many other wildflowers in the small clearings.[17]

By the late 1880s, dairying was emerging as an important industry in Victoria, helped along by the introduction of mechanical separators and refrigerated ships that made export of dairy products to Britain possible. The Victorian government promoted dairying and provided subsidies for cooperative butter factories and creameries to be built throughout Victoria. One was established in Traralgon in 1890.[18] Three years later, Andrew Galbraith stopped working as a baker in Traralgon and built a private butter factory in Tyers, with a guarantee from local farmers, who had been taking their milk into the factory at Traralgon, to supply the new venture. The small factory, A.L. Galbraith and Sons, was built next to the hall among the red box. Eldest son John was the manager, with assistance from his brothers Matt and Fred, who also continued to work on the farm. Butter from the Tyers factory received high awards from the Victorian Department of Agriculture and was exported to Britain and South Africa.[19] Andrew's entrepreneurial venture played a major role in the community. The factory was a hive of activity in the mornings when farmers in the district converged there after the morning milking and waited while their milk was separated, taking the skim milk home to feed to their pigs.

The Galbraiths' story – as well as the district's story – had moved from pioneering to farming. Dairy cows and sheep grazed on the flats and lower hills. The Galbraiths, though, had not been ruthless clearers of their land. They kept shelter trees of peppermint and box in the paddocks, a link with the original woodland cover, and there were still pockets of bush filled with pink bells, early Nancies, milkmaids, billy buttons, bluebells and everlastings. The open woodland, once purple and gold with chocolate lilies and wattle, was sown down with oats and grasses that added new colours and textures to the landscape. Now, silver waves of oats and rye grass rippled like the sea.[20]

The garden at 'Mt Hope' became one of beauty and productivity and sheltered the house and farm buildings on the ridge. The long, low house was surrounded with flowers. Jean described some of the roses growing there: 'pink and white Maman Cochet, Madam Rivers, Saffrano, Cloth of Gold, Souvenir de la Malmaison', to name a few. The orchard, planted with apples, oranges, lemons, limes, peaches, quinces and plums, was a worthy successor to its predecessors at 'Nithsdale' and 'The Pines'. Nearby was the vegetable garden and along the track linking the house with the farm buildings was a shrubbery that Andrew had planted, bordered by jonquils, irises and agapanthus.[21]

Andrew lived at 'Mt Hope' until his death in 1912, but Sarah had died in 1898. "'No wonder", Jean's mother said, "married at eighteen and with so much to do in the next forty years."'[22] An obituary in the *Traralgon Record* described Sarah as a 'very old and respected resident of the district'.[23] Although she was only 56 when she died, twenty years residence in Tyers made her an 'old' citizen of the district. Trees grown from seeds she had brought with her from Beechworth, including a blue gum, grew at 'Mt Hope' for decades, a legacy of her residence there. John Ross out-lived his daughter. He died in 1907 when he was 98, still taking an active interest in the farm he had helped to develop over the years.

Within the Tyers community, the Galbraith family had acquired an identity. Andrew had emerged as a community leader and entrepreneur and the family was also invested with cultural and intellectual leadership. They were regarded as learned and lovers of literature. In 1914, Matt was entrusted with £20 to go to Melbourne and buy books for the mechanics' institute library.[24] His choice of books, fiction and non-fiction, influenced what the community read. This perception of intellectual leadership may have led to a sense of Galbraith superiority that came with being 'bookish' and educated, a trait that younger generations of the Galbraith family have commented on, and one they felt Jean inherited.[25]

In her introduction to *Garden in a Valley*, Jean recorded the continuing ties of the next generation with Tyers. While her aunts Alice and Edith left the district when they married, only one of the five sons, Harry the printer, moved away when he was young. 'There is no work for a printer on a farm', she wrote.[26] After marrying, the adult sons built homes close to 'Mt Hope', satellites to the main house. Fred moved into a small cottage, 'Home', that was built next to the main house when he married. Later, he lived at 'Ingleside', another close neighbour to the family home. John, the factory manager, moved into a new house that was built down the hill from 'Mt Hope', fronting the Tyers River Road. The house was called 'Dunedin', a name reflecting the family's Scottish heritage. As well as working on the farm, Will ran the Tyers post office and store across the road from the factory and lived nearby. From these new homes, another generation of Galbraiths, Andrew and Sarah's grandchildren, walked to the Tyers school. They had inherited a collective sense of belonging and a love of Tyers and its landscapes that was evident in Jean, her brothers and cousins. Jean's new introduction to *Garden in a Valley* captured this; family and place were the backdrop to her story of the garden.

But being 'old' Tyers pioneers was only one strand of the Galbraiths' identity. Another was their faith. In 1893, the same year that the butter factory was built in Tyers, the Galbraiths became Christadelphians, and this profoundly affected the way they and their descendants continued to live in the valley.

From when they arrived in Australia, Andrew Galbraith and John Ross, deeply spiritual men, had been drawn to non-conformist denominations. They were members of the Congregational Church in Beechworth in the 1850s, before leaving to join the Baptist Church, where John Ross preached and lectured. But as they learnt more about the beliefs of Christadelphians, they decided that the tenets and structure of the faith agreed with their own reading and interpretation of the Bible. Although in worldwide terms the group was small, the Galbraiths had known Christadelphians in Beech-worth. Robert Tucker, who had come with Andrew Galbraith in the 1870s to select land at Tyers, was a Christadelphian.[27]

The Christadelphian faith had its origins in the mid-nineteenth century, and grew from the writings of John Thomas, an English doctor who was dissatisfied with the beliefs of existing denominations and migrated to America in the 1830s. Through intense Biblical study, Thomas sought ways of following a faith similar to the first century Christians and wrote on how existing Christian churches had moved away from the teachings of the Bible. 'To the bible, then, all must come at last if they would be truly wise in spiritual things', Thomas wrote in *Elpis Israel* in 1848. He was the originator of the name Christadelphian, Brothers in Christ. His ideas were further developed and expounded by Birmingham-based Robert Roberts. Roberts helped to define Christadelphian beliefs and promoted them widely through lectures, preaching and publications, including his influential *Christendom Astray From the Bible*. He was also founder and editor of *The Christadelphian*.[28]

By becoming Christadelphians the Galbraiths embraced new beliefs and ways of worshipping and living. Their lives were focused on the Bible as the revelation of God, which they considered completely free of error and the only source of knowledge of God and his plans. Systematic reading of the Bible was part of everyday life, as they sought guidance for living according to God's word. There was a reading plan for Christadelphians to follow, developed by Robert Roberts: they read the Old Testament once each year and the New Testament twice, beginning each New Year's Day with Genesis, Psalms and Matthew. Similar to the early Christians, Christadelphians had no clerical hierarchy. There was no centralised doctrinal authority. Each congregation, or ecclesia, was autonomous, and drew up its own statements of faith, all accepting the Bible as the only guide. Members often met in family homes for weekly memorial services where they shared bread and wine in remembrance of the death and resurrection of Jesus. Exhortations or sermons were delivered by members of the ecclesia or visiting brethren.

Fundamental to the Christadelphian faith, and therefore the Galbraiths', was the belief in the second coming of Christ, that Jesus will return to earth to establish the Kingdom of God. They believed that after death, people were at rest while they waited for Jesus to return and give the faithful immortal life. They were waiting for the resurrection, for the time when they would wake 'to perfection on an earth filled at last with the glory of the Lord, and see Him face to face', as Jean wrote in the late 1920s.[29] 'Greetings in our great hope', was the way many letters were prefaced to others who were in the Truth. Christadelphians rejected some of the beliefs that were fundamental to many other Christians, such as the trinity and immortality of the soul.

Baptism was the means to becoming a Christadelphian. In June 1893, at the Traralgon Temperance Hall, John Ross, who was 83, along with his son-in-law Andrew, grandsons John, Matt and Fred, and John's wife Clementine, were baptised. Through total immersion and a profession of their new beliefs, they underwent a symbolic death and resurrection to a new life. Five years later when Robert Roberts was on a visit to Australia, he came to Tyers to meet the Galbraiths and speak to the ecclesia. This was a significant event for the Galbraiths as Roberts' writing had greatly influenced their decision to become Christadelphians, and they were also contributors to his journal. Roberts expressed admiration for the Galbraith family, including the dedication that Brother Ross, then in his late eighties, showed for his religion. 'Stalwart sons share the grandfather's interest', he wrote, 'and the father [Andrew] is the centre of it all. It is a patriarchal establishment – a beautiful sight'.[30] Sarah did not become a Christadelphian.

As Christadelphians, the Galbraiths were entering a new community of brothers and sisters in Christ, and also withdrawing to an extent from the Tyers community where John Ross had preached. There were new expectations of how they would live their daily lives and who they would marry. They became pacifists or, though the term didn't exist at the time, conscientious objectors. They rejected political involvement and did not vote. Each night families came together to read aloud from the Bible. They gathered at the

Tyers River where baptisms were conducted by Andrew in its 'beautiful transparent waters'.[31] Daily, they were waiting for the return of Jesus, which altered their concept of time and the way they viewed death.

It was through the Christadelphian community that Matt Galbraith met Amy Ladson. Amy grew up in Beechworth, the same granite and cypress pine country that he had left as a small boy. Like Matt's parents, Amy's father Alfred Ladson and her mother Jane Taylor had come to Australia during the 1850s. Alfred Ladson became a storekeeper in Beechworth, where he ran several businesses.[32] Jane and Alfred had eight children of whom Amy was their fourth child. Where little was known of Jean's paternal grandmother, Sarah Galbraith, Jane Ladson kept a diary that provided insights to her daily life, her strong character and her hopes and fears for her family. In the early 1870s, Jane, a member of the Congregational Church in Beechworth, was given a Christadelphian booklet to read and immediately felt that she had to learn more. She decided to be baptised, a decision that, as her great-grandson wrote in his history of the Ladson family, showed her strength. She was acting alone and against the wishes of her mother and sisters, and joining an ecclesia where she was the only woman.[33] Her husband Alfred joined the Beechworth ecclesia a year after she was baptised. Jean knew her maternal grandmother well, as she lived until 1933.

Amy grew up in a family that loved music, poetry, gardens and nature. Her father was a gifted organist and her brothers and sisters played a variety of instruments. Among her siblings, Charlie, Bessie and Fanny were the family poets. Within the family, Amy had a reputation as someone with commonsense. She shared the same love of literature, nature and music, but was also an expert cook and housekeeper.[34] She was good at making things and her mother sent her to learn dressmaking in Beechworth. When Amy was twenty four, she moved to Melbourne with her younger sister Fanny. Alfred Ladson was not happy with the move, but, as their mother wrote in her diary, 'they made up their minds to make a start in life for themselves'.[35] In the city, they would have access to a wider Christadelphian circle and potential marriage partners.

Amy met Matt Galbraith after moving to Melbourne and they married in March 1905. Matt was 35, six years older than Amy. They moved into 'Home', the small cottage that had been built next to 'Mt Hope' for Fred Galbraith when he married in 1900. Sadly, Fred's wife died after giving birth to still-born twins. When Matt and Amy married, Fred moved back into 'Mt Hope' where his father, grandfather, uncle and youngest sister Jessie were living. Matt and Amy began making a garden around 'Home', including a rose garden that was Matt's special delight.

At the end of the year, Amy, who was six months pregnant, was away visiting her family in Beechworth, unaware of a tragedy that was unfolding at 'Mt Hope'. Five days before Christmas, another day had started routinely on the farm. Andrew was up first at 4.30, working in his large vegetable garden before the heat of the day. Matt and Fred had started milking and Will had come across from his home to join them. By 7.30 there was no sign of Jessie, who would normally be preparing breakfast. She was not in her bedroom, but a disturbing note was found recording her unhappiness and failings, and her fear that she was going mad. Her father and brothers found her body in the dam in the calf paddock.[36]

Three months later, on Wednesday 28 March 1906, Matt and Amy's daughter Jean was born, a joyful event for a grieving family.

Chapter 2

CHILDHOOD

Jean claimed she was born with a love of plants and gardens.[1] Her first flower adventures were at 'Home' where she was surrounded by the gardens her parents and grandfather tended. She could stand on the verandah with its passion vine and see an abundance of roses in the garden and clouds of pink and white blossom in the orchard. She could walk from 'our' garden, past her mother's perennial border and her father's roses, round a clump of shrubs and she was in Grandfather's garden, a long walk for a small child.[2] Her extended family shared their love of plants with her. Andrew showed her his special flowers. Her great aunt Kate who lived in a grey shingled cottage near her grandmother's house in Beechworth prepared a special child's garden for Jean when she came all the way from Gippsland to visit. It was in a big oblong box, and flower buds were starting to open.[3] One of Jean's earliest memories was of making a garden while she was on a holiday at the sea. She made sand gardens on the beach with flowers from the cliff tops, and remembered the satisfaction this gave her, a plump, contented two-year-old.[4]

As a small child, she found plenty to explore close to the house. She discovered birds in the garden – a spinebill in the daphne bush, a thrush she could see from the verandah. Encouraged by her mother, she began to observe their habits and recognise their calls. There were days of 'high adventure' in the orchard, gathering apples under the trees and biting into small crisp pears, 'Christmas pears' she called them, sweet even before they were ripe.[5] Further away from the garden and the orchard, along the road leading from 'Mt Hope' to the butter factory, was the bush. At first she found it dark and mysterious. She gathered buttercups on the fringes of its shadows, penetrating a little further as she grew older and then delighting in her discoveries. Finding her first pink bell was a 'wonder moment'.[6]

Lawrie [Lawrence] was born when Jean was two. They became close child-hood companions – so close that their names merged as 'JeanandLawrie'.[7] At night, Amy sang a special song to put the children to sleep. They called it 'the sleepy song'. Later, when Jean occasionally played it on the organ, the song brought back memories of the dining room at 'Home', 'with its red fire glow and gentle light', Amy holding Lawrie and Jean sitting on the rug between her parents. As Amy sang the sleepy song and children's hymns in front of the fire, Jean remembered being enveloped by a sense of comfort and absolute content, aware of a love that supplied every want and 'shut the outside world to oblivion'.[8] After being put to bed, she could hear her parents reading the daily chapters from the Bible, five verses each in turn. She couldn't hear the words but the sound of their reading gave her a sense of security. As soon as she and Lawrie could read, even haltingly, they joined in the nightly ritual of Bible-reading and read one verse each in turn, helped over the long words. Pasted on the wall of their bedroom was a picture of a shepherd and his sheep in a green meadow beside a pool, with the words of the Twenty-Third Psalm. Jean loved both picture and words.[9] In 1910, just days before Jean's fourth birthday, Lance was born and she welcomed another little brother into her life and routine.

During the day, Amy sang songs to her children about flowers and gardens. At night, many of the stories and poems Matt and Amy read to them were about flowers. For Jean, flowers, books, songs and stories fused. Her love of flowers, she thought, was set in her heart by 'song and story, as well as the living things' and it was no wonder her love of books and flowers grew together. From one of her first books, *The Three Little Spades*, Jean learnt that flowers were 'the radiant gifts of God' to be treated lovingly and always shared, and she also realised, from the daily reading of the Bible, that its whole theme was making the 'Garden of God'.[10]

But interspersed with memories of garden and flower adventures, and of warmth, peace and contentment with her parents, were also those of long hot nights when she suffered from eczema and asthma, of bandages being unwound on weeping rashes and soothing voices of her parents calming a frightened child in an asthma attack. Her father would read 'At the End of the Moonpath', a short story by the Australian nature writer and journalist, Donald Macdonald: 'And the white acacia was covering the room with scented snow …' She could smell it. [11]

Jean grew up in a Galbraith Ladson enclave surrounded by aunts, uncles and cousins. Down the hill at 'Dunedin', Uncle John's house, there were seven cousins, although the older ones had moved away for school and study. Her eldest cousin, Alan, was an engineering student at Melbourne University and the first of several Galbraiths of his generation to become engineers. Over at Uncle Will's there were three more cousins. The Galbraith family came together at 'Mt Hope' for major celebrations. Jean remembered the family meals, sitting around a table in a large shed in the courtyard between 'Mt Hope' and 'Home'. Ties between the Galbraiths and Ladsons strengthened. When Jean was two, her Uncle Fred married Amy's sister, Fanny. Just a track separated 'Home' from 'Ingleside', Fred and Fan's new home, and there was constant movement between the two households. Soon there were young cousins for Jean to play with. Violet was born six days after Lance, and Dick three years later. Another member of the Ladson family moved to Gippsland to live. Amy and Fan's violinist brother Tom left Beechworth and settled in Traralgon where he taught music.

The extended family was united in religion and met at the weekly memorial services. Matt's account of his nephew Alan's baptism showed the close involvement of the family in the ceremony. They gathered at the Tyers River among the wattles and manna gums to sing hymns and anthems. Andrew and Alan went into the water and Andrew baptised his grandson. 'As they were coming out of the water', Matt wrote in his letter describing the occasion, 'Will started the old Baptist baptismal hymn, "Praise the Lord, Hallelujah", which we sang'. The memorial service the next day was an emotional occasion for all the family, as Alan was the first member of his generation to be baptised.[12]

It would be difficult to call the Tyers that Jean knew as a small child a town, or even a township. There was no hotel or church and few houses apart from the Galbraith homes and the teacher's residence. There were saw mills in the hills to the north, but the rhythms of the day still revolved around the butter factory and the school, farmers arriving with their milk after the morning's milking and children riding their horses in from the farms to school. Later in the day, the 'quiet driver' of the butter factory wagon would set off to take the butter into the railway station at Traralgon and the school children would untether their horses in the horse paddock, ready for home.

When Jean started at the Tyers school, the original building had been replaced by a high ceilinged classroom with large windows facing south to the Tyers River road. The school's eight grades were taught by one teacher. It was a relief for the teacher when enrolments reached forty because then a sewing teacher or assistant could be appointed. There were forty children when Jean started and her cousin Ethel, Uncle Will's daughter, was the sewing mistress. Jean was a serious scholar who loved reading and learning but her schooling was interrupted by her childhood demons of asthma, eczema and bronchitis. She had few friends throughout her years at school, and later claimed she depended on books more than people. She felt she knew Elizabeth Bennet (of Jane Austen's *Pride and Prejudice*) better than she knew her schoolmates.[13]

Jean walked to school along the 'top road' that led from 'Mount Hope' to the butter factory and school. The next year she was joined by Lawrie, only four and a half but eager to start school. Trees arched over the road and one side was bordered with dense bush, still mysterious to a young child and 'so thick, that when we passed it on our way to school we would not go into any but a few open sunny parts, fearing we might get lost where the trees grew thick and dark'.[14] Masses of prickly bush pea grew along the road and Jean picked bunches of it for Amy on her way home from school.

Jean was six when Andrew Galbraith died in 1912. She remembered helping her mother to pick violets for the funeral. With his death came a loosening of the tight family unit that Jean described in her introduction to *Garden in a Valley*. The farm was sold, except for the five hectares around 'Dunedin'.[15] In 1914, John moved closer to Melbourne for his younger children's education and bought a farm at Werribee, leaving Matt and Fred to run the butter factory. Will also moved to Melbourne and bought a store in Camberwell. With the farm sold and John's family now living at Werribee, Matt, Amy, eight-year-old Jean and brothers Lawrie and Lance moved down the hill from 'Home' to 'Dunedin'.

'Dunedin', a tall narrow house, was built on a gentle slope of the valley. The house and its paddocks lay between two roads, the 'top road' that led to 'Mt Hope', and the 'bottom road', or the Tyers River road, and faced south across the valley to the Strzeleckis. As early photographs show, the house was bare and exposed when the family moved there, except for a windbreak of pines to the west, a young oak and elm that had been planted behind the house, and a struggling orchard to the east. There was a path running down to the front gate on the road where box trees grew. South of the road, there were still thickets of tea tree and paperbark dotting the river flats. Amy and Matt were too busy to start a new garden to rival the one they had at 'Home', although Amy grew flowers and vegetables. Matt tried to plant roses, but with little success. The heavy clay soil defeated the roses. Behind the house, the children had gardens and great care was lavished on these. Jean grew flowers from seed mixtures – lupin, nasturtiums, sweet peas, pansies, stocks, wallflowers and poppies – learning from Amy how to raise the seeds, transplant them into her garden and care for them. But soon Amy had less time to spend in the garden. Several years after the Galbraiths moved to 'Dunedin', Daisy Ladson, her brother Tom's wife, died after contracting food poisoning in the hospital where she had just given birth to her second daughter, Verna. Amy looked after Verna while she was an infant and the following year, 1917, her youngest child Angus was born. Gardening was put on hold 'till long afterwards'.[16]

'Dunedin', with four bedrooms, was bigger than 'Home'. The door on the front verandah opened into a central hallway, with bedrooms opening off to the left. At the front of the house to the right was the study. Its south-facing window featured a transfer of a hunting scene, the image much loved by children.[17] Matt, who was a capable bush carpenter, used glass doors recycled from a bookcase to build a bay window on the east wall and let in the morning sun. With its window seat covered by a mattress and cushions, and bookshelves built at each end, the new window became a favourite place for reading. Services were held each Sunday in the study for many years and there was also an organ in the room. Jean was a passionate lover of music and learned to play the organ when she was young, but she considered herself a 'poor player'. She was surrounded by musical aunts, uncles and cousins, and rarely sat down to play when she was young if there were other people around.[18]

Further down, the hallway opened into the hub of the house, the dining room, which was also the family sitting room. As well as the dining table – where Lawrie and Jean engaged in vigorous debates – there were armchairs around the fireplace and bookshelves lining the walls. Three foot logs burned in the fireplace, and the family gathered here in the evenings after dinner for the nightly Bible reading, then settling down with their own books. The bookcases were filled with poetry and English classics, books on religion, children's annuals, adventure stories and a growing number of *William* books, a great favourite with the boys. Often in the evenings, as they sat around the fire, Matt, Amy and Jean read about plants and dreamed of gardens.

There was a walk-through pantry connecting the kitchen and dining room, its shelves filled with jams and preserves that Amy cooked on the wood stove. A laundry opened off the kitchen and wood for the fire and stove was stored here. At the back of the house between the kitchen and back bedroom, facing north, was a porch where first Verna played as a baby and then Angus. When

Matt became a keen begonia grower, he extended the roof of the porch, using windows he had bought at the sale of an old hotel to make a glass roof, and placed his begonias there. Jean learnt about pollination and cross pollination as Matt tended them.[19]

A favourite place for games was a bush paddock next to 'Ingleside' on the top road. Going up to the paddock, Lawrie would swish the heads off dandelions and act out part of his favourite poem, Thomas Macaulay's 'Horatius', much loved by schoolboys of his generation. Lawrie was the hero Horatius, valiantly holding the bridge for Rome against the heroes of the Tuscan army, while tender-hearted Jean pleaded for the soldiers' lives. Little Lance came panting behind, calling out that he wanted to be Horatius too. They played hidey in the bush, Jean's brown plait always getting caught in twigs and scrub. Influenced by the stories of James Fennimore Cooper, they built wigwams by tying the wattle boughs together to make secret shelters, but careful not to break any branches. They felt part of the forest, 'of God's world that was given for joy', as Jean remembered. Their cousins Violet and Dick squeezed in too and shared the secret sanctuary. Surrounding them were prickly bush pea, pink bells, early Nancies, chocolate lilies, milkmaids, wattle blossom, bluebells and everlastings, depending on the season. In autumn they made gardens from mosses and lichen and created fairylands in an old enamelled basin. In spring they picked the wildflowers and placed them in a tin in the wigwam. When the flowers withered – and no-one was looking – Jean admitted to kissing them and telling them how lovely they had been.[20]

Christmas and birthdays were special occasions, as were family gatherings and other celebrations. There was a memorable occasion in 1915 when Uncle Charlie, Amy's brother, visited from England. After marrying Robert Roberts' daughter, he had gone to live in Birmingham where he was assistant editor of *The Christadelphian*. Galbraiths, Ladsons and other friends gathered at 'Ingleside' to welcome him. The Tyers River was a favourite place for family picnics. Photographs of these occasions show horses and jinkers on the bridge, while men in suits and ties and women in large hats are drinking tea down on the banks, with children paddling in the river.[21]

The children were infused with a strong work ethic and helped with the cows, pigs and poultry on the small farm. Because of her eczema, Jean was not able to milk but she went to bring the cows in with Lawrie early in the morning, 'through the mist when the sun had hardly risen', and helped with other farm chores while Lawrie milked.[22] Matt set a fine example of the value of hard work. He had loved nothing better than 'starting a day's ploughing with two good horses on a spring morning', he told his children, and constantly endorsed the value and dignity of working hard.[23] After an extended illness, when he went on a voyage to New Zealand in 1917 to help regain his health, he left letters for Amy, Jean and the boys, in case anything should happen to him while he was away. His letter to Jean contained praise, love and guidance on how she should conduct her life. He endorsed her love of nature – 'Keep warm your love of nature and the beautiful, don't read anything that will blacken the white of your mind' – and included a homily on the value of work. Though a keen reader himself, he advised against too much reading at the expense of work. 'Your love of reading while a wonderful power for good, can do you harm if it interferes with your doing'.

> Work is honourable and the commonest and humblest things, done well and heartily can rank with the most acclaimed services rendered to a King. Take time to be neat and thorough but do not be slow. Wasting time or dawdling about work is wrong. It also spoils the picture of one's life. The lines of one's life should be clear cut, not smudged as they are when we dawdle.[24]

He praised her study of the Bible. 'You have a good knowledge of your bible', he wrote, 'keep on and add to your knowledge … you may learn to love and obey God with your whole heart'. From her earliest days, Jean had absorbed all that her parents taught her on religion, unquestioningly accepting their faith as a template for her life. As her brother Angus wrote of their childhood many years later, 'we all shared the same faith in God as revealed in the Bible and have attempted to manifest that faith in our lives despite the frailties of human nature'. The hope of each member of the family, he continued, was the fulfilment of the words of the Lord's Prayer: 'Thy kingdom come; Thy will be done on earth as it is in heaven'.[25] Jean lived her life in prophecy – the Olivet prophecy – and looked to Jesus's return. These hopes were her 'most precious thoughts' and constantly in her mind, she explained in 1928.[26] The Olivet prophecy described the signs – war, famine, chaos – that would lead to Jesus's return: 'men's hearts failing them for fear' and people being more interested in themselves than in God.[27] Throughout her life, Jean felt that Jesus's return was imminent.[28] In 1920, when she was fourteen, she made the decision to be baptised and become a member of the Christadelphian community.

Jean's early love of flowers, discovered in the garden at 'Home', also spread to the bush. As a small child on picnics and family excursions, she began learning the names of native plants from her parents, observing them closely and noting their habitats. From early visits to the Tyers River she learnt about the manna gums that shaded the banks, and watched them shed great ribbons of bark in the summer and reveal white trunks. She soon recognised the woolly tea tree that flowered on the river bank. She saw the Victorian Christmas bush, a pale lilac mint bush that flowered at Christmas time along the river, and she learnt to recognise the fragrant scent of its leaves. And down low, at the water's edge, she didn't miss the small ferns dipping in the river. There were numerous family trips into the bush to find wildflowers and she began learning about families, species and varieties.

Jean's valley that she explored with her family consisted of the inner slopes of two roughly parallel ranges, the Strzeleckis and the Baw Baws, and contained a variety of vegetation communities. On the northern drier slopes behind Tyers, silvertop-ash, messmate, stringybark and box contrasted with towering mountain ash and cool temperate rainforest on the higher reaches of the Strzeleckis. On the valley floor, silver wattles and manna gum grew along the river banks, with swamp paperbark, tea tree and tussocks on the morass land. To the south east of the valley were hills of sand and gravel covered with banksia groves, grass trees, narrow-leaf peppermint and dense heathy undergrowth.[29] The roadside near Gormandale in the Strzeleckis became a favourite place for the young Jean because of the spectacular displays of wildflowers growing there. Long after the flowers had disappeared, Gormandale remained her benchmark when she assessed other places for their diversity of species and floral display. The area featured in a memorable childhood excursion: the day she saw her first correa, a local variety notable for its glowing red bells, *Correa reflexa* var. *cardinalis*. She was with her father returning from Blackwarry, high in the Strzeleckis, and driving towards Gormandale. The weather was atrocious. Ahead of them was a thirty mile trip back to Tyers in the horse and buggy, driving straight into freezing wind and stinging rain. But when she saw correa growing along the roadside, 'velvet bells woven of red fire', the rain was forgotten and she was out among them, turning to the flowers again and again, marvelling at their beauty.[30]

She started to keep field notes and recorded her sightings and descriptions. In spite of her poor eyesight – she wore glasses from an early age – Jean was an acute observer. When she was thirteen, she cut down an exercise book to make into a field notebook and wrote 'Notes on Plants 1919' on the front cover. For the next three years, she took this notebook on her excursions into the bush, recording all her observations, drawing diagrams of seeds and pods, noting her queries and identification dilemmas and resorting to invented names for plants she didn't know. Evident in the notebook were her attempts not just to keep a record of what she found, but also to capture the essence of what she saw:

> Aug 20 [1919] Found Everlastings and bacon and eggs. Golden wattle in full beautiful bloom. One tree seems to have bright red stems and is very beautiful. I wonder if it is a seperate [sic] species.

> August 21 Found a green orchid quite new to me. We call it the brown throat because each blossom is like a wide opened mouth with brown throat and tongue. The flowers are small and there are about a dozen on a stem.

Sept 25 We went to Lyre Bird gully yesterday. The Indigo and Golden Goodia are glorious clustering masses of gold and purple pink. Tree ferns water ferns and Lomaria and Lady ferns are beautiful and all well known mosses are carpeting the logs with green. The beautiful mint creeper climbs everywhere among the bracken. The musk tree is in bud but no sign of flower shows among the beautiful green and white leaves of the Blanketwood tree. Some of the musk is much more forward than other.

A week later, Jean crossed the Tyers River and went to 'the heath':

Oct 2 The other day Daddy took me to the heath for the first time. It is a wonderful drive. After we left the road the ground was almost purple with pink bells the two species growing together all very beautiful. It was broken everywhere with clustering bushes of small leaved parrot pea. The heath itself is a broad stretch of white, broken by a very narrow winding path of White titree and great masses of White Heath while the pink and white velvet flowers (Styphelia) grow in beautiful sheets. The pink one has not got pink flowers but pink stems and leaves which give the whole bush a most dainty pink shade. I wonder if they are different spiecies [sic]. The purple pink pyramid flower also grows sparsely here. I don't know what it is for none of us have seen it before and Pyramid flower is just an invented name.[31]

Jean went back to the heath the following winter and recorded her fascination with the place:

July 2 [1920] Went to the heath today……It is a curious place this heath, a space of 10 acres which for the last 8 years possibly the last 500 has no large tree on it. All round it rises a solid wall of tall box trees but on it is nothing but a few low gum bushes with peculiar golden white tops and a solid sheet of heath, Styphelia and wild hawthorn. There are no holes and no logs or indication of fallen timber. This and one similar place the "Bald Hill" are the only places we know where Styphelia grows.

The notebook didn't just provide a record of her early botanising – where she went and what she saw – it also recorded the botanical discovery of her place. It showed her developing an intimate knowledge of vegetation in the hills and valley – Little's Hill, Lyre Bird Gully, Hope's Hill, Bald Hill, the swamp at Dove's, just a few of the flower haunts that she visited and revisited.

She knew individual plants. She wrote of a clematis she had been watching for five years and recorded when it flowered for the first time.

There was no comprehensive field guide to Victorian wildflowers to help with identification of native flora. Her earliest botanical reference was a book she had been given when she was seven, *Nature's Little Ways*.[32] This helped her to study the shape of seeds and leaves, the parts of a flower, and to see how plants belonged to families. The reference books she gradually acquired described northern hemisphere plants. Jean couldn't believe her luck when she was thirteen and came across some tattered sheets of FitzGerald's *Australian Orchids* in the Beechworth library, while she was on a visit to her grandmother and aunts. The flowers were drawn by surveyor Robert FitzGerald, and published as folios between 1875 and 1894. Jean spent hours in the library studying the delicate hand-coloured plates of the flowers and dissections. She felt sure that no-one else looked at the folios and desperately wanted to buy them from the library.[33]

Jean gleaned whatever nature information she could find in the *Victorian School Paper*, the monthly magazines published in three graded issues by the Education Department and distributed to pupils in Victorian state schools at the cost of a penny per issue. The October issues always contained articles on birds, to coincide with Bird Day, while articles on trees featured in June to mark Arbor Day. Nature notes appeared sporadically throughout the year. Excerpts from *A Bush Calendar* by journalist Amy Mack were regularly included in the magazines published for middle and senior students, giving Jean an opportunity to read Mack's nature writing as she described the changing seasons and flora and fauna in the bush near Sydney, with particularly vivid descriptions of birds. As soon as Jean read about *Birds of Our Bush or Photography for Nature Lovers* in Lance's issue of the *School Paper*, she wanted a copy and was thrilled when Auntie Fan gave her the book for Christmas.[34]

When Jean became a senior student, though, there was less space in the *School Paper* for nature study. Articles on the progress of the First World

War, followed by the Versailles Peace Congress and memorialising those who served in the war, dominated the pages.

Of more botanical importance to Jean at that time were 'Nature Notes and Queries' and 'Nature Notes for Boys' by Donald Macdonald, the author of her loved childhood 'Moonpath' story. Macdonald's nature notes were published in *The Argus* for nearly thirty years and Jean, like many other country readers, 'grew up on them'. Readers sent in specimens for identification and their observations on local flora and fauna and described noteworthy happenings in their localities.[35] Macdonald's nature notes were so influential that *The Argus* noted on his death how many children 'who first saw their own country through the eyes of Donald Macdonald' had come to 'know it and love it through their own'.[36] Jean was a regular contributor to the columns.

Her interest in wildflowers extended to growing them in the garden. While she was out on flower excursions, she collected seeds from the bush and dug up seedlings to take back to the garden. She recorded their place of origin in her field notebook: orchids from Little's Hill, tetratheca and heath from north of the Tyers River, clematis from Lyre Bird Gully. She kept notes on their progress in pots and in the garden. There were many failures as raising seed and transplanting seedlings from the bush was a matter of trial and error, but soon plants such as daisy bushes and bottlebrush were thriving in the garden.

From when she was very young, Jean began writing descriptively about the plants she saw, searching for just the right words to convey colours, shapes and texture. 'No-one encouraged me to write. I just wrote', she explained of her early writing.[37] On days when her eczema was so bad that she couldn't walk, she remembered lying in the garden and writing 'descriptions' of what she had seen in the bush. She wrote of butterflies that danced above a 'yellow fragrant surge of Bush-pea', or recent discoveries of pink bells and bird orchids.[38] Her field notes included lyrical descriptions as well as botanical observations as she tried to capture what she saw, the texture of a styphelia, for example, with 'each flower looking like a tiny star cut out of velvet', describing sweet bursaria as 'a plumy mass of clusters of creamy blossom', and mistletoe whose 'red tassels hang like fringes of tapistry [sic] from their green waxy foliage'.[39]

Jean was influenced by the nature writers she read. While many girls her age were reading the immensely popular *Girl of the Limberlost* by the American author Gene Stratton Porter, Jean was studying Stratton Porter's nature writing instead. Inspired by a childhood growing up near the Limberlost Swamp in Indiana, Stratton Porter became a nature photographer and expert on moths as well as a writer and used her lucrative fiction to subsidise her nature books. Jean copied out numerous extracts of Stratton Porter's nature writing from *Music of the Wild* with the diligence of an apprentice writer. 'Since the beginning the forest has been singing its song but few there are who have cared to learn either the words or the melody', Jean copied into her notebook. 'The forest alone raises a chorus of praise under natural conditions. Here you can meet the Creator face to face if anywhere on earth!' Jean the music-lover was inspired to listen to the trees that Stratton Porter described as 'large wind harps, the trunks the framework, the branches the strings'.[40]

Jean's library of nature writing grew at each birthday. For her thirteenth birthday Auntie Em Ladson gave her Mary Milner's *The Garden, the Grove and the Field* featuring descriptions of English wildflowers that the author observed through the seasons. Another present that year was *A Year in the Woodlands* by English writer T. Carreras, full of fascinating diagrams, natural history and nature writing. When she was fourteen, Jean was given books by Australian nature writers: *Gum Bough and Wattle Bloom* by Donald Macdonald and *In Australian Wilds* by Charles Barrett.[41]

'Dear Cinderella', Jean wrote in August 1917 in a draft letter to the editor of *The Leader*'s children's pages, 'I noticed that the competition for this month is to be about "When Nature comes to Life Again", so I thought that I would try to tell you about Tyers when Nature has come to life again after its Winter sleep'.[42] *The Leader* was a pictorial newspaper published by *The Age* and each month Cinderella conducted essay competitions for young readers.

The winning entries won a prize of five shillings and were published in the children's pages. When Cinderella issued guidelines for August's competition, it was clear she didn't want any half-hearted contributions. 'I want my young friends to watch each day's change from the long winter sleep into the happy life of spring – how the birds arrive, the lambs and calves appear, the blossoms and the trees grow bright and so on … [The essays] must be sufficiently long to show good attempts at real work and observation'.[43] While the older children toiled away on worthy essays on Joan of Arc, the younger children looked for signs of spring. Jean was in her element describing Tyers: the colour of the hills, nest-building birds, fresh green leaves, wildflowers on the slopes and blossom in the orchard. There were also dutiful references to frisky calves on the flats and the light speck of lambs on the hillsides. 'And as the young birds learn to fly', her essay concluded, 'Spring merges into Summer'.[44]

She was joint winner of the competition and claimed this essay as her first published writing. It appeared in October, in an issue of *The Leader* that was filled with photographs of shelled villages, ruined churches and grave-strewn landscapes in France. Her essay, a response to Cinderella's 'happy life of spring', was juxtaposed with the grim realities of war on the Western Front. After this, Jean's contributions were regularly published in *The Leader*, and the prize money came in handy.

Jean began a more ambitious nature essay about the seasons several years later, written in pencil at the back of a school exercise book filled with compositions on the Versailles Peace Treaty, the Boer War and Charles 1, as well as dictation that showed she was not a perfect speller. She called her new nature essay 'The Seasons of Nature' and she dedicated it to her parents. Only autumn survives.[45]

A letter Jean wrote in her childhood revealed how she fashioned her own experiences into stories. 'Dear Daddie', Jean wrote in November 1917, while her father was away on his trip to New Zealand, 'I have had such a time of excitement this week'. The excitement included Flower Day, when she was up at half past five gathering flowers from the 'Ingleside' and 'Mt Hope' gardens, enough to make thirty bouquets. There was some exciting mail, too: 'a great big fat envelope' had arrived with 'an enormous sheet of paper on which the words To Miss Jean Galbraith with the compliments of the editor of the Leader and Cinderella were written and also a postal note for 2/6.' She had just returned from a rare trip into Traralgon and described for her father three 'adventures' on the way home. Adventure number one was seeing a blue wren and a firetail's nest when they crossed the Latrobe River. Adventure number two was observing three 'very curious birds', which she couldn't identify and described in detail. And adventure number three was being 'waylaid by a small highwayman by the name of Alec Archbold.' The young highwayman, a fellow pupil at the Tyers school, demanded newspapers.[46]

As an aspiring writer, Jean was fortunate in having J.W. Elijah as her teacher during her last years at school. He was appointed to Tyers in 1918 and taught Jean until she left in 1920. He became an important mentor who contributed greatly to her intellectual development and to her writing. Mr Elijah particularly encouraged student writing. He became the founding editor of *Echoes*, a school magazine of the Sale Inspectorate, that published contributions from teachers and pupils of the many schools within the inspectorate, an area stretching from Sale in the east to Wilsons Promontory in the south, and which included all the schools in the Traralgon district. As well as teaching all eight grades at the Tyers school, Mr Elijah was completing a bachelor of arts degree.

When he left in 1922 to lecture at the Teachers' Training College at Melbourne University, the Tyers community was sorry to see him go. During his four years there, he made an impact not only on his students but also on the parents who considered him an outstanding teacher. Their opinion was endorsed by Professor Smyth of the Training College who described Elijah's work at Tyers as 'brilliant'.[47] During his career as a lecturer at the Training College and later as a school inspector, Mr Elijah wrote *Principles and Techniques of Teaching in Elementary Schools* for student teachers – described as the 'teacher's bible for twenty-five years' – and a series of text books for school children.[48]

Mr Elijah became the writing mentor Jean needed, first as her teacher and then as a friend. As editor of *Echoes* he published her poems and he gave Jean the run of his library. After he left Tyers, she continued to send her writing for comment, while he kept her abreast of his college students' literary activities, discussed poetry with her and continued to encourage her. He joined her other writing mentor, Birmingham-based Uncle Charlie Ladson, who was a poet as well as working on *The Christadelphian*. Jean only met her uncle once when he came to Tyers in 1915, but after that visit, uncle and niece wrote regularly, and Jean began sending him her writing. 'I depend upon him to give me wholesome literary criticism when I need it', she wrote to a friend after some years of correspondence with Uncle Charlie, 'but I'm afraid he doesn't give enough … He hasn't seen his niece Jean for so long … that he has imagined a sort of fairy lady who is all he wishes her to be … I should be afraid to meet him now as he would be so disappointed'.[49]

It wasn't only Mr Elijah who was a great influence on Jean, but also his wife, Mabel, who had settled happily into the teacher's residence at Tyers and was particularly friendly with Amy and Fanny Galbraith. Mabel Elijah was an artist, a passionate gardener and a wildflower enthusiast. She joined Jean on many bush rambles and shared her knowledge of native plants. 'Mrs Elijah found the first Birdwing orchid today', Jean wrote in her field notes in August 1919. 'Mrs Elijah has the largest greenhood I have ever seen', she recorded several months later.[50] Jean was a frequent visitor to the Elijahs' home which was between 'Dunedin' and the school, borrowing Mr Elijah's books, admiring the beautiful flower arrangements that Mrs Elijah placed throughout the house and exploring her flower garden. Mrs Elijah also gave Jean painting lessons.

Mabel Elijah was a great fan of Flora Klickmann's 'flower patch' books, stories set in the Wye valley above Tintern Abbey. Klickmann, journalist and editor of the *Girls' Own Paper*, retreated to her country cottage for regular escapes from a stressful London life dominated by publishing deadlines. She wrote about her life at the cottage in *Flower Patch Among the Hills*, which became a publishing sensation and led to a long series of 'flower patch' books. Although saturated with British assumptions of class, the books provided a *mélange* of nature, people, gardening and life in the Wye valley. They had such an impact on Mabel Elijah that when she visited England in the late 1930s, she went to the Wye valley and tracked down many of the sites featured in the books. While Jean was later critical of Klickmann's writing, she read Mrs Elijah's copies and was introduced to garden writing through the 'flower patch' books when they were at the height of their popularity.

Mabel Elijah provided a significant friendship that was outside the Galbraith Ladson enclave. Within the family Jean was confident and enquiring, while outside the family she was suffused with shyness. '(W)e see so few people here' she wrote when she was twenty-one, 'and until I was sixteen I rarely left home at all, so many people still "fricht [frighten] me."'[51] She was self-conscious about her appearance and tried to fade into the background in many group family photographs, standing behind taller people or looking down to avoid the camera. But both the Elijahs penetrated this shyness and provided friendship and mentoring. In spite of their age difference, Mrs Elijah became Jean's friend and Jean felt closer to her than any of her classmates. When the Elijahs left for Melbourne – Mrs Elijah despondent at finding herself in the 'dustbin' of urban Brunswick – their friendship continued through letters. Jean helped to salve Mrs Elijah's homesickness for the bush by sending wildflowers. They gave her 'untold joy', she wrote to Jean after receiving one parcel. 'I seem again to live at Tyers and wander over familiar scenes'.[52] A poem fell out as she opened a box of heath, correa and wattle. It was one of Jean's:

> Wonderland a moment
> Greet you with these flowers
> Mingled scents and blossoms
> Rain and springtime showers.[53]

Jean left school after grade eight and the completion of her merit certificate. There was no further secondary education available locally. Writing about this over sixty years later, she explained that even though it would have been a drain on the family finances, she could have gone away to school in Melbourne but she didn't want to leave home. 'I felt I would only be half a person in the city', she said, revealing that at fourteen she was already melded to the valley. 'Well don't ever say you could not have the same opportunities as your brothers', she remembered her mother saying.[54] Jean became Amy's assistant in the house, helping with housework and cooking, making jam and bottling fruit, working on the small farm and continuing her self-education with Mr Elijah's books. She studied Latin, read the *Canterbury Tales* and translated some of Chaucer's Middle English. She continued to read voraciously, the books ranging from *The Woman in White, Last Days of Pompeii* and *The Merchant of Venice* to *Anne of Green Gables, Little Men* and Ethel Turner's *Little Mother Meg*. She read more nature books including Charles Barrett's *From Range to Sea* and eagerly read T.C. Wollaston's *Our Wattles*. When she was nineteen, she also attended two vacation schools at Melbourne University, where she studied philosophy and musical appreciation. In the music classes, she heard some of the iconic orchestral pieces of the western musical canon, an impossibility in Tyers where, without a gramophone or wireless, music was restricted to family music-making and community concerts at the Tyers hall.[55]

After leaving school she had more time for nature rambles and her bird and wildflower field notes became increasingly detailed. There were also trips to Melbourne and an abundance of relatives to visit. A letter she sent to her parents in 1921 while she was staying with her uncle in Wandin provides an insight to Jean, aged fifteen. She had been to a concert at the Melbourne Town Hall – 'too wonderful to describe' – and had eaten an expensive dinner at a café. She had made a cake for her young cousin's birthday and they had eaten some of the pears she had bottled. There were a few minor hiccoughs to report, such as spilling ink on her silk dress, but more urgently, she had run out of money. In her letter home she asked after the Elijahs and wondered, with the concern of an older sister, if Lance could do the eighth grade work. She also fired off a volley of questions about a Miss Hawking who was coming to stay at 'Dunedin'. The questions reflected her own interests and concerns: was she nice, was she well-educated, could she do housework?[56]

Her flower hunting range increased. She was now driving the horse and jinker and could go further into the bush with the pony, Midge. After Uncle Fred bought a car in the 1920s there were more frequent excursions into the Strzeleckis to visit Tarra Valley and Bulga Park, two national parks strung along the Grand Ridge Road and both botanical wonderlands for Jean to explore. To drive there, the Galbraiths crossed the Latrobe River and passed through Traralgon and the sandy heath country. Then they started climbing. The road to the parks was steep and narrow and best suited to dry weather. There were small farming communities buried in the forest and Jean saw areas of devastation where blackberries, ragwort and rabbits had invaded the steep slopes after the forest cover had been cleared. Preserved in the parks up near Balook were remnants of the magnificent forest that had once dominated the Strzeleckis: towering mountain ash, notable as the tallest flowering plant in the world; myrtle beech and sassafras; deep gullies filled with tree ferns; vines and creepers spiralling up the trees; scent from fragrant mint bushes and musk daisy bushes drifting along the moist paths. A photograph of a Galbraith excursion to Bulga Park in the 1920s shows Fred's car with a backdrop of the slender white trunks of mountain ash. The car's fender was decorated with wildflowers, a practice Jean would later deplore. Among the Galbraiths gathered around the car, Jean looks down, avoiding the camera.[57]

In 1921, the tandem lives of 'JeanandLawrie' started to diverge. Lawrie won a scholarship to Melbourne High School and left to complete his secondary schooling in Melbourne. Like their sister, the Galbraith boys were academically gifted. They were expected, more so than Jean, to go to Melbourne for secondary education and possibly university, and win scholarships to help finance their study. Jean was intrigued by Lawrie's experiences and reported on how strange it seemed to him after the Tyers school: three hours of homework each night and all sorts of bizarre rules.[58] Lance followed Lawrie several years later, and Angus left for secondary school in Melbourne in the early 1930s.

The same year that Lawrie left for school, 1921, Matt and Fred Galbraith sold the family butter factory. While Fred continued to work at the factory, the sale marked a new phase of living in the valley for the 'Dunedin' Galbraiths. Their attention was now focused on 'Dunedin' and the five hectares surrounding it. Matt developed an interest in herd testing and went in for a new line of pigs. He took the milk from his six Ayrshires to the factory where he had worked for the past twenty eight years.

Jean's girlhood was over. Many years later, when she was asked to complete a questionnaire about her career as a botanist, she entered the main elements of her childhood as part of her botanical training. They were a 'happy country home with nature loving parents who loved gardening and all outdoor nature, always a house full of books where reading was part of life, and sincere Christianity its most vital part'.[59] For Jean, these defining features of her childhood and girlhood were the foundations for her botanical career and the writer she was to become.

Chapter 3

BECOMING A BOTANIST

On 3 October 1922, Jean stood on the platform at the Traralgon railway station waiting for the early Melbourne train. Like many other Victorians in search of wildflowers in the middle of spring, she was not heading into the bush where they grew but was travelling instead to the Melbourne Town Hall, the venue for the annual wildflower show organised by the Field Naturalists' Club of Victoria (FNCV). Jean was sixteen, and this was her first solo trip to Melbourne.

One of her cousins met her at Flinders Street station, and together they joined the people crowding into the town hall. Only steps from busy Swanston Street, they were swept into another world. First came the scent of the bush, a tangy blend of gum leaves, wattle, damp moss and boronia.[1] Next came the visual delights. In pride of place on the platform, arranged under great festoons of foliage, were native flowers grown in the Melbourne Botanic Gardens: waxflowers, grevilleas, chorizemas, olearias and striking eucalypt blossom. Crowded onto display tables were wildflowers picked by country naturalists, teachers and school children from throughout Victoria, and sent from stations and railway sidings in special boxes addressed to 'The Town Hall, Melbourne'. There were spectacular varieties from the Grampians, rare flowers from the Mallee and delicate plants plucked from the Otway rainforest. There were intriguing Victorian orchids, some shaped like miniature flying ducks, others resembling young birds with open mouths demanding to be fed.[2] Wildflowers had been sent from other states as well, flowers that Jean and most of the other visitors had seen only in photographs: kangaroo paw from Western Australia and glistening red waratahs from New

South Wales. In yet another section were displays of native flowers grown in private gardens. Visitors were particularly impressed by the large lemon flowers of the bell fruited mallee, a Western Australian eucalypt that had been grown from seed in philanthropist Russell Grimwade's Toorak garden, and the vast array of flowers from J.M. Watson's Maranoa garden in Balwyn, the first dedicated native plant garden in Melbourne.[3]

Jean was entranced by the wildflower show, later describing it as 'a miracle'.[4] For several years she had been working alone in her study of botany and wildflowers. She had outgrown her parents' knowledge and also that of Mrs Elijah, who was more artist than naturalist. But here, all around her, was the information she was seeking. As the afternoon drew on, she was abandoned by her cousin who had to go home to cook dinner, but Jean couldn't tear herself away. In all the tumult and crush of the exhibition, organisers didn't fail to notice the young woman whose complete absorption, constant questioning and close observation set her apart. 'Is she still asking questions?' Jean heard someone call across the hall during a lull in proceedings. That afternoon, she met the show's chief organiser, noted botanist H.B. Williamson, and this marked the beginning of her botanical education and her entrée to the botanical world.[5]

By the 1920s, the wildflower show had become a major event in Melbourne's spring calendar and attracted huge crowds. The show had evolved from modest beginnings when it became a tradition for FNCV members to bring wildflowers to the October meeting. They started enlisting help from country friends to collect flowers and send them to Melbourne to augment the species on display, but the flowers were only viewed by a small group who attended the club 'Conversaziones'. In 1915, the FNCV decided to make the display available to a much wider audience and held the show in the Athenaeum Hall in Collins Street. An entry fee was charged, with the money going to a patriotic cause. Members were amazed to see over three thousand people crowd into the hall, eager to see Australian wildflowers. Boldly, they booked the Melbourne Town Hall, a large and prestigious venue, for the following year.

There had been an upsurge in interest in native flora during the First World War, a patriotic response where the flowers were not appreciated for their beauty or botanical interest but simply because they were Australian.[6] The opening speeches by dignitaries at the wildflower shows reflected this connection between wildflowers and nationalism. Perhaps only a brigadier general could find parallels between Australian wildflowers and Australian soldiers. When he opened the exhibition in 1919, Brigadier General Brand explained their similarities. 'While Australian wild-flowers were reputed to be the hardiest in the world', he told the crowd, 'the same could be said of the Australian soldiers and the Australian horses'. Like the wildflowers, Australian soldiers (and their horses) 'got on best without too much attention and too much coddling'. It was well known that the hardy Australian wildflowers endured harsh conditions, but so, too, had the diggers, experiencing the 'withering heat' of Egypt and the 'mud and cold' of Flanders.[7] Opening the exhibition several years later in 1921, Lady Stradbroke, wife of the governor of Victoria, emphasised the importance of nurturing a love of wildflowers among children, as this would extend to a love of the nation. 'It was the love of the buttercups and daisies of England', she explained, 'which had done so much towards making the Englishman love and be proud of his country, and Australian children should be taught to love and take an interest in their birds, their gum trees and their flowers, and all the blessings which they are privileged to enjoy'.[8]

While happy to capitalise on this patriotic fervour, field naturalist club members were more concerned with displaying wildflowers so that visitors could appreciate their beauty and even consider growing them in home gardens. Suburban gardens were full of neat beds of roses and chrysanthemums, dahlias and gladioli, carnations and daffodils. Very few Australian species were grown.[9] This made the indigenous plants seem more exotic than the introduced plants. The FNCV blamed the horticultural industry for neglecting Australian flora and tried to interest nurserymen in stocking Australian plants and seeds for home gardeners. Nurseries were invited to sell native plants at the wildflower show. They sold out so quickly that the club had to restrain its members from raiding display tables for specimens to sell on the depleted flower stalls.[10] Through the wildflower shows, members also wanted to dispel a myth that native plants couldn't be cultivated in home gardens. Displaying flowers from private gardens had become an important aspect of the show.

As chief organiser of the show, H.B. Williamson was probably exhausted by the effort of mounting the displays when he met Jean on her first visit in 1922. Flowers had been travelling to Melbourne the day before by train, car and ship – forty species had arrived by steamer from Perth, many with their stems stuck in potatoes. Club members assembled at the town hall to set up display tables according to Williamson's floor-plan, cover them with paper donated by *The Age*, and fill the hundreds of specimen vases with water. They were back early the next morning to take delivery of the flower boxes that were flooding in from Spencer Street railway station. Under Williamson's direction, the flowers were sorted into families and labelled for display, while the most interesting or rare specimens were selected for special displays. By early afternoon, with urns boiling on the afternoon tea stalls, the doors were opened and the crowds surged in.

When Jean met Williamson he was the headmaster of Dandenong State School, but most of his career had been spent in country schools, where he developed an early interest in botany and native flora, and had been greatly encouraged by the Victorian government botanist, Ferdinand von Mueller. Williamson introduced nature study into the curriculum at his schools and also encouraged students to grow native plants in school gardens.[11] When he moved to Melbourne, he was able to take an active role in the field naturalists' club and initiated a more systematic arrangement to displaying wildflowers at the exhibition.[12] Through years of collecting, Williamson had amassed one of the largest private herbaria in Australia. He was a fellow of the Linnean Society in London, and regularly sent Australian specimens to staff at Kew Gardens, the famous botanic gardens in London. He retired from teaching in 1925 and worked on his major work, *Revision of the Genus Pultenaea*, which included descriptions of sixteen new species of bush peas. He also became honorary curator of the herbarium at Melbourne University's botany school, and helped Professor Ewart to prepare a successor to von Mueller's outdated *Key to the System of Victorian Plants*, first published in 1888.[13]

Jean benefited from Williamson's dual roles as teacher and botanist, as he was keen to help young people learn about native flora. Within a fortnight of the wildflower show, Williamson began a weekly botanical correspondence with Jean that continued until his death in 1931. Each week, Jean sent specimens to be identified and he replied with botanical names, notes on the species, taxonomic information and answers to her many queries. He was pleased, he told her, that she was 'enquiring'.[14] Williamson sent her botany texts and guided her field work. He taught her to use Mueller's key to Victorian plants and instructed her on developing a herbarium. Within weeks they were discussing anthers and stigmas, notches in petals and juvenile foliage. Jean's anxiety to be accurate – heightened by her years of self-education without access to a comprehensive curriculum – was evident in her queries on terminology, citing and even pronunciation. Through the correspondence, Williamson linked her with the wider botanical world, to the identification dilemmas and debates that were raging. 'Oh those Olearias', he wrote in mock exasperation, as he outlined classification problems of Australian daisy bushes.

With Williamson as her teacher, Jean's knowledge increased markedly. A more rigorous approach was evident in the new set of field notes she started, using the numbering system Williamson instigated, and writing a detailed botanical description of each specimen he identified for her. But terminology didn't dampen her love of descriptive writing and she continued to keep informal field notes of plants she found, writing quick impressions of what she saw: 'Cherry Ballart and prickly Currant Bush bearing soft glowing fruits like crimson and orange beads', she wrote after a visit to Bald Hill. By keeping two sets of field notes, she could record the plants she found both botanically and lyrically.

By specimen 226, *Lomatia longifolia*, which Jean collected early in 1924, the correspondence became less formal. Instead of 'Miss Galbraith', Williamson began addressing her as Jean. Although school masterly – he always corrected her spelling mistakes – his letters reflected his sense of humour. Williamson also took an interest in Jean's brothers and their education: Lawrie's success at Melbourne High School and his enrolment in engineering at Melbourne University, Lance's transfer to Melbourne High School. He introduced Jean to the National Herbarium, founded by von Mueller in the 1850s and located in the Domain, outside the Botanic Gardens. It was a place she loved with its smell of dried plants and naphthalene, and the privilege of having access to the staff and botanical collections.[15] Jean became friendly with all of the Williamson family, often staying with them on visits to Melbourne and becoming notorious for leaving things behind – stockings, a navy blue dress left hanging above the bed. As a thankyou for her hospitality, Jean regularly sent bunches of wildflowers to Mrs Williamson. Not so successful, though, were the mushrooms she had gathered from the paddocks and sent to Melbourne. 'The mushies had arrived in a much mashy condition', Williamson reported regretfully.[16]

It wasn't only Jean who benefited from the correspondence. As Williamson had predicted in his first letter, their correspondence proved to be of mutual benefit. Jean collected specimens for Williamson's herbarium, and he learnt from her observations, valuable for a city-based botanist because they were 'straight from the field'.[17] The mutual benefit of their correspondence was evident at the next wildflower show in 1923. Wearing a large black apron, her hands full of flowers, Jean worked as Williamson's assistant at the classifying table in the Melbourne Town Hall, grouping into families named specimens of Victorian plants. The wildflower show became a permanent fixture and a highlight of her year.

In the letters she sent to Williamson, Jean wrote tantalising descriptions of the Tyers bush, 'word pictures', as he described them, where plants and place were intertwined.[18] Williamson was keen to visit. Was there a coach between the Traralgon railway station and Tyers? Was there a hotel at Tyers where he could stay? His questions showed how little the small settlement of Tyers was known. He came for a visit before Christmas in 1923, riding his bicycle from the train in Traralgon and staying with the Galbraiths while Jean took him to her favourite places in the bush. Four years later, her parents enlisted Williamson's help in choosing a microscope for Jean's twenty-first birthday. Williamson disguised his handwriting on the envelopes of letters he sent to Matt discussing the merits of various models. 'The conspirators had to "watch out" in case you "got wind"', he explained afterwards, as he congratulated her on her twenty-first birthday.[19]

Soon after they started corresponding in 1922, Williamson also suggested Jean join the Field Naturalists' Club of Victoria, which was the premier botanical circle in Victoria. For the shy girl whose social interaction had extended little further than the family, membership of the club introduced her to scientists, botanists, ornithologists, entomologists, naturalists and wildflower specialists. Some were her heroes, whose writing she had been reading from childhood. They included Edith Coleman, Edward Pescott and Charles Barrett, who joined Williamson as her mentors, encouraging not only her botanical study but also her writing.

Edith Coleman became Jean's orchid mentor. Her research on the role of wasps in pollinating three *Cryptostylis* orchid species had received international recognition and she became the first woman to be awarded the Australian Natural History Medallion. A former teacher, Mrs Coleman was also committed to writing for a general readership on natural history and protection of Australian flora. Her articles appeared in newspapers and magazines such as *The Age*, *The Argus*, *Victorian School Paper* and *Women's Mirror*. She often invited Jean to stay at her holiday cottage in Healesville where they went on orchid excursions. Mrs Coleman would spot gardens in the bush while they were out orchiding, and then send packets of seeds to the gardens' owners, anonymously. 'They don't know who sends them but I like to think of their surprise, and of my seeds growing in so many different gardens', she told Jean.[20] Jean approved of this.

Within a year of her first visit to the wildflower show, Jean began corresponding regularly with Charles Barrett, whose books were on her shelves. *Herald* journalist, author and nature writer, he was also editor of the FNCV's journal, the *Victorian Naturalist*. Where Williamson's correspondence was botanical, Barrett wrote to Jean about authors and nature writing. He introduced her to the Dunk Island books written by the Beachcomber, E.J. Banfield, and recommended she read the nature books of English writer W.H. Hudson, describing them as 'the finest thing of their kind in modern English literature'. Later, he urged her to read the books of plant hunter Reginald Farrer.[21] He lent her his much loved copy of *Walden*, Henry Thoreau's classic account of his two year sojourn in a cabin on Walden Pond in New England, living simply and close to nature. *Walden* had been Barrett's constant companion when he was serving overseas during the First World War, and Jean knew what the book meant to him. She treated it with special care, placing it on a table under a window where it rested between reads, 'looking over the peaceful garden like the wonderful serene book it is'.[22]

It was a red letter day when Barrett took Jean to Black Rock to meet Donald Macdonald, whose nature columns in *The Argus* she had been reading for years and whose 'Moonpath' story had been a childhood favourite. It was such a momentous occasion that she made sure she had a botanical souvenir to remember the day. On the way to Macdonald's house near Karkatta Street, she stopped to explore some of Black Rock's heath country and followed a track through the tea tree where she came across thousands of seedlings in ground that had been burnt, and were 'just the right size to move'. Jean took several wedding bushes to plant at home to mark the occasion.[23] Macdonald was bedridden throughout the time Jean knew him, but he was still writing his *Argus* column and articles. A close rapport instantly developed between the revered journalist and young woman, evident in their letters and Jean's descriptions of him to her Uncle Charlie. To Macdonald, Jean became the 'one in the world, the particular one, the very dear one to whom one's thoughts go thronging often'. Her letters were full of lyricism. She visited Macdonald on her trips to Melbourne, always bringing him the scent of the bush with her bunches of wildflowers, and dipping into her store of 'all happiness and beauty to tell over to him'.[24]

After several years of corresponding with Williamson and Barrett, Jean began contributing to the *Victorian Naturalist*, although she expressed some anxiety to Williamson about the extent of her knowledge. 'As to articles in the *Naturalist*', he replied, 'the matter of knowledge does not count for anything. Observation work with good common sense reasoning about the causes is useful and in fact necessary, just the kind of work you and others in the country can do'.[25] Her first contributions to the *Naturalist* were published in 1925: nest-building habits of fantails, magpies' methods of settling disputes. They were based on notes of the behaviour of birds in the Tyers garden and were published in 'Notes From Field and Study', which Barrett felt was 'brightened' by her work.[26] Her first article, 'Forest Regeneration in Gippsland', published in 1926, documented the gradual recovery of hilly country east of the Tyers River that had been burnt in a bushfire in 1923.[27]

Jean provided a link with the bush for her city-based field naturalist mentors. Like H.B. Williamson, Charles Barrett soon expressed an interest in visiting Jean's locality: 'You live in a delightful district for nature study', he wrote in 1923, 'and your description of birds and flowers and insects makes one wish to visit'. With fellow club member, Edward Pescott, a former principal of Burnley Horticultural College, senior pomologist in the Agriculture Department and author of *Native Flowers of Victoria*, Barrett organised a trip to Traralgon, hoping to combine 'a glimpse of <u>your</u> country of Tyers', with a visit to what he described as Jean's 'Promised Land', Bulga Park.[28] Members of the FNCV now recognised this part of the world as Jean's country.

Mr Elijah, lecturing at the Teachers' Training College, was also aware of her achievements, and wrote to Jean in 1925 that he was hearing 'good accounts of you in the botany line and feel rather glad that I can claim you as an old pupil of Tyers school'.[29] By 1925, Jean was corresponding with Reuben

Patton, botany lecturer at Melbourne University, and sending specimens for the University herbarium.[30] She also began corresponding with A.W. Jessup at the Burnley Horticultural College, who was later to become government botanist and director of the Melbourne Botanic Gardens. They exchanged seeds and sent each other plants and cuttings.[31]

Her growing reputation as a botanist led to an appointment with the Victorian Tourist Bureau as botanist-in-residence at nature study camps in the Grampians in Western Victoria. Her first trip was in spring 1928 when Jean was twenty-two, and where she helped a lively group of Fintona students and their teachers identify plants. As Jean's formal education had been at a small one-teacher school, camping with a large party of schoolgirls was a new experience:

> I had never been (except for a few odd days with guides) among other girls, and both eye and ear gained pleasure from the merry groups among the tents or climbing the steep valley sides, light heartedly teasing or helping each other, or sitting at night singing around the campfire while the tent light twinkled starlike behind …it was a joyous week that I love to remember but I am glad to be quietly at home now.[32]

Regular trips to the Tourist Bureau's nature study camps in the Grampians gave her the opportunity to botanise in one of Victoria's premier wildflower localities, a world of peaks, crannies and rock gardens.

While her increasing botanical expertise had led to friends and mentors among the field naturalists, botany also provided Jean with an entrée to her local community. Her first local contact through botany, and one that led to a lifelong friendship, was with Eva West, who was assistant shire secretary in Traralgon. Eva's father, Walter West, was nominally the shire secretary but as he was also the local Member of Parliament, it was Eva who effectively ran the council administration. She had trained as an accountant during the First World War, and was one of the first women to be admitted as an associate of the Incorporated Institute of Accountants.[33] After working at the Warragul Shire Offices, she came home to Traralgon and started her own business as an accountant and auditor, but returned to local government when her father was elected to parliament in 1922. Eva West was also active in the girl guides and the Traralgon Horticultural Society. The friendship with Jean began in 1925 when Eva sought her help to prepare the girl guides, especially the rangers, for their naturalist badges. Very few rangers in Victoria had been awarded this badge, she later explained to Jean, mostly because there were so few people qualified to train them.[34]

A nature study book that Eva West kept included details of the guides' botany excursions. Jean's first trip with the guides was to the sandy heath country of Traralgon South. 'Miss Jean Galbraith who is a member of the Field Naturalists Club came out with us and named the flowers', Eva recorded in August 1925. 'She also showed us how to press them'.[35] A memorable trip took place the next summer when Jean introduced the guides to the delights of fern gullies. Miss West, as Jean called her throughout the first twenty years of their friendship, packed six guides into her car and drove out to Tyers. They transferred into buggies driven by Jean and her father and headed up the Walhalla Road to Paradise Gully, passing the Tyers saw mill on the way. Miss West was impressed by its modernity – it was driven by electricity – but she also felt the loss of the forest keenly. 'It seems a tragedy to see some of the hills, which years ago, were also covered with this timber and thick forest, now all bare and abandoned and useless'. A little further on, the party left the buggies and scrambled down into a beautiful, aromatic fern gully: 'Really steep descent about a quarter of a mile, and the last part seemed perpendicular', Miss West recorded. 'It is simply beautiful…collected 11 different species of ferns which Miss Galbraith named'. Among the many guide excursions in 1926, Miss West noted one in early October 'to help Miss Galbraith gather wildflowers for the Wildflower Show on October the 5th'.[36]

Eva West was eighteen years older than Jean but the discrepancy in ages did not prevent them from becoming close friends. 'With all her business-like capacity', wrote Jean in 1928, 'she remains a dear bush loving girl'. Like Jean, Eva West was a seeker of beauty, finding it 'in the glimpse of branches and sky through her office window when the glory of the wider bush is crowded out of her busy day', Jean wrote.[37] Miss West was keen to learn from Jean and her nature study diary was full of information that Jean provided. Often when Miss West drove to meetings in remote parts of the shire, she took Jean as well and left her to botanise in promising patches of bush along the way, picking her up on the way home. Miss West loved Bulga Park, as Jean did, and was responsible for many of Jean's visits there. One trip was with nature-loving auditors who were taking a break from scrutinising shire ledgers and accounts. All members of the party were amazed by the vibrant red gum tips on the young trees as they drove through the hills to Bulga Park. 'None of us had ever seen such colour in any eucalypts', Jean reported to H.B. Williamson.[38]

Eva West introduced Jean to bush camping when she invited her on a trip to Tarra Valley with two ranger guides. The girls taught Jean how to make a stretcher, not altogether successfully as her poem, 'Song of a Stretcher, Being the Sad Story of Jean's Camp-Bed', revealed. Several more trips with the guides followed in quick succession, and some were further afield, including one to Lake Tyers in East Gippsland where Jean, Miss West and two rangers, Ethelwyn Leonard and Bertha Wigg, camped under the mahogany gums, close to the sea. Jean started to compile an album she called 'The Book of Our Camps' for Eva West and recorded their camping trips and nature experiences in stories, poems, photographs and sketches.[39] Each camp had its special moments. At Lake Tyers, it was watching a flight of swans pass over at sunset. A camp on the Morwell River, deep in the Strzeleckis between Boolarra and Gunyah, was memorable for the quiet evening walks on a track above the river, 'listening to the river speaking with its many voices, the cries and crooning of night birds, the little noises of the trees and leaves … evening scents …warm Pennyroyal, and cool fern and gum, and each separate tree outlined against the stars and silver sky a new delight'.[40]

Jean's growing reputation as a botanist stood her in good stead for duelling with senior guide, Gwen Swinburne, when Jean suggested some modifications to tests for the naturalist badge. Rangers had to know six trees by their leaves, fruit and twigs and be able to recognise them 'at 50 yards distance'. Jean questioned the merits of identifying a tree fifty yards away. Miss Swinburne defended the test, setting up a scenario of a ranger seeing a tree from a distance of fifty yards, identifying it and then knowing if she could collect firewood under it, inspect its flowers and buds, collect bark or rest under it. The test was international and more suited to identifying northern hemisphere trees – it was unlikely that Australian ranger guides would come across birch forests or elm groves when they were out in the bush – and Jean felt the test should be changed for Australian conditions. As she commented elsewhere about eucalypts, 'no experienced botanist would undertake to recognise a tree at fifty yards – and it cannot always be done with certainty even if one lived among the trees'.[41] Miss Swinburne agreed to modify the test, and asked Jean to contribute notes on tree identification for the guide magazine, *Matilda*.

As well as guides, Eva West began to involve Jean in other community activities. Secretary of the Traralgon Horticultural Society, she appointed Jean chief botanist of the local wildflower show. Jean attended some of the horticultural society's meetings, but her description of a meeting in 1928, when she went to hear a talk by an expert daffodil grower, shows she was more of an observer than a participant, an outsider looking in. The meeting was held in a local hall with the fire lit on a cold August evening. Jean noted the 'quaint asides between the secretary [Eva West], and the big smiling silver-haired president', the 'elaborately indifferent glances' of the people in the hall towards the table where their competition flowers were being judged, the friendly sparring between the 'lady-who-wins most of the prizes and the gentleman-who-wins the rest'. She wrote of the exchanges of roots and cuttings among members and the humorous stories they shared of gardening disasters. There were sudden interruptions to the meeting when the secretary was called away on urgent council business 'and so on … until the evening is over and the cups washed and packed away after supper'. Eva West locked the hall door. She was holding a special flower to take home to her sister

Vera, a daffodil grower whose deafness prevented her from coming to hear the expert's talk. Jean saw Brown, Eva's dog, race to meet her, as he did after so many night meetings, and escort her home through the quiet Traralgon streets.

Ahead of Jean was the ten kilometre drive back to Tyers in the jinker, wattles to admire in the moonlight as she crossed the Latrobe River, and plenty of time 'to remember and smile over the evening'.[42]

Chapter 4

MAKING THE GARDEN

In 1922 Jean embarked on her dual roles as botanist and gardener. The year that she travelled to Melbourne to visit the wildflower show and returned with an entrée to the botanical world was also the year she began to garden in earnest. In 1922, the Galbraiths started turning the rough land around 'Dunedin' into a place of beauty that would become the famous garden in a valley. Jean's roles as botanist and gardener were often intertwined in the garden and both would provide the raw material for a lifetime of writing.

All the Galbraiths were enthusiastic gardeners, even though 'Dunedin' had been neglected for the eight years they had lived there, but recent changes made developing a big garden possible. The sale of the butter factory gave Matt time to devote to gardening and Amy also had more time as Angus had started school.[1] Now sixteen, Jean had settled into her role as the daughter at home and had both the time and passion to realise the gardening dreams she had nurtured since childhood. The boys were also keen on gardening and even though Lawrie was away at school in Melbourne, he joined in the gardening adventures during the holidays and often undertook heavy jobs that were held over until he was home.

In 1922, the house still sat in bare surroundings, in spite of the oak and the elm that shaded the house to the north, and Amy's and the children's gardens. At the front, apart from a path going to the front gate, there were only docks and couch grass between the house and the road. The Galbraiths decided to begin their garden redevelopment in this front area and add two long pathways to the east and west of the existing one. Their plan, like the house itself, was long and narrow. The clay soil had defeated earlier gardening efforts, so their first task was to plough the new garden and dig drains. Lawrie and Lance laboured on breaking up the sub-soil, trenching the waste and preparing the garden beds.[2] They knew that water would be a problem as their only supply over summer had to be pumped from the well.

There were no plans for sweeping lawns in the new garden. Instead, wildflowers and roses were early priorities. Matt, Jean and Amy began with a long wildflower border in the east of the garden running between the path and the orchard. Here, Jean planned to grow native flowers on a large scale. She now had a book to help her, Edward Pescott's *Native Flowers of Victoria*, which she had bought soon after her visit to the wildflower show, and included instructions on growing Australian native plants. She described it as 'the book I began on' and it became an indispensable reference as she worked on the wildflower border.[3] She followed a regimen of only digging up small plants from the bush, taking care not to disturb the roots, then potting them in well drained soil and leaving them for a year before they were planted in the garden, with plenty of mulch to keep the roots cool over summer. The 'Dunedin' mulch was one of their secret ingredients. Rich and moist, it consisted of well rotted oak leaves from the tree at the back of the house, placed in a tank, watered, jumped on by young Galbraiths to compress it, and then left to decay.

Running along the east path, the wildflower garden was linear and ordered and in no way resembled the bush gardens that were developed in the 1950s, influenced by the natural landscape. Instead, Jean's vision was for a drift of wildflowers and shrubs forming a rainbow of colour along the path. Her first planting included wattles, pomaderris, hakea, grevilleas, correa and bush peas, interspersed with heaths and other lower growing plants. Combining her roles as botanist and gardener, she kept a record of where she had collected the plants and noted their progress in the garden, how long they flowered, when they seeded and the conditions they liked.[4] This mid-spring entry on the wildflower garden's progress in 1927 reveals her record-keeping. 'Bulbine, Arthropodium in bud, Boronia muelleri, Tetratheca ericafolia, Olearia,

Hibbertia in full bloom. Flowers still on red correa, Bauera, Kennedya, late flowers of clematis and wonga vine whiten the bush house'.[5]

With hybridising of native plants and seed selection well into the future, there were successes and failures in the wildflower border, and it didn't quite grow as she intended, with some plants adapting to the new soil and conditions and others dying. But Jean's description of its colours during late spring in 1929, when thirty species were flowering, revealed her success and the beauty she had achieved: the purple, lilac and mauve of mint bushes, red-brown of parrot peas, gold of pomaderris, blue of lilies, red and gold of grevilleas.[6] At the southern end of the wildflower border, close to the road, was the garden's crowning glory, an early black wattle (*Acacia decurrens*) native to the Sydney region, that Amy had spent several years nursing in a pot until it was ready to plant in the garden. The wattle grew into a 'forty foot pyramid of whispering gold' and dominated the garden in late winter. It became an attraction in Tyers. Every August, neighbours came to visit the 'queen wattle', as the family called it.[7]

While the wildflower border was being developed, the Galbraiths were also preparing the garden for roses, their great love. Under Matt's care, roses had grown abundantly at 'Home', the cottage further up the hill, but when they moved to 'Dunedin', his attempts to grow them floundered in the heavy clay. Now that so much effort had gone into preparing the soil, they decided roses would be the central feature of the new garden. The middle pathway would become a 'Via Rosarius' or Way of Roses, with a series of arches sloping in waves from the house down towards the gate, each one covered in roses. *The Australasian Rose Book* replaced *Native Flowers of Victoria* as the gardening reference to study each evening and agonising selections had to be made as they were restricted to buying only twelve new roses for the first planting. These would be augmented by a bundle of cuttings that had rooted. Once the selection was made, the Via Rosarius was underway and Jean became a rose grower. Assistant to Matt, she was constantly delighted by the colours, fragrance and beauty of the roses and their seductive characters. She steeled herself to become a more ruthless pruner. They began to learn the roses that best suited their soil, aspect and climate. From the initial twelve roses and assorted cuttings planted in 1922, the garden was home to over a hundred roses ten years later. They formed perfect bowers over the central pathway and climbers began rambling along fences and up trees. Bush roses filled the beds between the pathways, growing among perennials and bulbs, while overly rampant roses were banished to the orchard. Each year there was the annual ritual of studying rose catalogues that were kept on a shelf within easy reach of Matt's chair, and making careful decisions on what to order on a limited budget. Before long, though, the Via Rosarius fulfilled their expectations. 'We live in a bower of roses just now', Jean wrote at the end of spring in 1929, 'again and again we walk up and down the paths storing the flower beauty in our hearts'.[8]

Garden historian Richard Aitken has described bush houses as 'that most Australian of garden buildings'.[9] Popular in the 1920s as places where ferns and delicate plants could thrive in a sheltered and sun-filtered environment, they ranged from basic huts of tea tree and wire netting to elaborately latticed and lathed structures. Jean and her parents had always wanted a bush house and were now ready to build one in the new garden. Their version was vernacular rather than elaborate, and it had a chequered career. Matt built the frame and then waited for the school holidays when Lawrie and Lance would be home and could help thatch the walls and roof with tea tree and paperbark. Jean recalled guiltily that several of the boys' school friends, who had come for a camping holiday at 'Dunedin', also provided labour, carting loads of tea tree and paperbark from thickets near the river on scorching January days. When the walls and roof were finished, Jean described it as a Wendy house, with its pointed roof high enough for tree ferns. Jean and Matt raided the garden for suitable pots to place in their new structure, but the real work of filling it had to wait until the autumn rains when they could collect ferns from the bush. After a few days of wet weather in April, they set off in the jinker, armed with bags and a spade, and drove into the damp forest to

Plan of Garden in a Valley

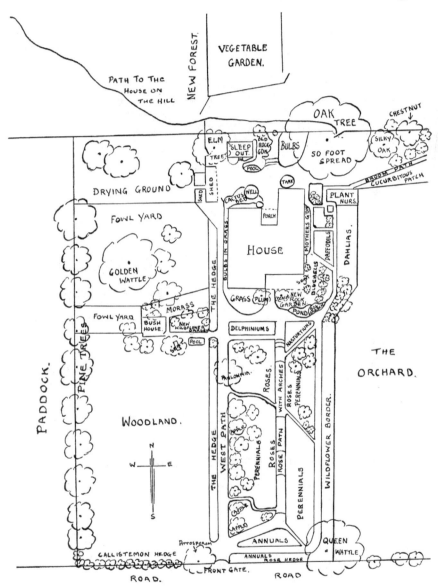

Plan of the 'Dunedin' garden, published in *Garden in a Valley* in 1939.

State Library of Victoria

the north of Tyers. When the track became too rough they left the horse and scrambled down into a fern gully where they filled their bags. The climb out of the steep gully, weighed down with ferns, was an exhausting one Jean did not forget in a hurry. Their bounty was planted in the bush house and seemed to thrive over winter and spring.

But in the summer, hot westerlies blasted through the tea tree walls and killed the ferns. The family felt remorse. 'When we thought of their cool gully home we felt we were vandals', Jean wrote later. The bush house was a dispiriting sight. Even worse, Jean's mentors from the FNVC, Charles Barrett and Edward Pescott, were coming to visit the garden. Urgent action was needed: dead ferns were removed and the boys were sent off with spades and sugar bags to the nearest fern gully. The replacement ferns were hastily planted and watered, and after a quick inspection the next day, Jean decided the bush house could pass muster.

After that, they boarded up the south and west walls and the ferns survived the hot summers. But Jean and her parents didn't follow all the bush house rules. '"Never plant creepers in a bush house", says every book on the subject', Jean wrote, 'and we agree that the rule is good, yet we do not observe it'. Instead, they brought creepers down from the hills, and soon the bush house was covered with crimson throated bells of the wonga vine and starry white clematis flowers. They also planted an East Gippsland passionflower that climbed around the door and added dashes of red. Their bush house was not perfect, Jean noted, but 'whatever failings there are inside, its exterior justifies its existence, so we would not change it'.[10]

An on-going project in the garden was reviving the orchard. When the family moved down to 'Dunedin', there were up to thirty stunted fruit trees growing to the east of the house. The pears were reliable bearers, but many of the other trees died before the Galbraiths began their garden development. After concerted ploughing and draining of the orchard area, as well as a strict pruning regimen, the survivors revived and gaps were filled with new trees planted under Amy's direction. These included eating and cooking apples as well as quinces, plums, cherries and citrus. They were unsuccessful with their first stone fruit, but tried again with different varieties of peaches and apricots.[11] The orchard at 'Dunedin' joined the long tradition of Galbraith orchards that had begun with the orchard planted at 'Nithsdale' in Beechworth.

Berries and nut trees were also planted in the orchard. A walnut was an early priority, as it was a tree Amy had wanted to grow since childhood, and Jean gave her one as a birthday present. 'I was not likely to forget it', she wrote as she described struggling along Elizabeth Street to Flinders Street Station in the heart of Melbourne with a five foot walnut tree in a pot, and then riding with it in the guard's van at peak hour.[12]

Jean delighted in the flowering cycle of the orchard. The white cherry plum blossom came first, followed by the plum trees, the pink peach blossom and the delicate pink of the quince. Then the apples started flowering, their crimson buds turning into snowy flowers. As both an aspiring orchardist and bird lover, Jean was prepared to share her produce with the parrots, lorikeets and currawongs, and reasoned that once the young trees grew there would be enough fruit for all. The trees' autumn colours added beauty to the garden, as did climbing roses that had been exiled to the orchard fence and the daffodils that were naturalising among the trees.

The family had brought two varieties of daffodils with them when they moved from 'Home' to 'Dunedin', and soon had enough to plant along the roadside as well as in the orchard. It was a revelation for Jean, though, when she walked into her first daffodil show, held in Traralgon in 1926, and was confronted by the alluring varieties on display. 'From that hour, I wanted daffodils', she wrote with steely determination, 'hundreds of daffodils, pale leedsii, short-cupped incomparabilis, poeticus and clustered poetaz, white and yellow bi-coloured trumpets, exquisite small barris, with their coloured cups …' The list continued. Most of the dazzling varieties at the show, she discovered, had been grown by Vera West, a sister of Jean's new friend Eva West. Vera was a passionate daffodil grower, with thousands of daffodils spilling out of the family garden in Traralgon during spring. An instant friendship was formed at the show as Jean rushed from daffodil to daffodil 'with the girl to whom these were all familiar friends'. The following autumn, Vera gave Jean a selection of bulbs – at least 24 varieties – to plant at 'Dunedin'. That first gift of bulbs – and the many more that followed – contributed to the glorious array of daffodils at 'Dunedin', filling the new beds and borders that were dug to accommodate them, and spreading throughout the orchard where they 'danced' in the spring.[13]

Jean had been making friendships among botanists but meeting Vera at the daffodil show was the first friendship she made through the garden. Vera was isolated by her deafness and Jean learnt 'finger talk' to communicate with her. They went on trips to Melbourne together, staying at the hotel favoured by country visitors, the Victoria in Little Collins Street. Vera was a frequent visitor to 'Dunedin' where she joined Jean on many rambles into the bush, and learnt about wildflowers. When Vera was away visiting friends in Melbourne in 1927, a year after the daffodil show, she wrote friendly letters to Jean about her activities at the club for the deaf in Jolimont, described Melbourne gardens she had seen and expressed her surprise that boys she went to school with had cars. The policeman in Traralgon had refused to issue her with a driver's licence. On this particular Melbourne trip, she had spent time in bookshops searching for books on Australian plants. 'There seem to be very few books written … When you find time amongst all your work I think you had better write one for us. You could do it beautifully', she predicted.[14] From Vera, Jean felt she learnt to see. 'I always leave her with an added feeling of serenity and appreciation of the loveliness of the world as seen through eyes alone', she reflected in 1928.[15]

It wasn't long before the house at 'Dunedin' was surrounded by trees, shrubs and flowers. Roses spilled over the arches, heath bloomed in the wildflower border, wattles added gold, and the orchard was full of pink and white blossom in spring. Cape chestnut, jacaranda, buddleia and paulownia added their colours. As the garden began to enfold 'Dunedin', Jean didn't feel that it was separating her from her landscapes. Instead, she saw the trees in the garden as a link with the valley. They were like outstretched hands, connecting the garden with trees in the paddocks and bush.[16]

Jean wanted to share the garden's bounty and began sending flowers to new friends and old. When the Elijahs bought a house in Camberwell in the mid-1920s, feeling rather countrified as they were surrounded by dairy cows and a flower farm, Jean sent cuttings for their new garden, both native and exotic, and regular supplies of cut flowers for the house. Mrs Elijah wrote to thank Jean for sending a 'box of sweetness', soon after they moved. 'The perfume of the roses went right through the house', she reported, 'a bowl for the front room, some for the bedroom and two red ones for Mr E's table, carnations for the wicker table in the front room'.[17] Jean sent flowers from the garden to Mrs Williamson, Mrs Barrett and other field naturalist club members.

She also wanted to join the hospital flower service and send boxes of flowers to Melbourne hospitals for patients to enjoy. The scheme was also known as the yellow box service because the boxes issued to gardeners – former kerosene cases adapted for flower transport – were painted a bright yellow, many with this inscription:

To brighten sufferings weary hours
Send sympathy expressed in flowers.[18]

The yellow box service had been initiated by the secretary of the Canterbury Horticultural Society, the eccentric and energetic H.A. Howard, whose enthusiasm had lifted the society from a nearly moribund state to one of the most active horticultural societies in Melbourne. Its calendar was filled with events, including a spring daffodil and wildflower show that Jean and Vera often visited, a show that seemed especially tailored for their interests. Jean even exhibited there in 1926, providing an installation described by a visitor as 'a scene of Wildflower Land in Gippsland, when touched with the brilliant heath blossoms in September'. It had a little stream running through a mossy valley of eucalypts, wattle and ferns, with colourful hardenbergia and heath.

There was even a grey fantail's nest hanging from a gum tree. 'The whole scene was a poetic fantasy, calculated to inspire city dwellers with a longing for the open spaces', wrote the observer.[19]

Four years after the garden's redevelopment, in 1926, Jean decided they had enough flowers to fill a yellow box every fortnight. The boxes travelled free on the railways and once she solved the problem of transporting them to the Traralgon railway station – by sending them in with the butter factory truck – she contacted Howard to ask about joining the scheme. His reply came on huge sheets of paper, with generously looped handwriting sprawling over them. Jean soon discovered that his idiosyncratic correspondence and flamboyant writing paper were cause for comment throughout the flower world. 'I have not read anything else that gives such an impression of breathlessness', she replied to Williamson's comments on the odd letters he had received. 'And the paper!' Jean continued. 'I had pink and yellow and yards of white from him and I remember Mr Pescott said he had brown – just ordinary brown paper!'[20]

The Galbraiths' flowers were sent to Ward XII at the Austin Hospital in Heidelberg, a men's tuberculosis ward with 40 patients, some of whom had little hope of ever leaving.[21] Jean soon fell into a routine of filling boxes every fortnight. Writing in 1927, she described her experiences of packing a box:

> It is a pleasure to pick the flowers in the evening and pack them, to line the boxes with cool damp paper and lay the flowers bunch by bunch, above the green that is to be put with them later, to hide here and there bunches of lavender and mignonette or treasured bits of heliotrope, wondering if they will be noticed among the brighter flowers … Then we fold the damp paper above them, lay a few more sheets on top, put in our return address label and they are ready for the morning when the kindly driver of the butter factory motor bus willingly carries them away to the station.[22]

The Galbraiths received courteous but brief replies of acknowledgement from the ward sister several times a year, but this changed when Grace Envall took charge of the ward. Sister Envall was a flower lover and wrote appreciatively to Jean about the flowers and their effect on the patients. This was the beginning of another friendship that sprang from the garden, as Sister Envall and Jean placed letters in the flower box that shuttled between the Austin and 'Dunedin'. Jean often included wildflowers in the box and Grace wrote of the 'whiff of the bush' when the lid was opened. She described the cheering effect the flowers had in the ward and the patients' sitting room and of the pleasure the patients received when they arranged the flowers.[23] She gave Jean insights to what the flowers meant to individual patients, some immobilised and at risk of haemorrhaging, others up and about, slowly recovering after long periods in bed. From Grace Envall, Jean was able to discover the men's favourite flowers, and she began corresponding with them, sending Christmas cards she made and contributing flowers and foliage to the decorations that were a feature of the ward's Christmas festivities. One year, it was a bush camp, right up Jean's alley.

'Dear "Flower Woman"', wrote recovering patient Eric Dane in 1929, in response to Jean's request to know of the patients' favourite flowers. He wanted to see Australian bluebells. He had only been in Australia for three years and had been told that wild bluebells grew here. From his hospital bed, Eric Dane also wanted to give her something in return for the pleasure her flowers had given him:

> I hope you haven't read anything of Mary Webb because I want to introduce her to you as a slight return for your flowers ... Of all things she loved flowers and birds and little things. I suspect all her books have the same dear atmosphere of Mother Earth. I feel somehow you will like her very much.[24]

It took some arranging, but Jean was able to present him with a bunch of Austral bluebells (*Wahlenbergia*). She had planned to visit the hospital for the first time in October that year, on her way home from a holiday in Beechworth, and organised a supply of bluebells that she could collect *en route*. She set off from Beechworth with Auntie Em farewelling her at the station and reclusive Auntie Bessie waving goodbye from the verandah as the train passed. Jean always enjoyed seeing the wildflowers that grew along the railway line between Beechworth and Wangaratta, but on this trip they were especially welcome: 'a real relief from the two women who sat discussing intimate details of embarrassing diseases'. At Wangaratta, she boarded the Melbourne train. Waiting for her on the platform at Seymour, and holding a large bunch of bluebells, was former Traralgon ranger guide, Ethelwyn Leonard, now living in Seymour. The handover took place as other passengers rushed past to fortify themselves in the refreshment rooms before the last stage of the journey to Melbourne. 'I had asked her for some bluebells for Mr Dane', Jean wrote to her family from the Victoria Hotel in Melbourne, 'and she brought me the loveliest bouquet of delicate big ones with Blue Pincushions and Shell Grass and fine Hair Grass'.[25] When Jean gave Eric Dane the bluebells, another friendship was started with flowers. Eric Dane was soon able to go home and he and his family also became close friends with Lawrie Galbraith, who boarded near them in Kew while he was studying at Melbourne University.

There was one patient in Ward XII whose favourite flower was snapdragons. This was Walter Thornby, whose job it was to unpack the yellow box when it arrived. Walter was English, but he had also lived in South Africa, and his plant associations ranged from the hop fields of his Kentish childhood to the vegetation of the Transvaal, before coming to Victoria where his brothers were farming in South Gippsland. Jean and Walter began corresponding frequently and Walter gave useful feedback on the condition of the flowers when they arrived at the hospital. They experimented with sending flowers in different stages of maturity. As their correspondence grew, Walter wrote more about himself and his life: how he had tried to overcome his rudimentary education through study and 'self improvement', his love of plants and of all the trees he had grown. He told Jean about South African plants and he discussed religion. Confined in hospital, he planned gardens in his mind, and wrote about them to Jean, such as his idea of replicating an English hedgerow: 'and then where the bank widens … there will be primroses and violets. Thyme and peppermint would be a necessity; thyme in any part and mint in the damper parts. Then when we come to the tiny brook there must be watercress … '[26]

He was firmly of the belief that an occupied mind was important for fighting his illness. This included reading, study and exquisite needlework. He wrote of causing 'some notoriety' when he sent his tatting into a competition. The only male competitor, he did extremely well.[27] And he wrote of personal things – of how the state of his health had made it impossible for the woman he loved to return his affection. He wrote of accepting that he would not work again and of his on-going battle with the Immigration Department and its threats to deport him because of his ill-health. Jean and Walter developed such a close friendship through their letters that she invited him to 'Dunedin', in the hope that one day he would be well enough to leave the hospital. 'Perhaps you will come some day and see the garden and your own snapdragon bed', Jean wrote.[28]

The garden structured Jean's time with its daily and seasonal routines. It became friend and companion. Most mornings she was out early before breakfast, looking for new buds and opening flowers, listening to birds rustling leaves as the sun began to light the dew. During the day there was a constant regimen of digging and manuring, raising seeds, planting, weeding, dead-heading and cutting back. Then there were the big seasonal jobs. Rose pruning was a strenuous task for Jean, balancing at the top of a ladder, struggling to reach roses on the archways and forcing herself to cut back their prolific sprays. Mulching before the hot weather set in was another important task in a garden that couldn't be watered over summer, spreading the mixture of moist decayed oak leaves to help the garden's survival. The orchard generated its own seasonal routines, from pruning through to harvesting, followed by bursts of jam-making, bottling and preserving. The garden infiltrated her evenings. Sitting around the fire in the 'Dunedin' dining room, Jean, Amy and Matt pored over plant and seed catalogues, making plans, drawing up lists, deciding what to order and imagining future beauty.

The garden became an important part of their celebrations, especially at Christmas when the extended family of Galbraiths and Ladsons gathered under the oak tree. There was one exception, the Christmas of 1928, when Lance was recovering from diphtheria. That year, as they emerged from a period of quarantine, Jean, Lance, Amy and Matt walked up to the 'Ingleside' garden fence in the afternoon. Their relatives had gathered on the verandah to play Christmas carols and hymns for them. The three violinists – Uncle Fred, Uncle Tom and Dick – with Auntie Fan at the organ, played 'Hark the Herald Angels Sing', 'While Shepherds Watched' and then 'O Come All Ye Faithful', and lastly 'Lead Kindly Light', 'Uncle Tom's favourite', as Jean remembered.[29]

Christmases returned to normal after the diphtheria episode, and an account Jean wrote in 1930 shows the important role the garden and its flowers played at Christmas. In the days leading to Christmas it was harvest time above her on the hills, where workers were busy stooking hay. Below her, the Latrobe had flooded and the flats were covered with water 'as blue as the sky and shimmering with silver'. Jean was immersed in flower preparations. Her first task was to make tiny bouquets of pansy and maidenhair for the patients and nurses of Ward XII at the Austin. The next day, soon after sunrise, she was out picking flowers to fill two yellow boxes for the ward's Christmas decorations, a floral clock. Jean placed the boxes in the jinker and drove them into Traralgon, stopping first at the shire offices where more flowers were waiting for her in Miss West's office, dropped off by local gardeners for the Austin's decorations: 'fragrant bunches of carnations and stocks and glowing snapdragons, and a bright multitude of pansies, which I especially wanted for Ward XII'. There were enough flowers to fill another three boxes and Jean delivered these with the 'Dunedin' boxes to the railway station. The frogs almost deafened her when she drove home along the causeway over the flooded river flats.[30]

On Christmas morning, Jean was up early picking flowers again. This time she was gathering roses for the West family, an annual tradition. Her

Uncle Fred delivered them when he drove into Traralgon after dinner to collect the Ladsons for the family celebration at 'Dunedin'. The focal point for the gathering was the 'Dunedin' oak. Angus had set out chairs, logs and rugs under its spreading canopy, and tables were scattered ready for afternoon tea. Thirty people gathered in the garden that year: 'Dunedin' Galbraiths, 'Ingleside' Galbraiths, Ladsons from Traralgon, and campers and relatives who had come to stay. 'We like to think that our campers have gone home refreshed', Jean wrote after Christmas, 'both the three white-faced city boys and the two older couples (aunties and uncles whom we rejoice to see on the rare occasions when they leave their suburban homes for the bush where they used to live)'.[31] 'Dunedin' with its country garden was an antidote to the stresses and strain Jean associated with city living.

The garden had been providing flowers to comfort people with debilitating illnesses; it was also becoming a restful place for the tired and convalescent. This was combined with Jean's new found talent for helping and comforting people, now that she had conquered her shyness and was making friends through botany and the garden. Returning from a trip to Melbourne late in 1931, she mused over the people whose hearts had been opened to her 'that I might enter and sympathise, each one a privilege, a responsibility and a new discovery'. Among them was Fanny Hodgson, whom Jean had met through the Field Naturalists' Club. Her husband had died after two years of illness, leaving Fanny exhausted and without hope. Jean thought the garden might give her peace and rest and she came to stay with the Galbraiths in January 1932.[32] On Jean's urging, Fanny went on to Inverloch where she could rest near the sea. Jean wrote a series of letters, suggesting strategies to help her deal with her feelings of hopelessness, ways of making her home less lonely, and encouraging her to find companionship in friendship. When Fanny returned to Melbourne, she wrote of her appreciation to Jean: 'You carried me over these few months. You have been so good, you made me try to pull through … I dreaded coming home but it was easier than I anticipated'.[33] Soon after her return, though, she discovered she had breast cancer and died several months later, possibly resorting to suicide. Her brother passed on a note Fanny had left for Jean, as well as a parcel containing all the letters she had received from Jean. Fanny hoped they could be made into a book 'to comfort others' – the way she had been comforted.[34]

From the mid-1920s, when Jean walked down the hill from 'Ingleside' to 'Dunedin' at night, she could see a 'city of lights long and low in the west'. It was Yallourn, a town that barely existed in 1922 when she had begun planting the first roses in the Via Rosarius. Underneath the tea tree thickets and swamps of the Latrobe River valley lay the world's largest reserves of brown coal, and in 1921 the State Electricity Commission of Victoria (SEC) was poised to exploit the resource and provide Victoria with a statewide electricity supply. That year, the chairman of the SEC, engineer and war hero General Sir John Monash, gathered with other dignitaries on a former dairy farm to witness a ceremonious turning of the first sod, as work began on building the Yallourn power station. The industrial complex of power station, briquette factory, open cut mine and model town built to house the SEC workers, became the 'city of lights long and low in the west' that Jean could see from her hill at night, and where machines and technology were dredging coal, generating electricity and bringing modernity to the state. The works whistle, souvenired from the *Emden*, a daring First World War German raider, was heard around the valley, including Tyers, as it sounded the shifts and smokoes at the power station and open cut, and provided a competing schedule to the daily routine of dairy farmers.[35] The process of digging up the valley had started.

Electricity was connected to Tyers in 1923 and wires like 'three silver cobwebs' dipped across the 'Dunedin' paddock to the house.[36] Life became easier with electric light and there was also the prized acquisition of an electric stove, a gift for Amy and Matt's twenty-fifth wedding anniversary.

It replaced the wood stove and became a 'wonderful boon' for Jean and her mother in summer as it turned the kitchen from the hottest room in the house to the coolest.[37] Although these comforts of electricity came courtesy of changes to the valley in the 1920s, Yallourn remained little more than a nightly twinkling of lights in the west. Jean, occupied with studying the native flora in the valley and tending her garden, was unaware of the implications of digging up the valley for coal.

Her dual roles of botanist and gardener were responsible for a garden that was different from many other 1920s gardens, due to its mixture of natives and exotics. Her love and knowledge of native flora sent her out hunting for plants and seeds in the bush and she reintroduced to the garden the wildflowers that had grown there before the land was cleared for farming. Her love of exotic plants led to arbours of climbing roses, dancing daffodils and garden beds filled with fragrant stocks and carnations. As a result, wattle and eucalypt shaded the garden with oak and elm; delphiniums and dahlias nodded to grevillea and bush peas; banksia roses and native clematis spiralled up trees. Jean's passion for botany and gardening were intertwined in the 'Dunedin' garden and would provide the inspiration and outlet for her other love: writing.

Chapter 5

CORREA

'I'm afraid all chance of getting the Town Hall for the next Flower Show has gone up in smoke', H.B. Williamson wrote to Jean early in 1925, after a fire had badly damaged the Melbourne Town Hall.[1] The club managed to book the St Kilda Town Hall instead, but members became increasingly concerned as the date of the wildflower show approached. It had been a dry winter and late spring, and many of the plants weren't in flower by early October. There were still many highlights, though, including the 'glorious' Sturt's desert pea sent from Broken Hill, making its debut appearance. Jean had extra responsibilities at this show. Williamson had given her space for a special Traralgon exhibit, and she had brought to Melbourne over 100 species of local wildflowers to display. She juggled the display with her usual role at the classifying table, identifying and labelling the flowers that arrived from around the state and the country.

In the crowds milling around the exhibits was Ralph Boardman, editor of a new gardening magazine, the *Garden Lover* (later renamed *The Australian Garden Lover*), launched in April that year.[2] The magazine was already well known in field naturalist circles, as several members were regular contributors. Edward Pescott solved readers' gardening problems in an advice column, while Charles French, who was also government entomologist, contributed a monthly 'Chat About Insect Pests'. Boardman was an accountant whose love of gardening and literature led to his work as a director of the Horticultural Press and editor of several horticultural journals. He was also secretary of the Nurserymen and Seedsmen's Association of Victoria, a group under attack from the FNCV for its neglect of Australian plants. But Boardman was interested in promoting native flora in the *Garden Lover*. During the afternoon, he was introduced to Jean, who now had a reputation among her fellow field naturalists as an experienced native flower grower. Boardman gave her a copy of his magazine.[3]

Jean wrote to thank him and their conversation continued by letter. 'We should like to do our best to encourage the knowledge and love of Australian wild flowers', Boardman wrote, 'and would appreciate the opportunity of publishing notes from you, on the subject'. He was impressed by her writing style. 'To have notes from you, written in the same happy strain as your letter … should assist, we think, in making known the beauty and utility of our native flora'.[4] By the end of December, he shelved the idea of 'notes' and instead asked Jean to write a series of monthly articles on Australian native plants. He suggested his nineteen-year-old contributor use a pen name for the series and cast around for a name that captured the essence of Australian flowers. Acacia, he considered, was overdone, and suggested Epacris.[5] But Jean chose her favourite local wildflower, a flower with vibrant red bells and a soft musical name: Correa.

When readers of the *Garden Lover* opened their February issue in 1926, eager for information on how to increase the productivity of their vegetable gardens, grow exhibition-standard chrysanthemums, or keep up a colourful display of annuals in their front gardens over summer, a new feature was waiting for them, 'Australian Native Flowers' by Correa. Drawing on her botanical knowledge and gardening experience in the wildflower border, Jean planned to introduce readers to Australian native plants and how to grow them in home gardens.

Her first article was colour-coded and described the blue wildflowers growing in January, and the pink wildflowers of February. The flowers that featured in this article mostly grew in the hills behind the Galbraith farm, or along nearby creeks. She described the native lobelias that could be found on dry hill tops in January, and encouraged the garden lover to collect seed to grow in the garden. She wrote about the Austral bluebells, so prolific that

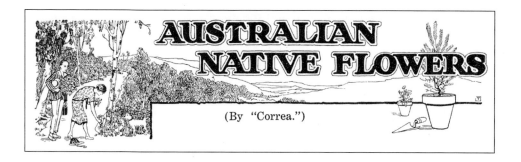

Masthead, 'Australian Native Flowers'.
The masthead for Jean's series in the *Garden Lover* showed the bush as a source of native plants for the garden.

Garden Lover, February 1926, State Library of Victoria

they made swathes of 'perfect blue' along roads and flat hill tops, and yet were unknown in home gardens despite being easily grown from seed. In February, the 'pinks' were in full bloom, including hyacinth orchids, their tall red brown stems ringed with pink flowers, but not suitable, she warned her readers, for transplanting. There were everlastings – flecked with pink, frilled with rose – soon ready for collecting seed. And even though they were not pink, she couldn't resist telling the readers about sweet bursaria because in February the riversides were filled with their creamy blossom and sweet scent. She gave readers instructions on how to collect sweet bursaria. Use a sharp trowel to lift the young seedlings growing under the older plants, she wrote. Wrap them firmly in moss or grass and take them home to grow in pots. A year later, plant them in the garden. 'Put them in a corner where they have room to stretch their thorny arms and they will give you the joy of blossom, and the scent of summer riversides'.[6]

Despite her inexperience, youth and shyness, Jean's writing was confident and assured. In the tradition of garden writers, she followed the flowering cycle through the year, but her rhythms were those of the bush: heath in June, peas in September, orchids in October and lilies in November. Jean had to combine the observation and training of a botanist with the skills of a writer as her articles were not illustrated and she was aware of the readers' ignorance of native plants. They knew all about popular garden plants of the 1920s, such as roses, chrysanthemums, gladioli, irises and dahlias. Iceland poppies were also a great favourite and many readers had watched their furry caps part to reveal slits of colour and release crinkled petals. But how many readers had observed a eucalypt bud open? How many had seen the cups and caps part to reveal neatly folded stamens that curled back to form a mist of pearl, red, pink or yellow around an upright style? The dresses of gumnut babies in May Gibbs' popular children's book, *Snugglepot and Cuddlepie*, may have been the closest many of Jean's *Garden Lover* readers had come to inspecting eucalypt blossom.[7]

Jean's inspiration came from her landscapes, and place and story began to supplant the botanist and gardener. The articles changed from garden writing to nature writing as she broke free from the template of the flowering year, and gave way to an irrepressible urge to write the stories of plants in places she knew intimately. After a visit to one of her favourite places, Tarra Valley in the Strzeleckis, story and place took over from flower description and helpful hints. 'I meant to write to-day of the varied beauty of Australian Daisies', she began her January 1927 article, 'In a Fold of Hills', 'but I have been among the hills, and the joy of their songs and silences must be told'.[8] There was an urgency to share this special place with her readers, and to write of her passion and joy.

Ditching the daisies, she took her readers to the hills of mountain ash and cool temperate rainforest instead, and wrote of flowers, ferns, berries, fruits, leaves and tendrils. Some of her readers may have known the Victorian Christmas mint bush that was flowering in the hills, but she also drew their attention to the blossom on the towering mountain ash, just visible far up the hillsides 'like dim white clouds'. It was easier to see the blossom floating in the still water of the creeks or as fallen flowers that spotted the roadside. She wrote about the creepers hanging from trees. The clematis, its flowers finished, now had a new beauty of feathery fruits. 'From tree to tree hang the long brown ropes of its stems and its green tendrils wreath the tree fern fronds'.

She wrote of the scent of the forest. There was Austral mulberry, which people who lived in the hills called orangewood, 'its orange scented leaves breathing sweetness as one brushes past'. But even more sweetly scented was the musk-daisy bush, 'with broad leaves dark above and silver below, with white Daisy-like flowers, whose starry florets have fallen now'. She told her readers of the purple appleberry, its flowers starting to fall: 'It is a strong and graceful climber, with narrow dark green leaves, and long bells, yellow green just touched with indigo, that in the autumn will be replaced by big berries of purple blue, even lovelier than the flowers'.

Many of the plants, she told the readers, were easy to grow. They had been carefully moved to the Galbraith garden, or had grown from seed collected in the hills. But although she was writing in a gardening magazine, her article didn't end in the garden. She took her readers back to Tarra Valley, the 'fold in the hills':

> I have told you of some of the treasures that enrich the hills; seek them, cultivate them when you can, but to know their full beauty, visit the stream sides where they grow ... where tree ferns mix with gums and maiden hair brushes the water ... and the silver air is tangled in mutable loveliness of scent and song.[9]

Her article, 'As the Days of a Tree', published a year later, also showed her shift from gardening notes to nature writing. It was a carefully constructed essay that began with Jean driving on a bush road through a peppermint forest on a sunny morning after rain, with the raindrops still glistening on the trees. The colours dazzled her:

> Orange twigs and ruby stems threaded the maze of leaves, and, in a mystery of colour, yellow deepened into green and crimson paled through pink to orange and bright gold or darkened into ruddy brown. Tremulous globes of silver and spots of shrill white fire threw lances jewel bright across the air as the sunbeams shattered their glory on the drops of rain ...

'That', she told her readers, 'was my first conscious awakening to the glory of the Peppermint'.[10]

From her memories of a magical drive through the wet peppermint forest, she then told the life story of one particular peppermint that grew in the paddock next to the garden, a remnant of the woodland that once covered the slopes around Tyers. She described its annual cycle: the round clusters of blunt-topped buds that burst into a creamy mist of stamens when the caps fell off, through to the seed ripening in the green and yellow cups in autumn. She wrote of the tree as shelter and shade but also as companion, as daily she saw its beauty in the morning sunrise and admired its glow in the last rays of light in the evenings.

Through the pages of the *Garden Lover*, and writing for home gardeners, Jean developed her own voice and style as she wrote about Australian flora. Without illustrations, it was only through her words that she could evoke the infinite variety and exquisite loveliness of the flowers for her readers. But she wanted her articles to be more than descriptions of flowers or even nature appreciation. She wanted her readers to experience the beauty of the bush through her writing, to 'know' the bush and feel that they were there, to hear its music and sense its rhythms.

As nature writer Mark Tredinnick argues, Australia, compared with America, has a very limited tradition of nature writing, a genre he prefers to call a literature of place. He suggests many reasons for this, including the absence of a tradition of essay writing in Australia. He asks if Australian writers had 'gone into the landscapes of a big and arid island armed too much with the literature of a small lush island', too steeped in the imagination of the English romantic poets. He questions whether the land with its sparseness and low relief defeated the lyricism and wonder of the nature essay. He considers the strangeness of Australia's flora and fauna, alien to European settlers, and he considers the impact of Australia's urban society, a nation whose literature belongs more to the city than to the country. Yet in 'Australian Native Flowers', Jean Galbraith was writing a literature of place infused with lyricism and wonder. She gave voice to place, told its stories and, as Tredinnick claims of nature writers, brought the landscape to a second life in the imagination of the readers.[11]

Although Jean hadn't read Reginald Farrer's books until the late 1920s, after she had started writing her *Garden Lover* series, there was some similarity in her articles with his writing style. Farrer, who was a plant hunter, rock gardener and writer, is credited with greatly changing the style of English garden writing, of having 'dragged garden writing into the area of *belles-lettres*'.[12] Among the garden writers he influenced was Vita Sackville-West, who saw him as half poet and half botanist and who admired his 'extravagance as well as his accuracy'.[13] Full of adjectives, well chosen verbs and metaphor, his writing evoked the character of plants, their colours and textures. 'His style is nearly perfect', Charles Barrett wrote to Jean in 1927, as he urged her to read Farrer, 'his enthusiasm for wild plants delightful'.[14]

Significantly, Jean was also writing differently from her mentor nature writers, Donald Macdonald and Charles Barrett, whose nature writing, as historian Tom Griffiths has argued, was pre-occupied with 'boys, nature, race and war'. Their promotion of a masculine culture of nature appreciation had been influenced by their war experiences – Macdonald in the Boer War and Barrett in the First World War – and the importance of defending the nation.[15] Jean's writing was not concerned with empire, race or the relationship between native flora and nationhood. Instead, she wanted to share the transcending joy that she experienced in nature, a joy of similar intensity to that experienced by William Wordsworth in the Lake District in England and John Muir in the Yosemite Valley in California.[16] Jean's passion for nature, however, sprang from her faith, from her love of the natural world created by God. Through her writing, she wanted people to see and experience the beauty that God had created; she wanted 'to tell the beauty of all those things which have their being in Him'.[17]

And she saw that beauty around her. Donald Macdonald, writing articles from his invalid's bed, was still dreaming of England. He wrote to Jean in 1932 – 'good Australian that you are' – of 'old England which was ever appealing to me as the cradle of the race', and described a walk he would like to take with her through English landscapes.[18] But Jean didn't dream of such landscapes. Nor was she interested in 'nationalising nature'.[19] Even when writing about wattles, a species potent with national symbolism, Jean's discussion was anchored by place, reflection and beauty. She delighted in the loveliness of the wattle, and she wanted to share her wonder at the many varieties that grew in one location. [20]

Sitting on a grey log on a hilltop near her home, Jean described in a *Garden Lover* article the different varieties of wattle she could see from her vantage point. Nearby were the varnish wattle with sulphur yellow bobbles and sharp, sweet scent; the golden wattle with the deepest of all wattle gold; the drooping bushes of sallow acacia; the long leaf wattle with its rich gold; and the feathery black wattle. Down by the Latrobe River flats she could see lightwoods. And on the sandy slopes on the other side of the river, she described the shrubby wattles that grew there: spike acacia, spreading acacia, juniper acacia and prickly moses. Her writing captured the place of the wattles in the landscape, their diversity and individual characteristics, their perfume, colours and beauty. Several months before her article was published, Melbourne nurseryman, W.R. Warner, had deliberately omitted recommending any gums and wattles in his *Garden Lover* article on small trees for the home garden because of the 'monotony' of native trees. 'With the majority of good Australians', he declared, 'I love the Gums and Wattles but then we can have too much of a good thing'.[21] Several months later, writing from her hilltop at Tyers and drawing on her delight in what she saw – rather than her duty as a 'good Australian' – Jean could dispel any perceptions of the 'monotony' of the bush. In her article she referred to T.C. Wollaston's *Our Wattles*, a book with helpful advice on growing Australian wattles, but she omitted the rhetoric on how wattles represented Australian national characteristics of generosity, youth, friendliness, optimism, prosperity and promise for the future, sentiments that permeated Wollaston's book.[22]

'Australian Native Flowers' continued from February 1926 to October 1935 and covered a diversity of topics. Now mostly forgotten and overshadowed by Jean's later garden writing, the series features nature writing that celebrates Australian plants. Although Jean later described this writing as immature, it merits re-appraisal as a significant and evocative contribution to Australia's limited nature writing tradition.[23] Importantly, the articles also express Jean's sense of botanical belonging and harmony with the local environment. They reflect her family history and connection through love of the landscapes and native plants. Jean was the granddaughter and great-granddaughter of selectors who had come to Tyers in the 1870s to establish a farm on timbered slopes stretching down to the Latrobe River. The landscape that she knew fifty years after they arrived was cleared farmland, bordered by roads that were fringed with remnant vegetation of the pre-selection days, and with pockets of bush. Her articles reveal how, as a young woman, she sought to bring the bush to her garden at Tyers, and re-introduce the trees, shrubs and flowers that her family had cleared. Australian garden historians have written of the significance of memory in the gardens planted by settlers. Through filling their gardens with the familiar plants of the homes they had left, memories of Britain and 'home' were perpetuated, and the 'unfamiliar was made familiar'.[24] For Jean Galbraith, a settler Australian who was gardening in the 1920s and felt at home in the Australian bush, the familiar was the Australian bush. While her garden, too, was a garden of memories, it perpetuated different memories. It linked her with the bush.

'Have we not learned', she asked her readers in 1927, 'that the glory of the garden is not alone of scent and beauty before our eyes, but also of memories and associations that cannot be numbered?'[25] She explained what she meant by 'a garden of memories', writing of a woolly pomaderris in her garden that came from a nearby riverside. 'We look at it and remember the mingled "sound and radiance" of the water, the hills, calm and green, folded endlessly one upon another, the Pomaderris itself a creamy golden cloud that rested in the valley … [W]e hoped to keep that beauty near us'. She spoke of a sheoak that she could see from a window and 'each year we remember a hill where its companions grow, a stony hill netted with the regal loveliness of Purple Coral Pea circled with Bursaria, blossoming now above the stream it loves, and crowned with Sheoaks like dark spires of pines'. A silky hakea in the garden takes her back to a day spent scrambling down Hakea Hill to a golden carpet of guinea flower, and looking over a cliff to a creek almost lost in ferns, pink bells and golden bush peas.[26] She doesn't just recall the occasions; the plants help her to relive them.

Her life and daily routine provided the material for her articles. Following her 'In a Fold of Hills', she wrote regularly about the rainforest in the national parks of Tarra Valley and Bulga Park, her special places.[27] The articles appeared after visits there with Miss West and the shire auditors, with mentors Charles Barrett and Edward Pescott, on guide excursions or after Galbraith family trips in Uncle Fred's car. Articles on the coast at Inverloch followed family camping holidays where Jean, now an experienced camper, was chief cook and bottle washer, but still had plenty of time to observe the vegetation in the dunes. The 'rainbow shores' of Tooradin found their way into an article after an FNCV excursion to the mangroves of Westernport Bay. Visits to her grandmother in the granite country of Beechworth provided material for articles, while the flowers and trees from the Grampians featured in the *Garden Lover* after Jean returned from her post as resident botanist at the Tourist Bureau's nature study camps. Most of the articles, though, were inspired by familiar haunts close to home: along the Walhalla Road or the Tyers River where she had been collecting specimens for Williamson; the heath lands in the hills near 'Dunedin'; the view from a log looking towards the Latrobe River; a peppermint tree growing by the west fence.

Through 'Australian Native Flowers', Jean was carrying out the aims of the FNCV: to promote knowledge and love of Australian plants and encourage growing them in home gardens. Her field naturalist mentors admired her articles and were quick to congratulate her. 'The articles are just what is required and should help the appreciation and the fostering of our natives',

Williamson wrote in February 1926, after reading her first article.[28] He took on the self-appointed task of reporting any printing errors, misspellings or inconsistencies of citing that he could find in the published articles. Edward Pescott recognised Jean as 'one of the leaders of the younger generation who will carry on our work – especially in the love and popularising of our beloved flowers … I'll watch with joy for the first book by Jean Correa Galbraith'.[29] Donald Macdonald also encouraged her, commenting after reading one article that 'it all strengthened my belief as to your destiny which is to write more and more and more and more'. He commented on how the 'Australian colour is all yours … You use it lavishly yet not in excess.' He also offered advice, reminding her that 'the touch of nature which makes the whole world kin is also the human touch':

> Don't crowd out the human element but look for it and risk having to drag it in by the neck to get it there … just life as you are privileged to know it in your Gippsland hills.[30]

The articles flushed out people throughout Australia who, like Jean, had been experimenting with growing native plants. C.R. Scott of Hampton, who had a large native section in his suburban Melbourne garden, wrote suggesting that a society of native flower lovers could be formed where members could exchange plants and seeds. T. Richardson from Western Victoria offered to send Grampians seed, while R.H. Fuller of Bowenville in Queensland, keen to grow grevilleas after reading one of her articles in the *Garden Lover*, offered to exchange Queensland plants for grevilleas. Reading Jean's article on waxflowers, Mrs Gannon from Artarmon in New South Wales sent Jean native seeds in her letter and thanked her for 'stimulating people's minds to the beauty of our Australian plants'. Hilary Dowling of Olinda in the Dandenong Ranges, an expert rock gardener, wrote to Jean about exchanging cuttings and told her that the articles 'do much to increase the love of our native plants'. Jean's wildflower garden began to reflect the gifts of her readership, with plants from other parts of Victoria and interstate adding to its beauty. The readers' letters revealed that around Australia there were dedicated native flower growers experimenting in isolation with seeds and cuttings in their own gardens, and learning from trial and error, as the Galbraiths had done. They were delighted with Jean's articles because she expressed their passion for native flora and was introducing Australian plants to a wide readership.[31]

Some of the readers, like Fred Barton, a young man from Sperm Whale Head on the Gippsland Lakes, became lifelong friends. Fred was an accomplished gardener and naturalist from a young age. His home was on an isolated peninsula on Lake Victoria where it hadn't been possible for him to row the long distances to the nearest school. Much of his boyhood was spent studying the wildflowers around his family farm, and he was influential in having nearby land reserved as the Sperm Whale Head National Park in 1927, to protect the ribbed thryptomene which was not found elsewhere in Victoria.[32] Like Jean, Fred had been influenced by H.B. Williamson. He became a keen member of the FNCV, an exhibitor at the wildflower show, and a passionate grower of native plants. After Fred Barton's first letter to Jean in 1927, they spent many years exchanging cuttings and seeds, and sharing information on cultivation methods.[33] Their correspondence, and that of many other *Garden Lover* readers who were experimenting with growing wildflowers, demonstrated the generosity and cooperation that existed between native flower enthusiasts, and the informal networks that began developing among gardeners who were inspired to grow Australian natives with little help from the horticultural industry.

Garden Lover readers also expressed admiration for Jean's skills as a writer and her ability to combine botany and literature, plaudits that had been extended in England to Reginald Farrer for his garden writing. In a letter to the *Garden Lover*, Helen White from Queensland singled out the 'graceful articles like those written by "Correa", to whom I should like to say a special word of thanks'. As another reader wrote, 'I wish I had the ability of your wonderful Correa that I could give you a description of the plants and flowers of the Grampians'. Further afield, a reader from Otago in

New Zealand wrote of receiving 'the greatest pleasure' from 'the charming literary (as well as botanical) articles by your contributor Correa'. Readers praised Jean's combination of natural history and writing: 'What a wonderful knowledge she has of natural subjects, especially of birds and plants. And her command of words to express her knowledge is truly remarkable', was one reader's opinion.[34]

Nurserymen also began corresponding with Jean. Some contacted her for seed supplies after they had received orders from readers of her articles. Was she the young lady who writes under the *nom de plume* Correa, nurseryman Charles Duncan wanted to know, and could she supply seed? Herbert Rumsey of Rumseys Honest Seeds in New South Wales wrote to Jean because he had heard from a 'mutual friend' that she wrote 'the "Correa" stories'. He congratulated her on the 'interesting way' she wrote about growing Australian plants. Jean was able to supply him with some Victorian seed that he needed, even providing seeds of sea box, boobialla and seaberry saltbush for a gardener from Florida who had read her *Garden Lover* article on coastal flora and had placed an order with Rumseys Honest Seeds.[35]

Showing a flash of entrepreneurship, Jean tried to develop her ad hoc supply of native seeds and plants to nurserymen into more of a business in the early 1930s. Unfortunately it was just at the time when Australia was plunging into depression. Acting on advice from Boardman, who suggested she try exporting to New Zealand, Jean secured an order from Harrisons' Nurseries at Palmerston North. She engaged a shipping agent and sent a consignment of 500 pots of heath and 24 pots of correa to Wellington. But although Harrisons were pleased to receive the plants, there were no follow-up orders. T.H. Brunn Garden Service in Melbourne took 50 correas in 1931. The same year, Law Somner, seed merchants and 'art florists', displayed sprays of her red correa in their window in Block Place in the city, but they did not receive any orders. '(T)hings are very slack in the plant trade in Melbourne at the present time', a Law Somner representative told her.[36] The depression challenged Jean's efforts to find a niche supplying native plants.

Her most successful venture was supplying a Melbourne nurseryman with pots of correa, heath, wattles and tetratheca to sell each year at the FNCV wildflower shows.

When Jean first started writing the articles, Edward Pescott wrote an appreciation of her work in the *Garden Lover*. 'I must express my appreciation and delight at the articles by "Correa", who writes on our native flowers. The articles are charming and accurate too. A stroll through the bush with Correa would be a great pleasure'. Possibly to safeguard her anonymity, he concluded: 'Long may he continue his enthusiastic stories of our bush wonders'. This unleashed discussion on Jean's gender. Readers wanted to believe that the ardent and sensitive writing of Correa was that of a woman, and many expressed their disappointment at discovering Correa was a man. Among them was 'Hortuland' who felt 'surprise and disappointment to know that Correa was a man. He writes more like a woman'. The editor had to intervene: 'We are pleased to be able to dispel Hortuland's disappointment – "Correa" is a woman, as her writings suggest', wrote Boardman. [37]

Jean's involvement with the *Garden Lover* increased, as Boardman recognised her writing talent. She was given the post as resident poet when Boardman tried to 'Australianise' Christmas, through celebrating the festive season with Australian plants, 'flowers of the colour of hope and joy', rather than 'dark drooping firs' of the northern hemisphere. He asked Jean to write a poem that would have 'happy thoughts' about Australian flora and Christmas in Australia to accompany an article on Australia's 'Christmas' plants, so-called because they flowered at Christmas. They included blandfordias, the reddish orange Christmas bells of Tasmania and New South Wales; the mauve Christmas mint bush in Victoria; and the New South Wales Christmas tree with its holly-shaped leaves and red fruit. Most dramatic of all, instead of a traditional holly wreath that had featured on the *Garden Lover* cover the year before, the December cover of 1926 featured the flaming orange flowers of the Western Australian Christmas tree, the *Nuytsia*. Accompanying the article was Correa's poem, 'A Christmas Prayer'. [38]

Soon Jean was writing two new series for the magazine: 'Australian Beauty Spots' and 'A Gardener's Bird Friends'. She was aware of the irony of compiling 'Australian Beauty Spots'. As she admitted to Williamson, 'it is rather ridiculous that I should write the series at all for I know very little of Victoria but the editor said "Write about the places you know and perhaps by the time you finish them you will have new ones"'.[39] Her aim in 'A Gardener's Bird Friends' was to increase the readers' appreciation of native birds in the garden by convincing them that any damage to flowers was easily compensated by the birds' regular feasting on insect pests. The first article focused on thornbills, voracious consumers of the rose grower's nemesis: aphids.[40]

Jean began publishing in other venues. In 1927 Charles Barrett commissioned her to write an article for a special bird issue he was editing for the *Victorian School Paper*. Drawing on her childhood experiences of exploring the tea tree thickets along the Latrobe River, she wrote an article, 'The Tea Tree World', that revealed the secret world of birds making their homes there. She received fulsome praise from Gilbert Wallace, general editor of the *Victorian School Paper*, who was greatly impressed by her writing and the originality of her contribution. 'You have filled my day with refreshment', he wrote after receiving her article. 'I read it aloud to a rapt audience which enjoyed to the full your true and delicate touch and the fine and emotional sensibility that prompted it. I have not seen for years a bird article that moved me so ... It will bring joy to thousands'.[41] The article was published in the October issue of the *School Paper*, to coincide with Bird Day, and attributed to '"Correa", a lady of Gippsland, Victoria'. Wallace requested more articles, and this set Jean on the path of writing nature stories for children. Jean also began writing regular nature articles for the *Leader*, which had been the venue for her first publication in the children's pages in 1917, and she contributed to *The Argus* and *The Age*.

By 1930 and approaching her mid twenties, Jean had settled into four roles. She was Correa, the garden and nature writer; she was a botanist developing expertise in Australian flora; she was an experienced gardener who had helped to transform a rough paddock into a beautiful and creative garden; and she was the daughter at home, running the house in tandem with her mother, caring for her brothers as they came and went from school, university and work, nurturing visitors who came to convalesce at 'Dunedin' and helping her father on their small farm. She constantly expressed her contentment with her life and surroundings. At her twenty-fifth birthday in 1931 she spoke of not wanting to be elsewhere than 'this perfect valley which becomes each year more beloved'. She found it 'beautiful beyond expression'.[42] Unlike many fictional heroines who needed to leave the confines of home to realise their ambitions, Jean accepted the role of the daughter staying home to care for parents and relatives. Yet at the same time she achieved a career from these very surroundings: the bush in her 'perfect valley' that led to her interest in botany, the home full of books that fostered her love of words and writing, the landscapes that inspired her and the gardening experiments that led to expertise in growing native plants and provided material for her first commissioned writing.

Arriving home from Lawrie's graduation ceremony in 1930, Jean wrote to H.B. Williamson: 'Here I am safely at home again, settling down to an accumulation of work – two articles to write, plenty of gardening, plants to mount, and visitors'.[43] Writing was now part of her routine. The *Garden Lover* and 'Australian Native Flowers' provided Jean with an apprenticeship that inducted her to the rhythms and discipline of writing monthly articles. The articles had encouraged the development of her own literary and autobiographical style as Correa, where she wrote not just about plants but about her landscapes and place. They gave her a readership and a reputation and became the venue for significant nature writing that helped gardeners around Australia to experience the beauty of Australian wildflowers and consider growing them in home gardens. The series also became the crucible for one of Jean's most significant relationships.

Chapter 6

GRANDFATHER

When Jean received her complimentary copy of the *Garden Lover* at the beginning of each month, she turned to the children's pages first. *Garden Lover* was committed to encouraging children to garden, as Boardman had promised in his first editorial. '[W]e must not forget the boys and girls', he wrote in April 1925. 'These young horticulturalists, and many are under ten years of age – are our coming citizens, legislators, and men and women of affairs. The love of horticulture implanted in the plastic years of youth will yield a harvest of public-spirited citizens with high ideals'.[1] 'Our Children's Section', edited by Uncle Dick, alias Boardman, made its debut in the *Garden Lover* in December that year. Uncle Dick invited young readers to send in letters and stories about their gardens and he also started a birthday club, posting packets of flower seeds to children during their birthday months. One of the first contributors to send in a story to the children's pages was not a child but, as Uncle Dick hinted, a grandfather. It was an engrossing story of a competition between four children and their grandfather to see who could grow the tallest sunflower. After this, young readers of the children's section were called sunflowers.

Grandfather continued writing to the children's section and became the oldest sunflower in the birthday book. Auntie Correa was also a contributor, and sent in poems and stories, including the Greek legend of the sunflower. In spring 1927, Grandfather organised another sunflower competition, not just for his grandchildren but for all the readers of the children's section. They were issued with giant Russian seeds and instructions on how to grow them. Throughout Australia, children planted the sunflower seeds, lavishing them with care and attention, constant watering and fertilising. Progressive measurements were published in the *Garden Lover* as stalks shot up and flower heads formed. At one stage Grandfather's was the tallest, but at the final tally, Mervyn Callender from Yea won with a 305 centimetre sunflower. Jean's young brother Angus was third; his sunflower measured 277 centimetres.

When Jean read the children's pages in March 1927, she was intrigued by a letter to Uncle Dick sent in by a young sunflower likening the feathery leaves in his carrot bed to a fairy forest. The image appealed to Jean, a lover of fairies and fairy stories, and she wrote a poem about vegetable gardens being fairy forests that she sent to him care of the *Garden Lover*. Grandfather – who, as it turned out, *was* the letter writer's grandfather – wrote to Correa and told her of the delight the poem had brought to all the family. Inspired by her 'Australian Native Flowers' series, he asked in a second letter for advice on establishing a native garden at his home in suburban Melbourne. 'Why not bring a bit of Correa's enchanting "bush" into my own garden even as she does so lovingly … ?'[2] Jean's generosity with supplying plants and seed swung into gear and she sent a box of wildflower seedlings, crowned with a spray of red correa. Grandfather was especially pleased to receive the spray of red bells. Although a devotee of Correa's articles, he was ashamed to admit he didn't know what a correa was.

John Inglis Lothian, alias Grandfather, was a Scot and proud of his heritage. He had worked in a Scottish publishing firm before coming to Melbourne with his wife and young family in 1888 to establish a business representing British publishing houses. This led to extensive travel throughout Australia and New Zealand, securing book orders for the firms he represented. His son Thomas joined the business in the late 1890s and expanded it to form a publishing arm, although his father was dubious about this development.[3] It became very successful and authors published by Thomas Lothian included well-known names in Australian literature: Miles Franklin, Henry Lawson, E.J. Brady, John Shaw Neilson. John Lothian retired from the business in 1912. A portrait painted by Frederick McCubbin shows a white-bearded elder statesman – or grandfather – with a kind and thoughtful expression. He had a lifelong interest in gardening and horticulture and had once owned an orchard in Ringwood.

When Lothian started corresponding with Jean in 1927, he was a widower in his seventies, living in a house in York Street, Mont Albert, called 'Tantallon' after a castle near his birthplace in East Lothian. The north end of York Street was a Lothian enclave. Living at 'Tantallon' were his sister-in-law and three daughters. Elizabeth was a classical scholar and teacher who was active in promoting tertiary education for women.[4] Lily was also a teacher and Isabella was soon to leave home to marry a Gippsland farmer and move to Bunyip. His son Thomas, daughter-in-law Effie and their four children lived several houses down the road, and there was much coming and going between the two households. Lothian's eldest grandson Noel inherited his grandfather's passion for gardening and studied horticulture at Burnley. He later became director of the Adelaide Botanic Gardens.[5]

Lothian led an active life and retained an interest in the family business. Gardening, reading and letter writing were staple activities, and to these was added the novelty of 'listening in' to the wireless. There were regular excursions into the city: visits to the Athenaeum to borrow books and read British newspapers, concerts at the town hall, trips with his grandchildren to the museum and the Botanic Gardens. On Sundays, he did the rounds of services conducted by Melbourne's prominent non-conformist ministers. A deeply spiritual man, he was in search of intellectual as well as spiritual nourishment. Every Sunday night there was a large family dinner at Thomas and Effie's house, where Lothian read aloud to his appreciative family after the meal.

Lothian's and Jean's correspondence sprang from a love of gardening and children, and from Lothian's desire to establish a native garden, influenced by Jean's articles and his admiration for her 'rare gift' as he described it – her nature writing. There was an instant and mutual delight in their letters. 'I had to go telling my people "Ah ha! I got a love-letter today"', Lothian wrote after receiving Jean's parcel of native plants and accompanying letter, 'and when they heard or read it, they all said "yes it is". And I know it is: for it has made a fine easy feeling round my heart ever since'.[6] They felt they already knew each other through the pages of the *Garden Lover*, and that they shared a spiritual commitment and a love of beauty. Their letters were long, frequent and full of joy.

They organised to meet for the first time in early October, when Jean would be in Melbourne for the 1927 wildflower show, and chose the Botanic Gardens as an appropriate venue, as well as meeting in the tumult of the wildflower show. There was nervousness on both sides. Jean let Lothian know that she was 'a plain ordinary spectacled person' and 'not lovely and graceful like the real Correa'.[7] Lothian set out to reassure her: 'Never mind the specs. You will always be "Bonnie Correa" to me'.[8] Jean also warned Grandfather that she would need something botanical to commemorate the occasion, similar to her first meeting with Donald Macdonald at Black Rock: ' … we must certainly steal seeds from the Botanical Gardens to mark the day!' she told him.[9] Lothian wasn't so sure …'I dinna ken about the stealin', he wrote in his 'auld Scots', but agreed to be an accessory to the crime: 'You do the stealin and I'll be Receiver and Pocketer'.[10] Jean was on the look-out for maple seed to plant at 'Dunedin'.

They met at the Office Gate, near St Kilda Road, and neither party was disappointed. The day started in sunshine but there was a quick shower that, as Jean remembered, 'turned the lake to blurred silver and left the gardens tender'.[11] Several days later, after staying in Healesville with her orchid mentor Edith Coleman, Jean was back in Melbourne, waiting to catch the 10 o'clock tram in Collins Street and spend the day with Grandfather. Lothian met her at the tram stop and escorted her to 'Tantallon'. 'And what is more', he wrote, 'to have had your bonnie meeting and parting kiss which came so quietly and maternally, like mother and child (though which was which t'were hard to say) made me feel both very blessed and very humble. It was a great gift and I shall try ever to be deserving of your loving confidence'. He had sent her his photograph several months before, and, like Jean, had been worried the original could be a disappointment. 'Happy me to have come through the ordeal', he wrote.[12]

Jean and Lothian soon discovered a shared passion for books and this became a major part of their correspondence as they discussed the literature they loved. Where H.B. Williamson's correspondence provided Jean with a botanical education, Lothian's contributed to her literary education and intellectual development, providing Jean with an opportunity to discuss what she was reading. They enthused about their mutual love of the romantic and Victorian poets; their letters were full of quotes from Wordsworth and Coleridge, Keats and Shelley, or from Lothian's beloved Blake or Jean's beloved Browning. Lothian even dubbed Jean the 'Shelley of the bush', so highly did he regard her writing. They wrote of their passion for Walter Scott's novels, and particularly of their admiration for the social thinker and art critic, John Ruskin, also regarded as an 'apostle of beauty'.[13] They read through much of the literature and philosophy of the ancient Greeks, enriched by Elizabeth Lothian's knowledge and commentary. They constantly revisited Dante and Shakespeare.

With a lifetime of reading behind him, his work in the book trade and his knowledge of contemporary literature, Lothian was able to introduce a conservative Jean, who had read very little modern fiction, to contemporary writers. He lent her books of essays and introduced her to travel writing. He sent her biographies. When he parcelled off a biography of William Morris for her to read, he described Morris as a man with 'a passion for all things bright and beautiful, as seen in our world of Nature's wonders and beauty, and in the common everyday life around us'. He felt Morris was someone with whom Jean had a lot in common: much of the same 'underlying spirit'.[14]

Like another friend, Eric Dane, Lothian urged Jean to read the contemporary writer Mary Webb, whose novel *Precious Bane* had received sudden posthumous acclaim when British prime minister, Stanley Baldwin, declared it a neglected work of genius a year after the author had died.[15] Lothian wrote of the resonances in Jean's writing with that of the internationally famous Mary Webb. Mary Webb's inspiration came from her landscapes, the Shropshire hills, and she wrote about them in her novels, poems and essays. Although much of her life was tortured by disfiguring illness and anxiety, her love of nature was transcending. Jean was seduced by *Precious Bane*, the book's heroine Prue Sarn, and Webb's depiction of early nineteenth century Shropshire. She even dreamt about it.

Lothian also urged her to read Webb's nature writing published in *Poems and Spring of Joy*. 'I wonder if you have seen it. If not you <u>must</u> as soon as you can, for she is very near to Jean, indeed like an Elder Sister', he wrote.[16] Mary Webb had written her nature essays in the early twentieth century, at the onset of her illness when she was in her early twenties, but, like her novels, they did not receive wide circulation until after her death. In the essays, she wrote about the healing power of nature, and how, steeped in beauty, joy and laughter, nature could be accessible to all.[17] Although their lives were very different – Jean happy and sustained by a deep faith – both spent girlhoods exploring their countryside, Mary the meadows, hills and lanes of Shropshire and Jean the hills, fern gullies and heathlands of her Gippsland home. Their close observation and delight in nature translated to fervent celebrations of nature's beauty and profundity, when they were in their early twenties. Their writing was filled with insights that helped people to see, share and enjoy that beauty. 'She is a "big sister" indeed', Jean replied to Lothian after reading *Spring of Joy*, 'so "far ben" that I can never hope to reach her, and how perfectly that she says all that I would say. She has written my thoughts (told far more perfectly than I could tell them) in her Spring of Joys'.[18] She was particularly struck by Webb's essay on an aspen that was full of colour, motion and music. 'The Aspen is particularly the full and perfect picture of what I have tried to say in many tree biographies, but especially in the first about the Peppermint some years ago and in the tale of the Sheoak (last year)'. Quotes from Mary Webb began appearing in her *Garden Lover* articles.

As well as books, Jean and Lothian shared a passion for music and wrote about it constantly. Jean's love of music had brought her to Melbourne in 1925 to attend a Melbourne University vacation school taught by Dr A.E. Floyd, a lecturer at the conservatorium who was also organist and choirmaster at St Paul's Anglican Cathedral, and a radio broadcaster. Her friendship with Dr Floyd endured after the classes finished, and on Melbourne visits she would often go to St Paul's, find a place near the stone arches of the darkened cathedral, and listen to the choir rehearsing or Dr Floyd practising the organ. Sometimes he gave her a private organ recital. She wrote about these special times to Lothian, of sitting on the high seat at the organ, feeling 'the world for the time being all music – you know how it is sometimes' and then leaving the cathedral to plunge into the late afternoon crowds and hurry across to Flinders Street Station to catch the Gippsland train.[19] In this way, many of her visits to Melbourne closed with music: 'music that sang in my memory as I watched the city change to town, the town to open fields, the fields to bush'.[20] In return, Lothian wrote regularly of the concerts he attended, the records he was listening to or the programs he heard on the wireless, including the regular commentaries of Dr Floyd and Fritz Hart. Both Jean and Lothian agreed with Floyd that music had the power to transform people's lives.[21] At her visits to 'Tantallon', Jean and Lothian always listened to records – Jean did not have a gramophone at Tyers. 'Music in its deepest joy is almost worship to me', Jean wrote.[22] She confessed to Lothian how much she missed music in the country. It was the one great joy of the city that she couldn't have in her valley, the experience of hearing 'real, revealing transcending music'.[23] Her kind neighbour, Mrs Ivey, often invited her to hear concerts that were broadcast on the wireless, but Jean was reluctant to accept the invitations, knowing that the only music Mrs Ivey enjoyed was community singing, and that she preferred talking to listening.

Few letters passed between Mont Albert and Tyers without discussion of the two gardens. Plants, seeds, tubers and cuttings passed between Tyers and Mont Albert, and formed a living link. Lothian reported on the progress of his bush garden, and the admiration it received from passersby in York Street, some of whom were invited 'to wander through and be introduced to our Coolgardie Gum ... which I call the "Shrine of the Bush"'.[24] Jean's letters described her garden with the same lyricism as her *Garden Lover* articles.

Lothian also became a writing mentor, encouraging Jean's writing and suggesting new publishing outlets. Impressed by her contributions as Auntie Correa in the children's section, he suggested to Boardman that Jean act as Uncle Dick while Boardman travelled to Hawaii and the west coast of America as a delegate to the Pan Pacific Conference on Education, Irrigation and Recreation, leaving his assistant, Winifred May, to hold the fort, including editing the children's pages. Lothian thought Jean could 'bring distinction' to the children's section, especially after he read Miss May's 'Cabbage', an article encouraging children to write a poem on a cabbage, which he found 'prosaic and helpless'.[25] Jean became Uncle Dick and thoroughly enjoyed writing gardening articles for children, answering their letters – trying to sound like bluff, hearty Uncle Dick as much as possible – and keeping her new role a secret from Angus and her young sunflower Ladson and Galbraith cousins who were contributors to the children's pages. When Lothian sent her notes to include in the children's section, he signed them 'your dutiful nephew, Grandfather'. He was disappointed when Jean wasn't asked to continue as Uncle Dick after Boardman's return from America.

'Jean it's a gem', wrote Lothian after reading her article on the lifestory of the peppermint, 'Of the Days of a Tree', and declared that few writers could do what she achieved, including Charles Barrett.[26] He suggested she write a series on gum trees, and she did write more 'tree biographies', as she called them, later discovering their synchronicity with Mary Webb's writing. After reading 'Rainbow Shores', he wrote of how he was dazzled by the colours in her article and linked Jean with Turner, Ruskin and Shelley as 'revealers ... of the beauty around us everywhere'.[27] Lothian was convinced Jean's writing deserved a wider audience than readers of the *Garden Lover*. When he read an article Boardman sent to the Melbourne *Herald* while he was away in the United States, describing the popularity of eucalypts and wattles in California, it set him thinking. 'Well what about getting in touch with horticultural papers and magazines in S. frisco and Los Angeles', he wrote to Jean. 'I can imagine American Nature lovers enthusing over Correa's writing and becoming quite a vogue'.[28] He discussed his idea with Boardman who thought it worth pursuing, and Lothian helped to see the idea through to fruition.

Although self-deprecating about her work, and also fearing rejection, Jean was keen to publish and in 1929 she wrote two articles she felt could be of interest to gardeners in America: 'The Flower Year in Victoria' and 'Australian Wattles'. The writing in these articles was more restrained than her *Garden Lover* series. Boardman had suggested the articles be illustrated, and she asked F.J. Bishop, a member of the FNCV and an enthusiastic native flower photographer, if he could supply the images she needed for the articles: wattle, heath, sweet bursaria, fringe lilies, native violets, mint bush and purple coral pea. Bishop was keen to collaborate and congratulated her on her intention to 'advertise our unique flora and also our country in that land of stuff and Bluster'.[29] From her small country post office in Tyers, Jean sent off a package containing the two articles and photographs, addressed to the *Gardeners' Chronicle of America*, 522 Fifth Avenue, New York.

Editor Dorothy Ebels sent a prompt reply to Mr Galbraith of Tyers, expressing her appreciation of the two articles, and inviting him to continue the series.[30] Where *Garden Lover* readers had been disappointed to think of Correa as a man, Ebels assumed the enterprising and knowledgeable writer was male. 'Australian Wattles' was published in September 1929 and 'The Flower Year in Victoria' appeared in November. Both were published under the name Correa. As the 'Flower Year in Victoria' contained more of an introduction – telling *Chronicle* readers that Australians had read of American wildflowers such as golden rod, purple asters and the pearly arrowhead, but that 'little of the radiance of our bushlands reaches you' – Jean may have intended this article to be published first. While the articles were heavy with names and lists, Jean was able to include enough description that, combined with Bishop's photographs, gave a sensory dimension to her writing:

> And so December ends the year with long, bright days when yellow everlastings flower. Burgan (Kunzea peduncularis) foams along the valleys and white Woolly Teatree (Leptospermum lanigerum) bends across the waters of every mountain stream. Christmas bush (Prostanthera lasianthos) is tall and gracious in her filmy robes of white and heliotrope, while her sister, the Balm Mintbush, fills green hillsides with her clear lilac blossom…[31]

Both Jean and Bishop were satisfied with the rates the American magazine paid, but the first payment, a cheque for $US11, had been made out to Mr James Galbraith, and was difficult to cash. After being informed that James was Jean, Dorothy Ebels sent international money orders to Mr Jean Galbraith as payment for the articles, and Jean/Correa continued to write regularly for the *Gardeners' Chronicle* during the 1930s, including articles on grevilleas, goodenias, gums, box, climbers, olearias, boronia, heath and correas.[32]

The international articles enhanced her reputation with her field naturalist colleagues and mentors, impressed that a young member of their club (she was 23 when she sent the first articles) was promoting Australian flora in America. H.B. Williamson was particularly responsive when she sent him the magazine containing her first article. 'It is no mediocre publication and you are fortunate in getting a footing in such a fine journal', he wrote. 'I am very pleased with your article, it is exactly what they want I should think'.[33] Soon, *Chronicle* readers in America were writing to Mr Jean Galbraith of Tyers via Traralgon with requests for seeds.

While Lothian had been instrumental in encouraging her to write for an American audience, he also sowed the seed for writing a book. 'Does Mr Boardman ever think of making a book from a selection of your GL articles?' he asked in 1931, commenting on the 'good material' that was available. 'I don't doubt but the book will come along in good time and may I be here to see and welcome'. Every year he raised the idea again. 'I would dearly like to see your Book (as Book it will be some day) before I go hence', he wrote in

1933, 'is there no prospect or word of it?' He continued to champion her work with Boardman, feeling that Jean had enriched the *Garden Lover* more than any other contributor. In a 'kind of farewell letter' he sent to Boardman when Lothian was in his mid eighties and felt he could no longer contribute to the sunflower pages, he wrote that 'the "Correa" articles had been the golden thread running through every number of the GL ever since I knew it to the present day'.[34]

Jean's response to 'the book' reflected her mixture of self-deprecation and quiet ambition that was fuelled by her need to celebrate the God-given beauty of flowers and show it to others. '"The book" is hidden in my mind', she wrote, 'and though perhaps I could bring it forth, very few, if any, would want it'. But also, aged 25, she was aware of waiting, hoping and learning and quoted some lines from Indian Nobel laureate Rabindranath Tagore's poem 'Waiting' that expressed how she felt:

> The song I came to sing
> remains unsung to this day.
> I have spent my days in stringing
> and unstringing my instrument.
>
> The time has not come true,
> the words have not been rightly set; [35]

In her letters, Jean was sharing with Grandfather her thoughts and, as she put it, 'all the details of my life'.[36] She liked writing to him on Sunday afternoons, in the quiet of her room, after the peacefulness of the morning service. Besides books, music, poetry and gardening, her letters were full of daily routines: early morning rising and how she appreciated the 'precious' hours between five and seven; of doing the housework that had become so routine it provided a good backdrop for reciting poetry. She told him of the electric appliances that were added to the home that made life more comfortable, mostly courtesy of Lawrie who was working in the engineering school at Melbourne University, and Lance, who had finished studying at

Melbourne High School and was beginning his training as a primary school teacher. Besides the electric stove there was the electric fan Lance gave the family, with its 'intelligent-seeming turning', and the feel of its breeze.[37] There was the electric radiator Lawrie gave her for her birthday, which meant she could write her articles and letters in a warm bedroom in winter, away from the distractions of the household and the sleep-inducing open fire. His gift of a typewriter for another birthday enabled her to type articles for publication, after first drafting them in longhand.[38]

Jean wrote to Lothian about the new friends she was making locally. Arriving in Traralgon in 1931 was Ree (Alice) Fry, whose husband had come to teach at the high school. Ree Fry was also a teacher, but had resigned when she married, complying with Education Department rules. This did not stop her teaching in an honorary capacity though. The Traralgon school now went as high as Intermediate [year ten], but students still had to leave for Melbourne to complete their secondary education and this, as Jean explained to Lothian, was too expensive for most at present. Ree Fry stepped into the breach, and began teaching the school's Leaving students in her home, among them Jean's cousin Verna Ladson. Jean was impressed by Ree Fry's selflessness, and soon discovered she shared a love of books, music and gardening. On visits to Traralgon, Jean often called in for lunch at the Frys' home in Mabel Street, high above the town, exchanging books and leaving with prized copies of the *Times Literary Supplement*.[39]

More intellectual stimulus came from another new friend, Anne Burnet, whom Jean met on one of Eva West's camping trips. Heading off to Eden and Twofold Bay in New South Wales, the party consisted of Miss West, Jean, Anne Burnet and a young Traralgon woman whom Jean described as a 'happy, healthy, unimaginative girl'. Besides writing about the joys of the holiday, Jean enthused to Lothian on 'the discovery of Anne':

> I had hardly expected to find – near here especially – a girl my own age, who has helped her brother turn an uncleared block into a farm, has built her own poultry houses and made her own garden from a rough bracken

patch, who ploughs and milks and keeps house for her brother, and who can discuss with intelligent interest Bergson or Haldane's or Eddington's books, colour problems or eugenics or medical research, her brother not the farmer is a doctor [Macfarlane Burnet], and who loves poetry as we do – can quote Browning almost as readily as I can – Shelley more readily and who enjoys or is familiar with all those books that are part of our very life.[40]

She wrote so often about the beauty of her valley that she had to ask if she wearied him. She also shared with Lothian the transcending joy she experienced from nature. 'Oh you Beautiful! You Beautiful!' she wrote of the beach at Inverloch as she described the full moon rise and light the waves from black to milky fire. 'The sunsets are wonderful here too – amber and rose behind the cleft rock of Eagle Rock – peach and amber reflected on the wet sands and in between a tumult of foam and broken fire'.[41]

Lothian visited Tyers on one occasion. It was stimulated by the momentous decision in 1928 to travel to Scotland to see family and old friends again. 'How is this sensational happening going to affect you and me?' he asked in February, and decided to make a quick trip to Tyers before he sailed.[42] His letters had been circulated around the family, and everyone – Galbraiths, Ladsons, the Wests, sunflowers – looked forward to meeting Grandfather. Jean was pleased that she could now show him her valley. Lothian took morning walks along the bush roads, trod the well-worn track up to 'Ingleside', and accompanied Jean to nearby bush haunts. The Traralgon flower show coincided with his visit and he made a guest appearance. Miss West drove them to the mountain ash forest and fern gullies of Bulga Park. Lothian was impressed by Jean's 'wistful but very capable companion Miss West', as he described her, and he was 'very proud' to have her as their driver. Only Vera West avoided meeting the visitor. 'Vera wishes that she could have met you, but was shy and afraid of troubling you by the difficulty of speech', Jean explained.[43] The three days were over too quickly and Lothian returned to Melbourne on the crowded Friday night train, sustaining himself with tea and raisin bread from the refreshment rooms at the Warragul station, and thinking back over his visit, appreciating how 'all your dear people had so lovingly entertained me'.[44]

Instead of writing to Mont Albert, Jean was now sending letters to Fremantle, Ceylon, Suez, London and North Berwick in Scotland, where Lothian stayed with his brother. He wrote to her about the countryside and flowers, visits to historic sites, people, concerts, books, long walks, excursions to his childhood home and the beauty of the English spring that delighted him when he arrived. Jean agreed it would be 'very bonnie to see England but while I am here I find beauty unfailing in our young eager land' and described sitting in mid-winter sunshine in her garden, watching a thrush take nectar from the red heath and poise to 'scatter his joyous silver music through the sunshine'.[45]

It was while Lothian was away – perhaps the physical distance gave her the impetus to express her thoughts – that she broached a subject that she knew they would not agree on, but one she felt she had to raise because it reflected her 'most precious thoughts'.

> I am moved now to say something of my most precious thoughts because they are so constantly in my mind … On details of religious beliefs I think that you and I differ in many ways – I have not spoken of these differences (to me often important) because I thought you preferred it so, yet in one special hope I would that we were one. Perhaps we may be – indeed probably for we both know the words "The son of man shall come in like manner as ye have seen Him go", and in those words is the thought and hope I mean. It is not to me a far off hope, but as certain as the night follows day – and is succeeded by day again; now it is something that may happen in the far future – but something very near – so near that it may be now or tomorrow or after a few years – but cannot be long.

This belief explained who Jean was, how she lived her life, her concept of time and her motivation for writing.

> So you see why I do not continually fear parting from you – for that parting may never be, why I do not sorrow more for a friend who cannot hear – for soon I may speak to her, why I do not seek to become popular through my writing – because my thoughts are but a feeble star soon to

be overwhelmed in the brightness of the sun. Yet as I said "it may be years" and in the times of waiting I would give you what pleasure I can, and take from you the refreshment that your letters always bring, even as I seek to put some more knowledge of beauty into the world through my writings and to enjoy in her silent years Vera's companionship.

I have no doubt expressed only part of what I mean – but it may explain why time feels so unimportant to me. Of course one cannot feel like that all the time. Even in my happy life, which in no way … would I wish to change, there are times of greyness and despair, when work seems useless and little daily interests but a weariness. But it does not last – hope and faith are too strong for that, and soon, knowing that "He who shall come will come and will not tarry" I am glad again and rejoice in the beauty of "the time vesture of God", and in my power, small though it is, of showing that beauty to others.[46]

From Scotland, Lothian struggled to reply to her letter. 'But Jean dear, I fear, – I fear, for I cannot say I see eye to eye with you on the question you ask'. He, too, had been aware of their difference during the 'blissful' year of correspondence. He stressed their underlying faith of 'believing that our chief blessing is in "loving and serving the highest and the best" and further that our fullest inspiration for that comes from our love of the Lord Jesus Christ'.[47] Ultimately, Jean had to accept this, writing '(w)hatsoever be your thoughts of this, in love of beauty and so love of Christ we are still undivided'.

Before leaving for Scotland, Lothian had expressed some disquiet that Jean, who wrote long, rapturous and intense letters, put so much energy in writing to an 'auld, auld man' – aware that he was 76 and she was 21 – and tried to limit their correspondence to writing fortnightly. Possibly he was concerned at the depth of his own feelings. He expressed his hope that a 'bonnie laddie' would appear on her horizon and constantly repeated this hope when he returned from his trip. 'You must not be disappointed if the dear life companion you wish for does not appear', Jean wrote in 1931.

Five and twenty may be over young for making pronouncements, and we cannot see the future, but so far there is not even "a little cloud as big as a man's hand". Or even the faint suggestion of anything to indicate the coming of such a companion … So let come what will come, I neither seek nor avoid it in this matter, being assured that "in whatsoever state I am in I shall be content". Because such companionship may be the greatest and fullest and most enriching way of giving oneself, lacking it one need not be unhappy – but rather greatly rejoice in all the other fair and lovable things of life.[48]

Jean was expressing to Lothian her contentment with her life, whether married or single, and drew on the quote from Philippians – 'in whatsoever state I am in I shall be content' – to emphasise her acceptance of her life. Unlike many young rural women of the 1920s and 1930s who regarded marriage as the means to a fulfilling life, Jean was not actively seeking a marriage partner. This was something Lothian conceded, telling Jean that she was 'not dependent as most women are on the man coming along', even as he continued to express hopes that someone was waiting in the wings.[49] As a Christadelphian, Jean was expected to marry within her faith but, as she explained, there was no-one presenting as a marriage partner.

In the 1930s, some members of her family thought her feelings for Walter Thornby, the flower-loving patient she had met at the Austin Hospital, were deeper than friendship.[50] When Walter was well enough to leave the hospital, he was a frequent visitor at Tyers and also became a Christadelphian. The family invited him to live at 'Dunedin' and built a sleepout for him in the garden. Walter had two happy years there, immersed in all the activities in the garden, but became very ill in 1934. He knew he was dying. His humour persisted in diary entries – 'did some needlework today with the idea of defying death with a needle and thread' – and he wrote of his regret that he hadn't planted all the avenues of trees he had planned, but his diary also recorded his pain and despair.[51] He was admitted to hospital in Traralgon in November. Jean went to stay with the Wests and sat with Walter at the hospital, reading to him. He died several days later.

When she told Lothian of Walter Thornby's death, she explained the nature of their relationship. It was not that of lovers:

To me, Walter was dear as a beloved son may be to his mother and to him his love for me was next to the love of God ... he was glad and content though he knew the limit of what I had to give. Surely I am richer for the perfectness of that companionship – richer for the very completeness with which he filled my thought though it was not with the passionateness of maids love for man, but only deepest tenderness. Had it been otherwise with me the wound must have been much sharper.[52]

Although she had lost his 'perfect companionship', she was relieved that Walter's suffering was over.

Her family continued to hold a range of opinions on Jean's attitude to marriage. When he was a teenager in the 1950s, her nephew Peter Galbraith asked why she didn't marry. Her reply was that she hadn't met anyone to whom she felt attracted in that way.[53] Her cousin Verna, however, believed Jean actively didn't want to marry. She remembered Jean saying that after she turned 25 she felt safe. 'No one will ask me now'.[54]

As a young woman, some of Jean's deepest emotional attachments were with her mentors, older men with whom she corresponded and who were prominent in their fields. Their letters provided her with education and guidance. Through her correspondence with H.B. Williamson she became a botanist; Uncle Charlie in England provided literary criticism; Charles Barrett guided her reading and writing; Donald Macdonald encouraged her inspiration from nature and her nature writing. When Williamson died suddenly in 1931, his family turned to Jean for advice on what to do with his botanical papers and famous herbarium. She left immediately for Melbourne. Jean, at 24, felt his loss deeply: 'every happiness had a heart of lead' was the way she described the year that followed his death.[55] When Donald Macdonald died nearly two years later, she felt herself more able to cope with loss. But while Williamson had been a 'teacher and beloved friend', her connection with Donald Macdonald was more intimate and complex. The year he died, Macdonald had written many times to Jean of what their relationship meant to him. Jean was 'the one in the world, the particular one, the very dear one to whom one's thoughts go thronging often', he wrote in 1932.[56] In another letter, he told her: 'It is odd Jean these moods in which I find myself wanting to talk to you like a godfather one moment and like a lover the next moment and knowing that you at any rate will find in it nothing incongruous or absurd for if there is one thing I do know that I understand in you my dear, it is your understanding'.[57] Jean felt a similarly deep connection with Macdonald, as she explained to her Uncle Charlie after Macdonald's death: 'Donald Macdonald was like another part of myself and seems to be part of me still'.[58]

Through letters, Jean had also established an intense relationship with Lothian that continued until his death in 1940. While they met several times a year when Jean was in Melbourne, their conversations were mostly through letters. '(S)urely we are more fortunate in our letter companionship than if we had only the more fleeting companionship of "face to face"', Jean told Lothian.[59] She often re-read his letters, and expressed what they meant to her: 'I thank you for them every time I read', she wrote after they had been corresponding for ten years in 1937, 'and sometimes wonder how much less of a woman – how much more undeveloped I might have been without these years of association with you … your wise and living mind … ever reaching out for beautiful and good things of all kinds, assimilating them and sometimes letting the essence of them blossom out into letters to me'.[60] She acknowledged Lothian's influence on her intellectual development and her writing. His encouragement had given her the confidence to send her contributions to new outlets, including introducing American home gardeners to Australian wildflowers. Through letters, he was someone in whom she could confide all the details of her life.

For Lothian, his first encounters with Jean were rejuvenating. 'It was you largely who at a period of low humdrum level I had come to – a kind of sere and yellow leaf time, wakened me up to a fresh wonder and apprehension of the mysterious wonder and grand order of the bonnie world around us – full as it still remains of sorrow and suffering'. The wonder, passion and energy that were stirred through their correspondence gave him 'new vigour of body, soul and spirit', released creative outlets and revived 'latent powers and a fine appreciation to what had become dormant and unused, with all the resultant pleasure and satisfaction that has given me'.[61] But aware that the correspondence between a young woman and an old man had become too intense, he tried to impose limits and rein it in.

Lothian turned 80 in 1931. As the 1930s progressed he became increasingly frail and tired. His eyesight deteriorated and letter writing became a burden. Their relationship was a great comfort as her letters and thoughts continued to flow to him. And, as he predicted, 'with a quiet relaxation old age entails, we will still go on to the end of the chapter; still interested in each other's doings and thinkings and readings and mutual welfare'.[62] His encouragement of her writing didn't waver.

Chapter 7

WRITING THE GARDEN

After five years of writing 'Australian Native Flowers', Jean confided to Lothian that her work was becoming stale, repetitive and 'written out'. It could only be revitalised by exploring new regions – especially the mallee and alpine areas – but because of the depression and the need for strict economy in the Galbraith household, this was not possible. The last article, she told Lothian in January 1932, had been 'so slight that it hardly seemed worth reading. As for the next one – it must be sent by tomorrow's mail – and I've not thought of a subject yet!'[1] She wrote to Boardman to tell him she wouldn't continue with the articles after March. This was not an easy decision to make as she greatly enjoyed writing them, but she didn't want to produce 'second best work'.

Boardman urged her to continue and suggested widening the scope of the articles. He also offered to pay fifteen shillings for each article.[2] Before this Jean had received a £3 stipend each year in addition to complimentary copies of the *Garden Lover*. Jean agreed to continue, and hoped the money could pay for trips to 'new flowerlands'. Boardman also began using F.J. Bishop's wildflower photographs to illustrate her writing, just as they were illustrating her articles for American readers in the *Gardeners' Chronicle of America*.

Still writing the series in the mid-1930s, a conservation thread was becoming evident in her articles. This hadn't been present in an article she wrote in the *Garden Lover* in 1928, when she waded into the debate on whether wildflowers should be protected by legislation. 'Are we such barbarians that our own flowers are not safe from our careless hands?' she asked. She was concerned at denying children the delight of picking wildflowers that she had experienced in childhood. Instead, she promoted 'responsible' flower picking and told readers to gather wildflowers as though they were flowers from their own gardens, just carefully taking what was needed and leaving the plants unharmed.[3]

During 1931, a wildflower protection act was passed in Victoria, to combat exploitation of many of Victoria's wildflowers and making it illegal to pick certain species. Protected were all the Victorian wattles, ferns and orchids and other popular flowers such as boronias, thryptomene, waxflowers, red correa and the silver daisy. Some of the lilies, mint bushes and myrtles were protected, and so was the Gippsland waratah. The FNCV supported the act and member Edward Pescott had acted as an advisor on framing the legislation. 'The Act is to be administered sympathetically', Pescott told Jean. 'It is the destroyer, the ruthless tearer and the iconoclast that we will be after'.[4]

Jean now became a committed supporter of protection. After the legislation was passed, she devoted a *Garden Lover* article to explaining the new legislation. 'Since we have wasted the riches we inherit, since we have been careless because the gift is free, our wild flowers are being lost', she began.[5] This was a significant shift. The 'responsible' picking Jean had advocated several years earlier was no longer an option. Neither was digging up seedlings from the bush to transfer to the garden, as Jean and many other wildflower growers had done year after year, their only means of obtaining many native plants for the garden. With her article on wildflower protection, Jean began using her *Garden Lover* articles as a platform for conservation.

The legislation also had implications for the FNCV wildflower shows. After spending fifteen years arranging extravaganza displays to promote Australian wildflowers and educate the public about native flora, the club's methods had to change. It could no longer be associated with mass pickings of flowers from the bush. The club now had to educate people about the vulnerability of wildflowers and the need for their protection. Instead of holding the annual wildflower show in 1931, a Wild Nature Exhibition was held instead. A key feature of the exhibition, organised by Jean, was a 'Protected Flowers' display, consisting of specimens of the protected species, picked from private land and exhibited so that the public could recognise them. The display emphasised the conservation of native plants.[6]

In 1935, Jean began her own conservation project, as well as writing about protecting plants. When Fred and Fan Galbraith decided to sell 'Ingleside' and move to a larger poultry farm at Brown Coal Mine, a mining settlement near Yallourn and ten kilometres west of Tyers, Jean approached the new owners to see if she could buy a section of the treasured bush where she, Lawrie and Lance had played as children. Fred had tried to preserve the bush by fencing it with rabbit proof wire netting but Jean was sure the new owners would clear it. They agreed to sell her a section for five pounds. 'There are delights in plenty there now', she wrote to Lothian in July as she took possession of her bush, 'a big open glade, a tea tree thicket carpeted with moss where a honeyeater nests every year, brown capped fungi – grey lichened wood.'[7] She set to work to restore it, with visions of bringing back the wildflowers that were disappearing from the bush and roadsides around Tyers, and providing a sanctuary for birds.

As she negotiated to buy the bush, she wrote a forceful article about the destruction of the Tyers River. Published in the *Garden Lover* in 1935, 'The River's Tragedy' carried a passionate environmental message as she described the eroding of the Tyers River, caused by 'men's blindness' and greed. The Tyers River had always been a special place for Jean. Not far to the west of the original Galbraith farm, she had known it as a fast mountain stream with banks of towering manna gum and wattle, woolly tea tree, fragrant mint bush and ferns lining the water's edge, the scene of family baptisms and picnics, and a favourite place to swim. But in the last ten years, forests had been burnt in the river's catchment to provide feed for a small number of stock, while downstream trees along the banks were ringbarked and vegetation cleared to make way for grazing and crops. She wrote the article from the river's perspective and there was an undercurrent of anger. The river protested at the clearing, warning that spring floods would break its banks: '[D]on't you know that with unclothed banks I must work my own destruction, washing away, scouring out?' it pleaded. The warning was ignored. Then came a week of rain. The riverbanks were washed away, houses were flooded, fences and bridges were destroyed. When the floodwater subsided, the river was choked with debris from the ringbarked trees, its banks were eroded and the paddocks were covered in sand. Three more floods followed in quick succession, increasing the damage.

> For beauty there was desolation, for fruitfulness barren sand, for riches poverty. The water catchments were denuded to make men rich, the lowland banks were cleared for little gain, and the result filled the valley with fear.[8]

Three months later Jean's final article in the 'Australian Native Flowers' series was published. Calling it 'A Wider Path', she took her readers into the hills, crossing the flood ravaged Tyers River, and stopping along the track that led to the pink and white heath lands. 'We have come to say goodbye for a time to old paths, for next month we shall begin to tread other ways', she wrote in the article. It was time to write about her garden and all the plants that she loved in it.

> We have never lived the full life of the garden together, we have only unwoven one thread from its tapestry, a rainbow thread, yet incomplete because the garden world … consists not in bush alone, nor wholly in exotic flowers, but in both these and much more …

For nearly ten years Jean had written about Australian native flowers for a gardening readership, some of the most sustained writing on native plants published in the 1920s and 1930s. Her articles had inspired readers, Lothian included, to reach out from their neat beds of exotic plants and grow natives as well. Other readers had enjoyed the articles for their lyricism. For some time, though, as Jean told Lothian, she had been waiting for the 'next treasure' to come – stringing and unstringing her instrument – and now it had arrived.

'Next month', she told her readers, 'we shall meet in the valley and see how the garden was born'.[9]

In the November issue of the *Australian Garden Lover* in 1935, under the heading 'A Garden in a Valley – Always Growing – Always Changing', Jean promised her readers a story: 'This is a story of a garden and sometimes of those who live in it, humans, birds, fur folk, as well as flowers'.

> It is not a model garden of terraces and peaceful lawns, rarely alas is it even orderly, for we – Father, Mother and I – are the only gardeners, except when the three tall brothers come home for holidays, and the garden is frankly too big for us. Yet we love it and learn much from it, and we think that perhaps others might love it and learn from it too.

'Story' was the right word to introduce the new series. But it would be more than the story of a garden; it would also tell the story of the family who lived in the garden: the parents and their four children who grew up to be Correa, the Engineer, the Teacher and the Student. The series would tell of the people who moved in and out of the garden and of the garden's place in a wider setting of relatives, friends, neighbours and landscapes. It would be full of dialogue and ideas. And it would be reflective, exploring the role gardens play in people's lives and capturing the experience of gardening.

By now, Jean had read about other people's gardens. Among them was Marion Cran's *Garden of Ignorance*, an immensely popular story written by a journalist who had moved to Surrey to start a garden. Jean had read the 'flower patch' books by Flora Klickmann about her cottage, garden and community in the Wye Valley, and she had read the masterly English gardener Gertrude Jekyll's writing on her house and garden at Munstead Wood. She had also been reading monthly issues of a new English gardening magazine, *My Garden*, with the seductive subtitle *An Intimate Magazine for Garden Lovers*, founded by journalist Theo A. Stephens. Stephens wanted to produce a magazine where gardening advice was not the main reason for publication but where contributors wrote about their plants and gardens, in articles notable for 'the charm of their writing'.[10] In choosing to write about her garden – and her life – Jean may also have been influenced by some advice

Donald Macdonald had given her several years earlier when he told her to consider 'the human touch' in her writing, 'just life as you are privileged to know it in your Gippsland hills'.[11]

At 29, Jean was young to be launching into gardening autobiography, but she was someone who carefully collected and stored her memories, nurturing a cache and resource that she dipped into many times. In 'Australian Native Flowers', she had already described her garden as a 'garden of memories' and here, surrounding her, was a living archive. The plants themselves were receptacles of stories while the different sections of the garden, such as the wildflower border, rock garden, orchard and lily pond, were historical records that documented the ideas, hard work and people who had brought them into being. Jean, seeming older than 29, was reflective. She spent a good deal of time looking back and revisiting her stored memories, savouring the experiences they unlocked, as well as looking forward, as gardeners do.

Although she claimed she was taking a wider path in the new series, there was continuity with her earlier articles which had also been reflective and autobiographical. In both series, she was drawing on her place. In her first series, she had written of the landscapes she knew intimately and used her skills as a writer to take readers to the hills, the heath, the river. Now she invited readers into her garden that reached out to the same hills, heath and river and described the garden plants – native and exotic – with the delicacy evident in 'Australian Native Flowers', still sharing her experiences and love of beauty.

Her first article was a reverie of childhood and garden, of adventures with plants at 'Home' up on the hill before moving to gardenless 'Dunedin', of starting small gardens with packets of 'Children's Garden Seeds', and recalling the intense excitement of nurturing the seedlings and the wonder when they flowered. She called these the 'years of dream' before they started the garden in a valley, and ended with the ploughing, draining, digging and trenching that were the preparations for the new garden. 'Thus the garden began', she concluded, and she gave her readers a glimpse of what was to come:

> I have shown it to you, an untrained child garden almost without promise, but now I look down that long path, where the ploughing used to be, through arch after arch of roses. In spring they make it a rainbow path with fallen petals. Primrose and Polyanthus, white and blue and crimson, purple and tawny and gold, border it thickly, clustering in their crinkled leaves, while above them ranunculus look up to the roses and all the mixture of bright flowers that makes the spring air glow. The orchard beyond is full of fruitful trees, the wilderness has become the woodland. But that is today …[12]

Early articles focused on developing the wildflower border at 'Dunedin' and establishing the bush house. They were written as stories with dialogue and action. But when it came to telling the story of roses at 'Dunedin', it was impossible for Jean to confine it to one article. How could she, she asked her readers, when the roses were crowding around her, and 'every one for some reason asking to be spoken of'.[13] She spread the rose story over two issues and divided it into eras, first of planning and developing the rose garden and then of describing the roses that were now established and abundant. Both instalments were peppered with successes and failures. The roses emerged as characters whose personalities were formed by their colour, shape, perfume and growing habits. A few months before, *Garden Lover* readers had been introduced to a bare paddock that was the repository of garden dreams. Five articles later, they were savouring visions of roses rioting over archways, covering fences, shooting up trees and filling garden beds, their fragrance drifting up and down the paths.

Just as 'Australian Native Flowers' was an innovative contribution to nature writing and promoting Australian flora, 'Garden in a Valley' was also breaking new ground. Although Jean was writing about subjects that were bread and butter for the *Garden Lover* – roses, garden plans, caring for flowers – her articles, as stories, stood out from the others in the magazine and in other Australian gardening magazines.[14] Also, Jean did not set out to impose any gardening views on her readers.[15] And unlike the stories of gardens she was reading about in *My Garden*, there were no gardeners to carry out the orders and directions of the literary owners. 'Dunedin' was Jean's and her parents' garden, a combination of their visions, plans, hopes and hard work. Any 'help' was provided by brothers and friends and the occasional itinerant worker looking for odd jobs.

Increasingly, Jean began writing her life into the garden. Soon, Walter Thornby appeared in the articles. He was the Artist in 'The Garden Claims a Friend'.[16] In telling the story of how Walter came into the garden, Jean wrote of the hospital flowers and discussed the link between friendships and flowers. She wrote about building the sleepout for Walter in the garden, so that he could move to 'Dunedin', and of his contributions to the rock garden, the lily pond, the hedge and the vegetable garden that were the subjects of articles that followed.

From childhood, Jean had dreamed of rock gardens, and when she visited the Grampians for the first time in 1928, she encountered a vast rock garden that was 'more wonderful' than her dreams. This trip provided the catalyst for planning the rock garden at 'Dunedin'. But before she could start, there were two main problems to overcome. First was her ignorance – Jean had seen very few domestic rock gardens and she had limited information on how to make one – and secondly, she lived in an almost rock-free environment, a rounded valley with gentle slopes and smooth fields. But when her father dumped a load of rocks under the oak tree as a surprise, the foundations were there, and she was ready to create cliffs, valleys, clefts and ridges between the oak tree and the elm, where her childhood garden had been. Once she started, Jean became immersed in digging, draining, laying foundations, carting sand, gravel and soil, arranging and re-arranging rocks. Lance, who was teaching nearby, was the hero of this story. He worked as chief rock mover, concreter, stone mason and pipe layer. Work halted while the sleepout was built for Walter right next to the site. When it resumed, Walter also became involved in the rock garden, contributing his aesthetic sense. When they made a pool at its base, he masterminded a waterfall and directed the artistic placement of rocks. He brought two goldfish, Gregory and Gwendoline, back from Melbourne to release into the pool, and designed the sundial that was built near it. Spread over a number of articles, the combined efforts of Correa, the Teacher and the Artist in planning, building and planting the rock garden became an engrossing saga for the readers.[17]

Jean also wrote about the vegetable garden, another of Walter's legacies. He was 'shocked', she wrote, to discover that although the Galbraiths lived on a farm, they bought most of their vegetables in Traralgon. He set to work planning a vegetable garden, overseeing its digging, ordering seeds and then directing the planting. But this was spring in 1934, and he had only a few months to live. 'He went away from us after a weary illness, smiling, into peace', Jean wrote in her article on the vegetable garden, published two years after Walter died. She carried on his work. From a reluctant vegetable grower, Jean now became a passionate one. 'Does a miner weary when he finds gold?' she asked as she described the thrill of harvesting potatoes. No gardening achievement gave her more satisfaction than reporting to her mother that there were 'peas, beans, carrots, parsnips, red beet, silver beet, white turnips, radish and celery, all ready to use'.[18]

Angus, who had left school and was studying agricultural science at Melbourne University, now appeared as the Student in her writings. Home on a university holiday in 1935, he helped Jean to make a garden seat by the lily pond. She wrote about it in 'The Seat', and turned the construction details into another engrossing story. Jean designed the concrete seat, while the Student worked on its construction. When she printed words with a stick into its wet concrete, she felt that she had given the garden a voice: *Wenn ihr stille bleibt, so will euch geholfen worden* (If you would be quiet, then would help come). 'That was the motto for our garden seat; the message of the whole garden made articulate', she wrote. The seat became a well-loved garden feature as people sat there watching the lily pond and fountain: visitors convalescing at 'Dunedin', babies watching the interplay of water and light, lovers seeking peace and seclusion.[19] Later, it was one of Edna Walling's favourite places in the garden.

In 1936, soon after her thirtieth birthday and when she had settled into the routine of producing monthly 'Garden in a Valley' articles, Jean wrote to Lothian, reflecting on the rhythms of her life. She felt she was navigating a series of lakes and streams. There were quiet wooded lakes where friends walked, but suddenly the banks became narrower and the lakes crowded into fast flowing streams that seemed never ending, sometimes with rocks and the 'bitter spray of a waterfall'. But just as suddenly and unexpectedly, the streams always widened again into peaceful lakes. At the time of writing her letter, she was busy navigating a fast flowing stream with narrow banks, looking after two invalids who had come to convalesce at 'Dunedin', and with little time for reading and writing. As well, Matt's health was deteriorating – he suffered from angina – and Amy was experiencing the symptoms of rheumatoid arthritis, giving Jean more responsibilities in the house and the garden. 'I hope it will be by happiness and not sorrow that the stream widens into a shining lake again', she wrote.[20]

With her hands full running the house, caring for her parents and other invalids, Jean's involvement in FNCV activities lessened. There was no time to attend meetings and excursions, or even to contribute to the *Victorian Naturalist*. Between 1925 and 1935, sixteen of Jean's notes and articles had been published but in the next ten years, she only contributed three. At times, she told Lothian, she was so busy that the only time she had for reading was in the morning when she plaited her hair.[21] Strict economy was also necessary in the Galbraith household and for Jean this meant no unnecessary trips to Melbourne. Lawrie helped out by paying Angus's expenses at university in Melbourne. Jean had no difficulty accepting a life of economy. After all, as she explained to Lothian, they had all they needed for physical comfort and they had limitless beauty: 'a whole world full of trees and flowers and birds, a whole heaven full of love, as many books as we have time to read, and friends that we would rather have than any in the world'. She was content and would 'not change my happiness so full it is, for any other'.[22] Jean, at thirty, was already expressing her endorsement of a simple life. Material possessions were not highly valued or sought after, while appreciation of beauty was transcending. She threaded her joy and celebration of beauty into her 'Garden in a Valley' stories.

'Here I stay', Jean wrote in 1937 in an article she called 'Garden Adventures', 'like a spider in its web, waiting for adventures to come to me'. She celebrated the riches she received from her garden, the network of sharing through giving and receiving and the unspoken messages that accompanied gifts of plants and flowers. 'Our flowers seemed ready to give us some part in everything', she wrote. 'They were always ready to speak for us when we had few other words and whenever we sent them as our messenger it seemed as if they gave us a share in a new experience'.[23] The flowers provided an entrée into other people's lives and experiences, enriching those of the giver and receiver. Through the garden, Jean was integrated further into her own community as people came to 'Dunedin' seeking flowers to celebrate births and weddings, or to find comfort in times of illness and death.

Among the lovers visiting the secluded garden seat by the lily pond were Lance and May and Lawrie and Lin. In 1936, when Lance was appointed head teacher at Ni-Ni-Well near Nhill in the Wimmera, he became engaged to his cousin May Ladson from Beechworth. The next year, Lawrie was also engaged. Now a lecturer in civil engineering at Melbourne University, he had spent the summer holiday gaining practical experience with the Country Roads Board, working on the new bridge over the Latrobe River at Rosedale, where he fell in love with Linette Siddle. The two couples planned a double wedding in Melbourne in late August, 1937. It would be daffodil time and Lance requested a daffodil wedding.

The day of the wedding began early for Jean in Melbourne, as she dressed in her new costume and went over to Kew where Lin was staying. She saw Lin standing at the window, looking across the Yarra valley with its silvery river and wattles, and 'hoped the days before the bride and groom would be as fair and fruitful as the view before them'. Back at 'Dunedin', at the exact time of the wedding, Amy, who now rarely left the house, planted a may tree and a linden tree in the garden with her sister Fanny.[24] The wedding reception was held in Malvern in a room full of daffodils. Vera West had sent masses of her loveliest flowers and Matt had brought down great bunches from 'Dunedin'. After the reception, Lance and May left to catch the train to Adelaide for their honeymoon, while Lawrie and Lin drove off to the Dandenongs. The daffodil wedding, as Jean called it, appeared at the end of the two articles she wrote about growing daffodils at 'Dunedin'.[25]

During 1936 and 1937, while she was writing articles about the hedge that Walter Thornby had inspired, the woodland, lilies in the garden, winter flowers, the sleepout, the pumpkin patch and the lily pond, Jean had been busy on another Herculean development, a second rock garden. The first rock garden had been the biggest of her gardening adventures, and she had tried to explain to her readers the 'magic' that was in it. She continued to love the rock garden, but was aware of the mistakes she had made. It needed daily rescues from drought and invasive plants. The second rock garden would replace an untidy mound in front of the study. Jean also hoped it would give width to a garden that was essentially long and narrow. She was only able to contemplate undertaking such an ambitious project when Lance's friend, Ivor Crampton Smith, offered to help. He appeared as 'John' when Jean wrote about the new development in the *Garden Lover*. Ivor was energetic, enthusiastic and not deterred by the back-breaking project, working early in the morning and setting up reading lamps so that he could continue late into the night. They worked together excavating, carting stones, mixing cement and building terraces, a waterfall and a top and bottom pool. There were cascades to make, cliffs to build, crevices to mould and moraines to create. And for Jean, there was the intense joy of planting. By early spring in 1937, just after the daffodil wedding, many of the plants had started flowering. 'It was worth all the work', Jean quoted Ivor as saying when he saw the rock garden flowering. A month later he was killed in a motorcycle accident, and Jean felt her resilience fall away. Writing became hard work, she told Lothian, 'as if the spring of joy had been clogged with mud and clay'.[26]

Ivor's death may have contributed to a reflective article, 'The Golden Hours', published in January 1938, where she explored the spiritual dimensions of the garden, its place in daily life, joy and suffering, and its healing powers. 'There are sorrows in most of our lives and for many, physical weariness or pain dull the edge of our happiness', she wrote, 'but the gardener's world is not barren because of these'.

> The joy may go from it but the beauty stays, with the wholesome work to increase beauty, and out of this, though it may be slowly, the golden days are reborn. They come first in a moment here, a moment there, with wonderful surprise until joy is ours again.

And even though people experience pain, she wrote, they find that beauty stays with them, for the seasons come 'as radiantly' whether they are welcomed or ignored, and they make people glad again.

> No one who has lived close to a garden could desire that the flowers should fade to match his sorrows or mark his annoyance. The succession of spring and summer, the fruition of autumn and the winter rest are his consolation.[27]

After this, Jean began writing about the second rock garden. It took four articles to tell the story. Re-reading them as a whole, John Lothian could see their potential. 'They would make a 'delightful chapter in The Book that is to be', he predicted. 'You'll see'.[28]

In March 1938, Jean was preparing for another camping adventure organised by Eva West, packing items such as citronella, wire for hooks, milk jug covers, enamelled basin, hairpins and safety pins, as well as her naturalist equipment: plant press, census, bird book, camera and binoculars. With Miss West driving, and passengers Miss Ethel (Miss West's other sister), Jean and Anne Burnet, they planned to drive along the Princes Highway to Sydney. The Wests left Traralgon, picked up Jean at Tyers and Anne at Glengarry, and then headed east, planning to camp the first night at Cann River. It began raining steadily. Passing through places with ringing East Gippsland names like Toorloo and Tostaree, the rain became driving and relentless. They didn't think of floods until they crossed the Snowy River at Orbost, and looked down on the flats to see cattle sheltering on high ground and houses marooned on rises. They battled on through the deluge until they reached Cabbage Tree, little more than a clearing in the forest on the Princes Highway. They couldn't go any further and stopped at a road workers' camp. The workers had retreated to Orbost earlier in the day but the foreman was still there and gave them shelter in one of the tents. 'I'm ashamed to offer you this place', he said. 'I wish I could offer you my camp but look at it!' They looked – and saw a neat galvanised iron shed with three feet of water flowing through it. It made them grateful for what they had. With the help of kerosene, they managed to light a fire in the tent's tin chimney, even though water was streaming down on to the hearth. Anne Burnet valiantly cooked bacon and eggs as the water splashed over her. 'We rested if we didn't sleep', Jean wrote of their first night. The roar of the Cabbage Tree creek drowned out the rain.[29]

The campers were marooned. The highway was impassable to both east and west where bridges had been washed away. They were offered accommodation at the school and settled down in the classroom with a big fire to dry out their clothes and bedding. 'We had plenty of wood, plenty of books, plenty of provisions and waterproof shelter', Jean wrote later. 'We were well content with our lot'. They couldn't leave Cabbage Tree for four days, and then had to retrace their route to Orbost as the highway was still cut further east. They decided to drive to Canberra via Bonang and the Monaro high plains, and then continue on to Sydney.

'I shall always be glad I travelled up that road as it is one of the most beautiful I have ever known', Jean wrote to Lothian. 'For miles and miles it runs hand in hand with streams, sometimes beside them, so that one can almost touch their ferns, even see every pebble of their little beaches'. It was a winding road that led north to the New South Wales border and climbed through the wonders of East Gippsland rainforest and wet eucalypt forest, past the Errinundra Plateau and shining gum, southern sassafras, black oliveberry and mountain plum pine.

They were fourteen kilometres south of Bonang when the car stopped 'with a little gasp'. Jean and Anne set off to walk to Bonang, fortunate to get a lift for most of the way, and the car was towed to the guest house where they spent the night. A local managed to start it in the morning, and they set off to drive over the Monaro high plains. Ever the botanist, Jean would have liked to stay longer at Bonang. She was told of a place nearby where thousands of East Gippsland waratahs grew, along with creepers, ferns and trees that made her 'botanist self eager'. They reached Bombala on the Monaro high plains where the car was checked and pronounced fit, but it broke down near Bibbenluke. They waited for a mechanic to come and fix it after telephoning for help from a nearby farm house. Jean, the rock gardener, didn't mind the delay at all and delighted in what she saw. This section of the high plains was like an endless rock garden, with wildflowers growing in crevices and sheltering among the rocks. They camped the night at Nimmitabel and arrived at Canberra the next day, pleased to have an opportunity to look around the fledgling national capital. But after leaving Canberra and driving east towards Goulburn, the car faltered again. This time a mechanic from Canberra managed to identify and fix the problem, and the travellers finally reached Sydney, staying there for three days. With the Princes Highway now open for traffic between Melbourne and Sydney, they were able to drive south along the New South Wales coast and camp for several days at Jervis Bay where Jean spent her thirty-second birthday. The sea was sapphire and beryl, and the heath near their camp was full of 'the loveliest New South Wales wildflowers': flannel flowers, Christmas bells, boronia, waxflowers.

They arrived home on Easter Sunday with tales of floods and breakdowns, high plains and a harbour bridge, forests, wildflowers and sapphire seas and, for Jean, a new cache of memories and experiences to store, ready to use in articles. It took her two evenings to write an epic letter to Lothian, recounting her holiday. 'It is a birthday I shall not forget', she wrote of her time at Jervis Bay, before putting down her pen on Monday night.

But the letter didn't end there:

Tuesday 5am

So much I wrote last night, and I wish I could end there, but you would hear the next news anyway, so it's better for me to tell it. Do not be too saddened for us Grandfather, when I tell you that we had bad news this morning (2am) that Lawrie had been killed by a snowfall on Mt Hotham. We are all thinking of Linette. She will be brave we know – but it will be worst for her. We are so thankful there is the little one coming to plan and prepare and be brave for …

I am going to Linette at once, though I shall probably return home the same night. You know all our hope and joy (ours and Lawrie's and Linette's also) is in the thought of the return of the Lord Jesus "who shall so come in like manner as ye have seen him in heaven", and because we, living in the light of prophecy all our lives, we feel that the parting may not be for long. Do not be too sad for us: the world is still beautiful.

With all my love to you,

Jean.

Lawrie had set out with a colleague from the engineering school at Melbourne University, Mansergh Shaw, to hike from Harrietville to Mount Hotham during the Easter holiday. Lin, who was four months pregnant, stayed home in Melbourne.[30] Lawrie was an experienced hiker and the veteran of many bushwalks in the Victorian Alps. It was not known, though, that he had a heart condition. Leaving Harrietville, they climbed up to Mount Feathertop, and then down the Diamantina Spur to the West Kiewa Valley where they spent the night at Blair's Hut. The next day they followed the snow pole line up to the high plains. On Easter Sunday they climbed down into the Cobungra Valley and stayed at Dibbins Hut. When they woke on Monday morning, the weather had deteriorated. They set off in the rain for the long haul up Swindler's Spur to Mount Hotham. The rain turned to heavy snowfalls and they were determined to push on to the Mount Hotham Hospice They climbed over Loch's Spur, following the snow poles, and then began their descent in deep snow, but missed the turn-off to the track leading to the Hospice. They had to retrace their steps up the steep spur, slipping and falling in the snow. They found the track, but Lawrie began to show signs of exhaustion, stumbling and falling, until he was unable to continue. He lapsed into semi-consciousness. Mansergh Shaw feared Lawrie had had a heart attack, and dragged him to the shelter of a snow gum where he made him as dry and comfortable as possible before setting off on a frantic dash to get help from the Hospice. When the rescue party reached Lawrie, he was dead.

Jean set out immediately for Melbourne to support Lin, while Angus went to Bairnsdale to identify Lawrie's body. Lance was hundreds of kilometres away at Ni-Ni-Well. Amy's niece Verna Ladson, then a music teacher in Melbourne, hurried down to Tyers to be with her uncle and aunt. She was very close to them as they had cared for her when she was a baby, after her mother's death. She described the scene later to her son. 'Auntie Ame threw her arms around me and said, "Oh my dear, we knew you would come when our other children couldn't be here". Uncle Matt stood there, clad in a great oilskin coat and carrying a kerosene tin in each hand to feed the pigs, and the tears ran down his face, but he couldn't say a word'.[31] On the day Lawrie died, Amy wrote in her diary: 'They that wait upon the Lord shall renew their strength'.[32]

Jean, glad that Verna was with her parents, stayed in Melbourne where Lin gained comfort from her presence and turned to her for advice. There was a calmness about Jean as she drew on her faith and conviction that the parting from Lawrie would not be for long. In a letter to her parents, she wrote of telling concerned people that they would not deny their faith by 'overmuch sorrow'. She was 'not finding everything hard – perhaps I will later – but I don't know whether the future meeting hasn't become to[o] real for the present to have lost its worst power to hurt. I feel so at present'.[33] She wrote about the kindness of others, including the proprietor of the Hotham Heights Accommodation House who had driven Lawrie's car down from the mountains to Melbourne and made sure he arrived after dark so that Lin wouldn't see it pulling up at the house.

Lin moved to her parents' home in Rosedale and Jean returned to Tyers, where there was a mountain of mail to respond to, as relations, Lawrie's university colleagues, students, friends, field naturalist club members – he had helped out at numerous wildflower shows – and many, many people wrote to the Galbraiths to express their sympathy. Replying to the letters was mostly Jean's task. She received a particularly comforting letter from her Uncle Charlie, her literary mentor in England. It was full of kind and wise support, with special encouragement for Jean because he knew she would be helping others. 'I remember warning you to prepare for sadness because of the dear friends you had all so much older than yourself', he wrote, 'but I did not think of so great a loss among those younger than yourself'.[34] A letter from her cousin Arthur Galbraith, who was helping with Lawrie's affairs, summed up how many family members were feeling: 'We look forward to seeing Lawrie at the Resurrection. But for the time being, it is hard to bear isn't it'.[35]

Jean continued with her 'Garden in a Valley' articles. Early in September, she wrote an article about the bush she had bought three years ago and her efforts to restore it. It was both homage to Lawrie and a story of regeneration. Published as 'The Paddock' in October 1938, she drew on her memories of Lawrie as she wrote of their childhood in the patch of bush, playing hidey among the wildflowers, building wigwams from the wattles, and remembering an 'erect brown-eyed schoolboy' acting out 'Horatius at the Bridge'. Then she told of the Engineer walking through the bush paddock after she had bought it, remembering those adventures and helping Jean with her plans to restore the bush. 'We must bring a whole lot of little Wattles and the prickly bushes', he said, 'and set wild Boronia in it. Remember how it used to be.' He went hunting for bird orchids to plant near the stump where they used to grow. He spotted the special log where they used to hide and dragged back the part that wasn't rotten, placing it in the tea tree grove. 'It was not the paddock of the years of dream, but it was safe, the trees were growing up, birds were unmolested', Jean wrote of her bush sanctuary.

In the article, she also told readers that the Engineer had died, 'leaving us with memories that are more to us than the hurt', and told them about a newcomer in the garden story, Peter, the Engineer's son, who was one week old. '[A]nd it may be that when the Paddock has grown up into some likeness of our place of dreams there will be children to play in it, to build wigwams in the undergrowth, and play breathless hide and seek, to chase the Dandelions among the grass and step softly between the Blue Stars'.[36]

Late in 1938, Ralph Boardman, editor of the *Garden Lover*, wrote to Jean suggesting the Horticultural Press publish a selection of her 'Garden in a Valley' articles as a book. John Lothian was delighted with the news: 'Will I not be a proud prophet when I get a copy in my own hands?' he asked.[37] Jean began work on selecting articles, amalgamating some to form chapters, revising the text and working out an order to give the book structure and cohesion. The 'Background of Years', an article reflecting on change in the garden, home and valley during the twenty five years the Galbraiths had lived at 'Dunedin', and written soon after Lawrie's death, became the last chapter in the book, an interweaving of past and present where 'yesterday lives in today, today is inherent in yesterday', and an inventory of loss and gain, 'where forest has been replaced by pasture and new homes and families have come to the valley'. The article she wrote after Ivor Crampton Smith's death in 1937, 'The Golden Hours', with her reflections on the healing dimensions of the garden, formed a moving epilogue.

Garden in a Valley appeared in December 1939. Published several months after war had been declared, the book reflected wartime austerity. Its green and brown cover featured a sketch of a 1930s-style house in a sparse garden, with '2/6' prominently displayed on the front. Illustrating the book were the few photographs that had appeared in the *Garden Lover* articles, taken by a friend, Harry Boss Walker, who had first come to Tyers to convalesce from tuberculosis. As one reviewer remarked, it was 'an unpretentious-looking little book'.

Jean had written the preface in April that year. The civil war in Spain had just ended, Japan had invaded China and world war was looming. In the preface, she addressed issues of war and peace. 'We need to remind ourselves', she wrote, 'that there must still be gardens in China and Japan, that even in tortured Spain there are trees and flowers blossoming, and round innumerable homes in Germany and Italy, as in England, flowers are tended and loved by peaceful-hearted folk who want nothing but to live quietly and grow their flowers …

> Yet because there are others who care little for beauty or growth or gentleness the world lives in fear. If we have to face the horror of war, let us remember that there are flower-loving hearts all over the world. That knowledge makes war more horrible, but it should also make it impossible for us to hate any nation.

> More could I say, since peace is become so precious to us all, but you may think it outside the scope of a garden book.[38]

Through a gardening medium, she had the courage to remind readers of a common humanity.

The book also had a foreword by Jean's friend and mentor, Edward Pescott, by now author of many gardening books, who suggested that her writing could be compared with that of the noted English plant writer and collector, Reginald Farrer. Pescott recognised that Jean was doing something different in *Garden in a Valley*. Even as Australia was developing its own literature and where many new books 'of character and type' were being published, he wrote in the foreword, Jean's book was breaking new ground. It was a book where everything was 'so simply and so joyfully' pursued, a book permeated with literary merit and love of nature. 'The garden lover, the wildflower lover, the bush walker, the bird enthusiast and others, will read this book with pleasure and they will read it and read it again', he predicted.[39]

As Pescott had written, Jean's book was breaking new ground. Few garden books in Australia had offered such an intimate portrait of a garden where readers felt comfortable and at home. Few books had woven a garden story so skilfully and compellingly that readers were kept enthralled by the narrative and inspired to go out into their own gardens and create their own beauty. In Australia, there had been few garden writers with the literary skills to evoke the flowers so beautifully, or to reflect on the act of gardening and its part in people's lives, and to celebrate the pursuit of beauty and friendship in the garden. Because of its links with nature writing, it would also appeal not just to gardeners but to lovers of nature. Jean's book was also a simple profession of her faith where the Galbraiths, as gardeners, were working with God who had given 'every tree to bear fruit after its kind'.

Jean dedicated the book to 'the Two at Home who lived the garden story' and to John Inglis Lothian. Since 1931, Lothian had been suggesting her *Garden Lover* articles be published in book form, and now he had the results of his vision. He read a chapter each morning, sitting up in bed and balancing two pairs of glasses to read the text. 'This morning my sermon was your "Epilogue" of which I am very fond', he wrote early in 1940.[40] He died six months later. The Lothian family returned all Jean's letters, the record of their deep relationship, and she stored them with his.

Although there were positive reviews of the book – 'if you don't enjoy it, see a doctor', wrote one reviewer, 'there must be something radically wrong' – it would be over forty years before *Garden in a Valley* received recognition as an Australian gardening classic.[41] In 1943, Boardman sent Jean a rather dispiriting letter about its progress. Even though all the copies had been sold, there was no profit after expenses were paid. He would not be reprinting. 'Your book has considerable literary merit', he wrote, 'and I understand you have received very many appreciations. Friends of mine who read the book were extremely appreciative. This must be encouraging to you and may point the way to further efforts on your part'.[42] His lukewarm appreciation of *Garden in a Valley* would not have softened the impression conveyed in his letter that the book had not been much of a success.

Chapter 8

FROM THREE TO ONE IN THE GARDEN

'I used to be proud of my vegetable garden', Jean Galbraith wrote in the *Garden Lover* in late 1943. 'Sometimes, not often, it was weedless. But now the calves and hens have stolen my garden time, and I am ashamed when I look at it ...'

> There are thistles among the potatoes, Prairie Grass dropping seeds among the beans. Onions and parsnips that have been left in the ground are going to seed amongst a tangle of Fog Grass and Chickweed. Even the silver beet, which always flourishes, is overgrown; the strawberries are a tangle of runners; the rhubarb needs watering.[1]

In her first 'Garden in a Valley' article, Jean had admitted that the garden was too big for the Galbraiths, although there were three people tending it. Now, in the early 1940s, with Matt's angina worsening and Amy's rheumatoid arthritis greatly reducing her mobility, Jean had become the main gardener. She was also cook, housekeeper and carer and had taken over management of the animals on their small farm. And now there was a child living at 'Dunedin'. With a young son to support, Lin had decided to train as a nurse and arranged for Peter to go to 'Dunedin' while she moved to the nurses' home at the Sale Hospital. Peter brought great joy to his aunt and grandparents. He explored in the orchard, collected eggs, helped to harvest the potatoes and feed the calves and pigs. He went to the shed with his grandfather when Matt was still able to milk the cows. He listened delightedly as Auntie Jean and Grandmother read an inexhaustible supply of stories and recited poems. And now that they had a wireless, part of the Galbraiths' daily routine included listening with Peter to 'Kindergarten of the Air'. Jean wrote special poems for him, putting his activities into verse, just like A.A. Milne's *Now We Are Six*, a favourite book. Jean called them the 'Peter Poems'.

Down in the orchard the daffodils grow,
Daffodils yellow in springtime aglow,
Apple trees blossom and oranges swell,
Down in the orchard that Peter knows well.

Down in the orchard when summer is near,
Raspberries yellow are ripening here,
Under the fig tree a hen hides her nest,
Peter and Grandfather find all the rest.

Down in the orchard on dull winter days,
Wattle is yellow; a little wind plays,
Shaking the jonquils and laughing at me,
Who could be dull with such flowers to see![2]

Writing had to be fitted into this crowded routine. In October 1939, two months before *Garden in a Valley*'s publication, Jean began a new series for *Garden Lover* readers, 'Two – and a Garden', a story of restoring a neglected country garden. As Jean told a friend later, with war imminent, she didn't feel she could continue writing about the happy things happening in her own garden, so concentrated instead on writing a story about a garden's regeneration.[3] Although the garden restorers, Christine and John, were fictional, the series was closely based on the experiences of Jean's old Tyers friends, the Elijahs, who had bought a property, 'Doongalla', in the Dandenong Ranges. Deep in mountain ash forest, its once grand homestead had been destroyed in a bushfire and the garden was a sleeping beauty, waiting to be brought back to life. Mabel Elijah, the reluctant city dweller, now had a garden in the bush and spent weekends and school holidays there with her husband, Jean's former teacher. Their first task was to restore a cottage on the property which had survived the fire: 'There has been so much to do at the cottage that we are not able to spare more than a hurried look around the garden, before we start for home', Mrs Elijah wrote to Jean soon after the purchase.[4] The Elijahs pressed Jean to visit 'Doongalla' after Lawrie's death, and she stayed there in 1939.[5]

With Mrs Elijah's letters detailing their progress and Jean's own experiences of working in the garden, she had ample material for what turned out to be several years of articles. In the new series, she captured the hidden magic of 'Doongalla'. On the drive into the property, eucalypts and wildflowers gave way to an avenue of elms, an expansive park of deciduous trees and conifers, camellias, rhododendrons, terraces and neglected gardens. The rather stiff characters, Christine and John, conveyed Jean's attitudes to gardening, quoted her favourite poetry and expressed her spirituality. John Lothian commented on the new series in a letter to Jean. Although not so 'at home' with the new series, it was growing on him with every instalment, and he enjoyed 'the moralising and quiet conversation of the married couple'.[6] Enclosed with his letter was one from his grandson Noel, describing his hair-raising exit from Germany when war was declared.

In 1943 however, Jean was back in familiar territory, writing about her own garden, when she began a new series for the *Garden Lover*, 'From Day to Day in the Garden'. As with 'Australian Native Flowers' and 'Garden in a Valley', where she had drawn on nature writing and story in her gardening articles, Jean was again breaking new ground. Where 'Garden in a Valley' had been a series of stories on how a garden developed, 'From Day to Day in the Garden' was a continuous story of life in a garden and the life of a gardener, spreading out to Jean's circle of friends and their gardens. The series was not a simple recording of monthly happenings as the gardening year progressed, underpinned by seasonal gardening advice. Instead, it was crafted by a writer with a distinctive voice and style and an acute sense of her audience. The writing was intimate and generous, for readers were invited into Jean's garden and life. Her words made the garden – its plants and features, its seasonal joys – come alive in the reader's imagination.

The new series contained the hallmarks of her earlier writing: celebrating the beauty of God's creation and the inspiration she derived from her place. She never tired of admiring its beauty, and this slipped into her articles. 'Coming home', she told her readers after visiting her neighbour Miss Anderson who lived behind Jean on the ridge where Andrew Galbraith's house had been, 'I face the whole wide view of our valley, with its blue surrounding curve of hills, a view so beautiful that I do not try to describe it'. But she did:

> (E)veryday I am surprised at how fair it is: coloured fields, its clustered trees, the river outlined with wattles, the serene blue of the hills, the towns, smudges of red and white in the distance, with roads connecting them, their trees making dark patterns against the pastel shades of crop and pasture.[7]

An important component of the new series was celebrating the beauty of everyday life. Morning and night, it was part of Jean's routine to separate the milk from the cream, rhythmically turning the handle of the separator, 65 turns a minute. For many women on farms, this was a laborious task, but for Jean, it was an opportunity to appreciate the progression of beauty through the seasons and reflect on what she could see through a small window and door at the back of the house, as she steadily turned the separator.

> At regular intervals, I change to the left hand and, half turning, face the open door. It is a narrow door used for bringing in wood, but it is much more than that. It brings me the world outside. Through it I saw the first jonquil, followed by more and more till there was a whole galaxy of white and gold, then the daffodils came, and I hardly realised that the jonquils had faded because the accent had moved to the golden trumpets in front of them. The oak branches stretched above them, and next their buds were swelling, while away beyond I looked up the green pasture to the road and saw a *Prunus pissardii*, virginal against the gums. Now its bloom has fallen and its dark leaves melt into the shadows. The daffodils have gone, but white irises bloom where the jonquils were. Above them the oak leaves are pale gold, and the catkins have come back again with their bees. The yellow Banksia Rose drops through them like sunshine: the lowest spray is just outside my door.[8]

The delicate, evocative descriptions made it easy for readers to share Jean's view and savour the beauty of a seasonal progression of plants and flowers, as seamless as a symphony where one set of instruments fades and another rises to take over the theme.

She wrote of friends and community. The close gardening bonds with her friends 'Jane', 'George' and 'Mary' featured in 'From Day to Day'.[9] 'Jane' was Jean's friend Anne Burnet and 'George' was her husband, Charles Hawkins. When Jean first met Anne she was helping her brother to develop a farm to the east of Tyers at Glengarry. Charles was an engineer who had moved to Traralgon to work at the newly established Australian Paper Manufacturers, but decided he wanted to farm instead, and came to the Burnet farm to gain experience.[10] When they married, Anne and Charles moved a short distance to a new farm they called 'Narkoojee', in red box forest. Jean helped them to start a native garden at their new home. 'Mary' was Anne's sister, Marion Burnet, known as Marzie, who lived in Traralgon. Jean and Marzie shared a passion for succulents and Marzie also became an enthusiastic grower of native plants and a bird lover. The three gardens, Jean explained in her articles, formed a triangle, and there were constant exchanges of plants and gardening intelligence.

Despite her joy in the garden and nature and her constant thankfulness for the beauty that surrounded her, there were times when Jean felt overwhelmed by the tasks ahead of her. Neglected parts of the garden were growing wilder, and finding time for picking and preserving fruit and keeping the vegetable garden in full productivity was difficult. There were fewer visits to the new garden at 'Narkoojee'. When she was finally able to visit Anne and Charles, cycling through gentle rain in June, her description in the *Garden Lover* recorded the sheer pleasure at being out and about, enjoying the countryside: a robin flying from post to post beside her, calves keeping each other warm in the rain, mist drifting in the valleys between the hills to the north. There were cockatoos feasting on onion grass along the roadside. As she came closer, they rose together, flying low across the road in front of her, circling and soaring until they dropped into the branches of several dead trees, 'filling them with whiteness like the breaking of a *Magnolia* into flower'.[11]

The war was present as an undercurrent in her writing. Her daily visits to the post office where she took bundles of letters to mail, and where letters and enticing parcels of plants and seeds were waiting for her to collect, brought her close to the war. Everyone standing in the room while the mail was sorted anxiously monitored the arrival of letters from those serving overseas, 'knowing how letters keep the unnamed dread at bay'. There was a release of tension once the mail was sorted and the letters that meant so much to her friends and neighbours had arrived. She wrote of the woman who lived further up the hill, whose son would not be coming home. She wrote of the joy of the young couple next door when they were together during the husband's rare periods of leave, and she wrote of the young postmistress who sorted the mail, always looking out for letters from her husband who was 'in the islands' somewhere. She wrote, too, of Fillipo, the Italian prisoner of war who was working for Anne and Charles on their new farm.

Jean was also involved in wartime correspondence. She wrote weekly to Les Morgan, a family connection who was serving overseas and had survived the retreat from Greece. 'You have no idea how much I look forward to getting your letters', he wrote to Jean in 1940. He had treasured memories of the garden at 'Dunedin', memories, he told Jean, that 'kept me clean in mind and stopped me from many a slip'.[12] Jean also wrote regularly to her English cousin Edith Ladson, Uncle Charlie's daughter, who was experiencing terrifying bombing raids in Birmingham. Edith had been circulating copies of *Garden in a Valley* among her friends where the gentle story of garden-making contrasted with the destruction around them. Edith was sure the book would sell well in England, she told Jean.[13] Soon after writing this, she endured a night of 'indescribable terror' when her house was almost destroyed in a bombing raid.

Seasonal produce, the wonder of sunrises, comparison of leaf forms, Red Cross bazaars and descriptions of flowers opening were all part of 'From Day to Day in the Garden'. So were many anecdotes of Peter's exploits in the garden, but these ended abruptly when Peter went to live with Lin's parents. For four years he had been at the centre of life at 'Dunedin'. His departure was much sooner than Jean had anticipated. She made an oblique reference in the *Garden Lover* that the Galbraith household was now back to three. 'It is just a year since I began to tell you these day-to-day garden happenings', she wrote in 1944,' and, despite all change, despite all hurt and happiness, here are we three in the garden still'.[14]

After this difficult time, she went for a holiday to Tasmania early in 1945. Marzie Burnet had moved to Hobart, and Jean flew over to visit, while her sister-in-law, Ella, who had married Angus in 1940, held the fort at 'Dunedin'. For *Garden Lover* readers, Jean wrote of the old house and garden on the slopes of Mount Wellington that Marzie was restoring with her brother and sister-in-law; she wrote of wildflower gardens she saw among the rocks on Mount Wellington and of the exhilarating views of the Derwent estuary.

From childhood, Jean had been fascinated by mountains and alpine plants and had created her own alpine landscapes in the 'Dunedin' rock gardens. Here in Tasmania, she could explore the alpine world of Cradle Mountain. She stayed at 'Waldheim', an accommodation house built by Gustav Weindorfer, the great campaigner for Cradle Mountain's reservation as a national park. Set on a ledge surrounded by a natural rock garden, and with Cradle Valley sweeping in a wide curve below, 'Waldheim' in the 1940s was a cosy mountain retreat run by the Connells. Jean went exploring on the high moors of Cradle Mountain. The alpine anemones were like 'flowers of a dream and the buttercups that lie on the margins of sunlit pools stir one like a miracle', she wrote.[15] The cushion plants of the high moors that fused together to form clusters of boulder hardness, fascinated her. Here was grandeur, wonder and isolation. She brought home memories 'to be taken out and rediscovered and enjoyed in the quiet hours of home'. The memories also provided material for articles.

During the war years writing became an increasingly important part of Jean's income and she began publishing regularly in new venues, including the Australian nature magazines *Walkabout* and *Wild Life*, despite her increased workload at home. *Walkabout* described itself as a 'geographic magazine' dedicated to publishing 'the most interesting features of Australia and the South Seas', and provided absorbing reading for armchair travellers. Many of the articles described people's lives in remote parts of Australia, New Guinea and the Pacific, illustrated by impressive photographs. Among the women contributors to *Walkabout* in the 1940s were Ernestine Hill, Henrietta Drake-Brockman and Mary Durack, writers who drew on their experiences of living and travelling in remote parts of Australia. *Wild Life* had a stronger natural history focus. Published by *The Herald and Weekly Times*, it was edited by Philip Crosbie Morrison, the distinguished naturalist, conservationist, science journalist and broadcaster. *Wild Life* was also lavishly illustrated with large photographic spreads.

For both magazines, Jean drew on her experiences and the places around her, as well as mining her carefully stored memories to produce cameo pieces on plants, birds and landscapes. Her first articles for *Wild Life*, published in 1939, were on birds. 'Miss Galbraith lives with her birds; they are part of her day, and of her life, and she writes of them not as specimens identified from a book, but as the intimate companions of her home in a Gippsland countryside', Crosbie Morrison wrote in his introduction to her first article, 'Bird Calls in a Gippsland Garden'.[16] She shared with her readers the birds she saw during a day in the garden at 'Dunedin', weaving in descriptions of calls and the birds' colours and habits as they darted among the natives and exotics in the garden. In spring 1940 she moved on to wildflowers and began a series, 'Flowers of the Wayside', that celebrated wildflowers growing close to 'Dunedin', simple flowers that were easily overlooked. She told readers of the wonderful spring they had experienced in 1939, when chocolate lilies had been 'waving tides of purple bloom', and the roadsides were carpeted with milkmaids, early Nancies, buttercups, field daisies, violets and pea flowers. 'I thought that the marvel and delight of childhood, the carpet of wayside flowers, had gone … but it came again in every least detail and beauty as it used to be'.[17] The series continued with seasonal descriptions of summer, autumn and winter wildflowers. Another set of articles she wrote for *Wild Life* was 'The Bush Road', where she described the vegetation on a nearby road during the seasons. The idea for the articles came as she was cycling back early one morning after staying with Anne and Charles and marvelled at the eucalypts lining the bush road: red and yellow box, mountain grey gum, manna gums, stringybark and peppermint. Her articles were illustrated by F.J. Bishop's photographs.

Jean's experience of caring for an orphaned sugar glider was fashioned into a story for *Wild Life*, and published in 1941. A limb from a tree in the garden had come crashing down in a storm and killed a family of sugar gliders, except for one. The tiny fellow – he measured about an inch and a half in diameter – was brought inside and revived with a syrupy mixture of sugar and milk. For the next two months, she told her readers, he spent most of his days sleeping under her collar, a substitute for his mother's pouch. To Jean, he was Little Chap, and to two-year-old Peter, who loved him, he was Squirl. Much revived, Little Chap came into his own at night, leaping and 'flying' from table to curtain, bookshelf to picture frame. When Jean had to go to Melbourne, Little Chap went too, travelling under her coat collar on the train. Her *Wild Life* article didn't mention the mayhem in the carriage when he appeared from under her collar.[18] Soon Little Chap was big enough to sleep on a rug in the dining room by day, snapping at moths and spiders by night and making the room cobweb-free. Jean planned to release him after winter, but he disappeared one night when a door was left open. She could only hope that he found a safe sleeping place and could cope with life outdoors.[19] A photograph of Peter and Little Chap illustrated the article. It was a soothing contrast to graphic photographs of Australia's venomous snakes and spiders that were regular fare in *Wild Life*.

A holiday to the Wimmera to visit Lance and May and her young niece Marjory at Ni Ni Well in spring in 1941 provided material for both *Walkabout* and *Wild Life*. 'In the Wimmera – Now', an article published in *Walkabout*, was both nature essay and travelogue where Jean wrote about the colours of a landscape dominated by cereal crops.[20] For *Wild Life*, she wrote a series with more of a naturalist bent, 'Flowers of the Wheatlands'. In his introduction to the series, Crosbie Morrison described the author as one who 'writes in such a fascinating personal manner about her friends among the flowers and birds of the bush'.

Jean had been regularly drawing on her memories in her gardening articles, and now, with much less time for botanical exploration, she relied increasingly on memories for her nature articles. In 1943 and 1944, she contributed articles to *Walkabout* based on her camping trip to Sydney in 1938 with Eva and Ethel West and Anne Burnet. She wrote of the deserted homes she had noticed on the uplands of the Monaro, of the natural rock gardens she found when the car broke down and on the abundance of wildflowers at Jervis Bay, where the party had camped on their way home from Sydney, a celebration of wildflowers, rock pools, sea and beauty. Other articles mined further back to childhood, such as her wonder at seeing her first correa on that cold sleeting drive home from the Strzeleckis.

Jean reached out to a new international readership during the war years when she began writing for *My Garden*, an English magazine which Jean considered her favourite. *My Garden* was a natural outlet for Jean's writing, because of the emphasis its editor placed on garden writing as a genre. It had a devoted readership in the U.K. and North America of people who wanted to immerse themselves in gardens, rather than read instructional articles. With her acute sense of audience, Jean crafted her writing on Australian native plants for a northern hemisphere readership. 'Epacris Impressa, Who Grows it Now?' was published in 1941, its title containing the hint of a challenge. 'I have just been plant hunting in Gippsland … which has a climate nearer to that of southern England than any other part of the mainland. The result is this outburst about epacris', she wrote. She drew on information from an 1852 issue of the *Scottish Gardener*, that recorded heath from Victoria growing in greenhouses in Edinburgh, and wondered if it was still grown in Britain. She discussed how she grew it in her garden in Australia, but much of her

Matthew Galbraith, Jean's father, known as Matt.

Ian Hyndman Collection

Jean's mother, Amy Ladson.

Ian Hyndman Collection

The Galbraiths' butter factory at Tyers among the red box trees, 1912. The mechanics' institute can just be seen on the right.

Ian Hyndman Collection

Harrowing at 'Mt Hope', with Matt standing on the right.

Ian Hyndman Collection

Jean with Auntie Em's chooks during a visit to Beechworth.

Ian Hyndman Collection

Jean with her father

Ian Hyndman Collection

Jean aged 7, dressed for a school concert, standing on the verandah at 'Home'.

Ian Hyndman Collection

Lawrie and Jean with their cousin Douglas Galbraith in the middle.

Ian Hyndman Collection

The Tyers Timber Mill in the 1920s, showing forest to the north of Tyers.

Traralgon and District Historical Society

A view of the Latrobe River in flood, looking north to the Tyers hills.

Traralgon and District Historical Society

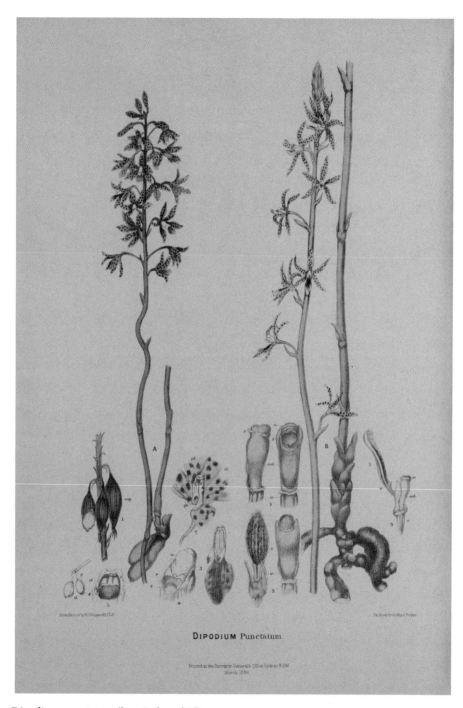

Dipodium punctatum (hyacinth orchid).
Jean came across several folios of FitzGerald's *Australian Orchids* in the library on a childhood visit to Beechworth and spent much of her holiday studying the illustrations.

R.D. FitzGerald, *Australian Orchids*, volume 1 part 7, Government Printer, Sydney 1882.
State Library of Victoria

A bare 'Dunedin' in 1914 when the family moved there.

Ian Hyndman Collection

Galbraith family and friends at the Tyers River, photographed by Jean's aunt, Fanny Galbraith, c. 1917.
Lawrie Galbraith is on the far left and Lance Galbraith is at the front right. Jean is not so easy to spot. Her head can just be seen behind the woman in a white blouse in the centre.

Ian Hyndman Collection

Correa reflexa var. *cardinalis*.
Jean saw her first red correa near Gormandale – 'velvet bells woven of red fire' – a memorable moment.

Photographer, Ken Harris

Matt, Jean and Lawrie out collecting for the garden on the Walhalla Road.

Ian Hyndman Collection

Tarra Valley Park.
The mountain ash forest at Tarra Valley and Bulga Park, high in the Strzeleckis, was a wonderland for Jean. Charles Barrett described this country as her 'promised land'.

Accession no. H91.330/4593, Pictures Collection, State Library of Victoria

Grandfather, John Inglis Lothian, inspecting a rose in his garden.

Jean Galbraith Papers box 3462, MS 12637, Australian Manuscripts
Collection, State Library of Victoria

Angus Galbraith was an enthusiastic participant in the *Garden Lover* sunflower competitions.

Ian Hyndman Collection

The Australian GARDEN LOVER

A MONTHLY NEWSPAPER DEVOTED TO AUSTRALIAN HORTICULTURE

Vol. 2, No. 9   CHRISTMAS NUMBER   December, 1926

The Christmas Tree of Western Australia (Nuytsia floribunda)
Republished by courtesy from the book "Wildflowers of Western Australia," by Mrs. E. H. Pelloe

[PRICE 6d.

Australian Garden Lover cover, December 1926, featuring *Nuytsia floribunda*, the Western Australian Christmas bush.

Editor Ralph Boardman wanted to promote celebrating Christmas with Australian flora, rather than 'dark drooping firs' of the northern hemisphere.

Flowers in the bush and the garden.
The gardener in the Via Rosarius (above) and on a trip to Gormandale (below) renowned for its wildflowers.

Ian Hyndman Collection

The fountain and the seat at 'Dunedin'.
The subject of a 'Garden in a Valley' article in 1935, and photographed by Edna Walling in the 1950s.

Ian Hyndman Collection

The Tyers River was a favourite place for swimming.
Walter Thornby ('the Artist'), Fred Galbraith, Daisy Galbraith, Jean, Dick Galbraith, Lance Galbraith and Verna Ladson c. 1933.

Ian Hyndman Collection

'Garden in a Valley'.
Artist Peter Cuffley's painting of the garden at 'Dunedin' in the 1930s, based on Jean's writing, photographs, a 1939 garden plan and the plants still growing *in situ* in 1984.

Peter Cuffley

The first edition of *Garden in a Valley*, published in 1939.

Family group at 'Dunedin' c. 1948.
At the back are Verna Hyndman [Ladson], Jean, and Linette Galbraith with Peter. In the front are Grant Hyndman, Amy in her wheelchair and Robin Hyndman.

Ian Hyndman Collection

Jean's two collaborators on *Wildflowers of Victoria*: botanist Jim Willis of the National Herbarium of Victoria and Winifred Waddell, founder of the Native Plants Preservation Society.

Photo of Jim Willis courtesy of State Botanical Collection, Royal Botanic Gardens Melbourne

Photo of Winifred Waddell © of Bauer Media, State Botanical Collection, Royal Botanic Gardens Melbourne

Morning tea in the Australian Room c. 1950.
Jean often brought a fruit cake to share with the friendly staff while she was working at the Herbarium.

State Botanical Collection, Royal Botanic Gardens Melbourne

'The Baron's Couch'.
Jean's bed at the Herbarium, and still in use in the staff tea room in 2013.

State Botanical Collection, Royal Botanic Gardens Melbourne

Top: Moira Pye, illustrator of *From Flower to Fruit*, with Jean at 'Dunedin' c. 1965.

Photographed by Edna Walling Accession no. H96.150/233, Edna Walling Collection, State Library of Victoria

Bottom: Photograph of chamomile sunray by Edna Walling for 'The Harvest of a Quiet Eye'.
Jean's caption reads: 'In the north-west the pale Chamomile Sunray (*Helipterum anthemoides*) runs up to the trees like the foam patterned shallows of a wave'.

Jean Galbraith Papers, box 4098, MS 12637, Australian Manuscripts Collection, State Library of Victoria

BELL-FRUITED MALLEE
E. PREISSIANA

I 126

Eucalyptus preissiana **(bell fruited mallee), c. 1950–1969, Stan Kelly.**
Jean first saw this mallee at the FNCV wildflower show in 1922. Over forty years later, she was
thrilled to see the trees flowering near Ravensthorpe in Western Australia.

State Botanical Collection, Royal Botanic Gardens Melbourne

Photograph by Edna Walling of 'pink bells, gum and rock' for 'The Harvest of a Quiet Eye'.

Jean Galbraith Papers, Box 4099, MS 12637, Australian Manuscripts Collection, State Library of Victoria

Jean Galbraith was awarded the Australian Natural History Medallion in 1970.
Variations of this photograph taken in 1969 were used to accompany articles celebrating her achievement.

Ian Hyndman Collection

Jean Galbraith and Bill Cane photographed at a wildflower show in Sale, *Gippsland Times*, c. 1975.

Jean Galbraith Papers, box 4092, MS 12637, Australian Manuscripts Collection, State Library of Victoria

Wildflowers of Victoria, Colorgravure, second edition, 1955.

Collins Field Guide to the

WILD FLOWERS

of South-East Australia

Jean Galbraith

Including the temperate regions of N.S.W., Victoria, Tasmania, South Australia and Queensland

Field Guide to the Wild Flowers of South-East Australia, Collins, 1977.

Epilobium tasmanicum, Gentianella diemensis, Wahlenbergia ceracea, Epilobium curtisiae,
Epilobium gunnianum, Wahlenbergia gloriosa, Viola betonicifolia, Elizabeth Conabere.

While Jean worked on her field guide to the wildflowers of south eastern Australia for
Collins, her botanical artist friend Betty Conabere was painting wildflowers from the same
region for a Nelsons publication. Jean helped her to select specimens and provided restful
accommodation.

Print by John Turner of Jean Galbraith's famous picket gate at 'Dunedin'.

Ian Hyndman Collection

A familiar sight to visitors: Jean standing at her picket gate.

Ian Hyndman Collection

Jean setting off on a Latrobe Valley Field Naturalists' Club excursion on the Lost Plain near the Tamboritha and Howitt roads.

Photographer Mary Austin

Garden in a Valley (second edition), Five Mile Press, 1985.

Jean Galbraith at her table c. 1990.
People flocked to visit 'Dunedin' after *Garden in a Valley* was republished and found a magical garden and welcoming host who was still writing articles on nature, plants, her garden and memories.

Photographer Barrie Turpin

Prostanthera galbraithiae, **the Wellington mint bush, endemic to Dutson Downs and the Holey Plains State Park. This beautiful mint bush is a nationally threatened species.**

Photographer Kylie Singleton, Department of Environment and Primary Industries

Boronia galbraithiae, **aniseed boronia.**
Found only between Stockdale and Dargo, this boronia is considered a nationally threatened species.

Photographer Kylie Singleton, Department of Environment and Primary Industries

Jean Galbraith Rose.
This rose was discovered growing as a sport on a David Austin rose bush 'Abraham Darby' at Nieuwesteeg's Rose Nursery in Coldstream, Victoria. The rose with cupped blooms of deep buff apricot pales to a soft beige with age and has a rich fruity fragrance. It was propagated at Nieuwesteeg's Rose Nursery, where a staff member, Linda Bullen, was a friend of Jean Galbraith's, and then registered and released in 2000. With the permission of Jean Galbraith's family, this beautiful rose was named in her honour.

Photographer Janice Chesters (with thanks to Linda Bullen and John Nieuwesteeg) article was also concerned with describing the beauty of the heath flowering among the hills near her home. 'It ran like fire under the trees', she wrote. 'It covered whole hillsides with snow – it lay like a carpet as far as we could see, red and pink and white'.[21]

A request from a nurseryman to send correa airmail to England was the stimulus for an article on correas. Australian nurserymen, she wrote, did not stock correas, claiming there was no demand for them because they were an Australian native. 'Yet we who live near one of the comparatively few colonies of the finest form of it … grow a dozen plants together and it thrills us with delight the winter through'. She counted the red correa as one of the loveliest Australian plants to grow in the garden and described a cliff in her rock garden that was hung thickly with the correa's scarlet lanterns. 'In texture they are like fine velvet, and under the low pressure of the microscope the velvet resolves itself into translucent scarlet hairs, rising starlike from crystal globes which are living cells'. She told readers that it had been known for a long time in England where it was described as the 'Australian fuchsia'. 'Perhaps the plant I sent will bring it back to English gardens'.[22]

A particularly beautiful article celebrating the bark of Australian gum trees was written in response to a plea in *My Garden* for growing trees with coloured bark, such as birches and willows. Jean had visions of other trees whose bark she loved:

> I thought of blue gums, columnar and pale … How many readers of *My Garden* have ever seen a Blue Gum … its white trunk spinning up 50 feet unbranched; its milk white boughs lost in its shadowing leaves? The smooth trunk is rounded like flesh, with the colours of sunsets and sunrises upon it, chill grey melts into blue, blue into lavender and rose, here comes a streak of amber or warm brown running half the length of the tree, shading through creamy gold to white.

She wrote of manna gums, shedding their bark in January to reveal the flawless warmth of their creamy boughs, the old bark dropping in ribboned heaps around the bole of the tree. She described the beauty of snow gums in autumn, when their branches were 'flushed with rose or afire with red'.[23]

In June 1942, her topical 'Onions for England' was the lead article of *My Garden*. She described participating in a scheme where Australian home gardeners grew onion seed that was sent to England by the Department of Agriculture. Even onions became a subject for lyricism as Jean described their place in her garden in the southern hemisphere. They were planted in August, 'when rain drenched the yellow wattle bloom'. In September, the green spears came up, along with the daffodils. The seed ripened in the warm weather and Jean began harvesting on a hot day in March. 'We grew them to help you but we grew also beauty for ourselves'.[24]

Similar to her *Garden Lover* writing, her articles were laced with reflection. In 'A Garden and a Child' where she wrote about memories of her grandfather Andrew's garden, she reflected on what gardens mean to children and how even the smallest garden could be a fairy land for a child.[25] In 'Autumn Trees' when she described the deciduous trees in her garden, she meditated on the beauty and generosity of trees: 'they do not fail us when in times of stress we fail them'.[26] Her *My Garden* articles had all the hallmarks of her *Garden Lover* writing: lyricism, passion, evocative descriptions of flora that provided word pictures for her readers, reflections and a sharing of her love of plants and beauty. And she was also introducing readers to Australian flora.

Jean was the only Australian to be published in *My Garden*. As a contributor she was among distinguished company, her articles sitting comfortably with writers such as Beverley Nichols and Constance Spry; Captain W.E. Johns of *Biggles* fame; novelists H.E. Bates and Compton Mackenzie; and Eleanour Sinclair Rhode, famous for her writing on herbs and garden history. There was a difference between Jean's contributions and those of some of the other *My Garden* writers, many of them titled landowners employing teams of gardeners. In their articles, the gardeners were often represented as obstreperous, cantankerous and uncomprehending when it came to carrying out instructions. But there were no class assumptions in Jean's writing, no underlying condescension. She made it clear that her garden was not large, grand or costly, and that a family had planned and planted it. Now, it was cared for by one woman, 'giving it a few spare hours from crowded days'.[27] *My Garden* also had a small readership of discerning gardeners in Australia, including Edna Walling who regularly quoted from it in her *Home Beautiful* gardening articles.[28]

During the war years, Jean also began writing for the *New South Wales School Magazine* in addition to her regular articles for the *Victorian School Paper*, drawing on her distinctive style of writing about nature for children. She did not write instructional articles or nature notes. Instead, she wrote child-centred stories about children exploring the natural world, playing in the bush and discovering orchids and birds or the marvels and varieties of seeds. The stories were usually narrated by children, giving them agency, and the contents were influenced by autobiography and place.

Her series for the *Victorian School Paper* that began as 'Wigwam in the Tea Tree' provides an insight to her nature stories for children. Appearing monthly throughout 1942, the series began with a sister and brother, Betty and Tom, building a wigwam from wattle and making a secret hideaway in a beautiful patch of bush, just as Jean and Lawrie had done when they were children, after reading the Pathfinder stories of James Fennimore Cooper. In the series, Betty was the narrator. Besides enthusing about their games and adventures, Jean wrote about wattles, heath and nesting birds, about sundews and orchids in their bush, all crafted as stories. The series continued in 1943, but the title changed to 'Betty and Tom in the Wimmera' and the story focused on Betty and Tom's experiences in western Victoria where they had gone because their father was not well and needed a drier climate. Now Betty told stories about an environment where the plants needed to protect themselves over the dry summer, about dust storms, wheat crops, and the explosion of flowers in spring.

The series continued in 1944, again with a difference. Fortunately Dad had recovered and they returned to Gippsland, but Betty wasn't home for long. There was no secondary school near their farm, and she went to live with her aunt and uncle in north east Victoria to attend school there. In the articles, Betty wrote to Tom about exploring the granite country in the mountains: plants growing in rock crevices, the flowers and birds she saw, about looking for myrtles, oil glands on leaves and how the spring flowers differed from those in the Wimmera and Gippsland.

Through the Betty and Tom series, Jean was able to write about three environments that she knew well: her home base of Gippsland, the Wimmera that she had come to know through staying with Lance and May, and the granite country near Beechworth that she had explored since childhood. She could discuss plant adaptations and the differing characteristics of the vegetation. Over the years, Jean wrote countless articles in a similar style for children. They were often about a sister and brother, reminiscent of the 'JeanandLawrie' of her childhood. They were always set in the country and all explored some aspect of natural history: how seeds spread, gum nuts, banksia groves, orchids, a dragon fly shedding its skin. There were numerous bird stories.

The first article she sent to the *New South Wales School Magazine* reflected its wartime context, and was called 'A letter to Dad'. Published in 1943, the story was told by Barbara, whose father was away fighting in New Guinea. She and her brother Billy found it hard writing letters to him because nothing seemed to happen at home. Then Barbara had an inspired idea: she would take a notebook with her around the farm and record what she saw so that Dad could share it too. When the children took notebooks to the creek on Saturday where they went to grill some chops for a picnic lunch, Barbara noted the blossom and bark she saw in the apple gum, the toadstools along the track, a golden whistler in the paperbark, a description of the creek. The children sent their letters off to Dad. 'You can guess how we waited for an answer to our notebook letters', Barbara told the readers. 'When it came it made us gladder than ever that we had written.' Extracts from Dad's letter were included in the story, and extended the nature information for the readers:

I went with you to our creek, away from the heat and the mud and flies of New Guinea. I could hear your voices when Billy skipped the stones, then the whistler singing. You made me *hear* him, Babs, when you said he "sounded like sunshine", and Billy made me see him "white bib and black tie above his yellow breast!" I heard lorikeets shrieking in the apple gum blossom and saw the white limbs and thick white bloom ... and as for that lunch – well, I want one just like it when I come home.[29]

Comments from the editor of the *New South Wales School Magazine*, J.W. Hayes, showed how impressed he was with the story and its originality. He asked her for more contributions, telling Jean the *School Magazine* was keen to encourage Australian writers of children's stories.[30] With this invitation, Jean contributed prolifically to the magazine for the next twenty years, writing stories for all primary school grades.

'I began this just after the first wireless announcement, "Japan has offered to surrender"', Jean wrote in the September issue of the *Garden Lover* in 1945.[31] On that evening of the 'promise of peace', she put aside a scientific journal she had been reading and turned for inspiration to Ruskin. She reflected on the individual's responsibility for whether a state of peace or war existed. 'In every least thing in which we seek our own good at the expense of others we are asking for war', she wrote, influenced by a quote from Ruskin: 'So far as you desire to possess rather than to give ... to seek supremacy instead of love ... to command, instead of to bless'. She summed up: 'The choice is ours and every hour we build foundations of war or peace'. The next day, when the war was officially over, Jean sent daffodils to the young postmistress whose husband would now be returning, while the woman from the hill whose son had been killed brought sweet peas and celery down to the Galbraiths, to show her welcoming of peace. That night there was community singing at the Tyers hall. In common with many other gardeners, Jean started planning her own memorials to peace. She would plant a larch, a tree she had wanted to grow for some time, as well as an almond for blossom and nuts, a grapefruit for beauty and a Californian Redwood for its long life and wide span. Jean was generous with the number of peace trees she planned, but, as she reasoned, 'when should we plan new beauty if not now, and it is trees, not flowers, that one should plant for peace, long lived trees, deep rooted, wide spreading in maturity'.[32]

Matt's angina had been steadily worsening. By the end of October, when he was gravely ill, Jean spilt boiling water on her legs and badly scalded them. She kept going with all her household work and was left with severe scars. Matt died in November, less than three months after the war ended. In his history of the Galbraith family, Ian Hyndman described the scene when Matt's coffin was taken out of the house and carried down the 'Via Rosarius'. It was late spring. The roses he had planted, tended and loved were in full bloom.[33] Amy stood on the verandah with her niece Verna, Ian's mother. As she watched the coffin leave, Amy quoted from a poem by Ednah Proctor Clarke:

> Bear out his body when ye will,
> He stays – my love, my bridegroom still,
> God made us one – the living God,
> Death cannot make us twain.

Matt had been a passionate gardener. His greatest possessions, after his Bible, had been the plant catalogues that he kept within easy reach of his chair. Where there had been three in the garden, now there were two, Jean told her gardening readers. He was not in the garden now, 'but the garden blooms and we are not desolate'.[34]

Jean was delighted when Verna, with her husband Jock Hyndman and young family, came to live next door in 1946. Verna and Jock appeared in many *Garden Lover* articles as 'the Musical Cousin' and 'the Scotchman'. The following year, Fred and Fan Galbraith returned to Tyers with their daughter Daisy, after selling the farm at Brown Coal Mine. They moved into a cottage

Jean owned on the top road, once used for housing butter factory employees. Amy and Jean, the two in the garden, were now surrounded by relatives.

Once again, the garden was full of children. The Hyndman boys were in and out, Peter came to stay during the school holidays and at Christmas, and there were visits from Lance and May's children, Marjory, Geoffrey, John and Tim. The garden at 'Dunedin', with its narrow paths and secret places, was a wonderful place for adventures and Jean devised a special game for her young relatives, 'Under Sealed Orders'. Peter Galbraith remembers it well:

> Jean explained that agents in the Secret Service did not know what they had to do until they received their 'sealed orders'. The game would start with a message in a sealed envelope saying something like "Sweep the leaves from the western path for 10 minutes, and then have two biscuits from the biscuit tin". In the tin there would be something like "Look in the hollow log under the oak tree". There would be the next order such as "collect eggs from the near orchard" and directions to where the next message was hidden. This would go on for a couple of hours.

According to Peter Galbraith, the game was a win-win situation. The children had great fun, tasks were completed around the house and garden, and Jean was able to enjoy a few hours of undisturbed writing time.[35]

Jean had a natural affinity with children and several generations of relatives who visited 'Dunedin' when they were young emphasise this. They felt she treated them with respect and without condescension. She made them feel special and valued. She knew what activities would interest them: writing clues for 'Under Sealed Orders', leaving out sheet music for a musical child to play on the organ, taking very young children to see the goldfish in the lily pond or teaching them to make daisy chains. She gave children time and attention. Peter Galbraith remembers that Jean spent hours in the back of his 'car' (an old bedstead with a pram wheel attached as the steering wheel), describing for him the scenery that was flashing past, or climbing into the oak tree that had temporarily become a fort or a ship to share in the adventures.[36] Above all, she created a wonderful environment for children. For one young relative, Jean was a 'fellow traveller' in the world of imagination and a visit to 'Dunedin' was like slipping into a magical space where fairies and talking trees really could exist.[37]

On her visits to 'Dunedin', Marjory remembers a special smell inside the house, a combination of fresh and dried flowers and old books.[38] Still sitting on the shelves were Jean's and her brothers' childhood books that succeeding generations loved to read. Jean encouraged their reading and always gave books as birthday presents, as well as other thoughtful small gifts. On Peter's and Marjory's visits, Amy, who was now using a wheelchair, was always ready to recite poems or tell stories to the children whenever they asked.

Amy's rheumatoid arthritis had become more severe and she was often bed ridden. Yet although busy caring for Amy, Jean still managed to produce a stream of articles for the many magazines to which she contributed, writing them at the dining room table. In a poem he wrote many years later, Geoffrey Galbraith recorded an enduring image from his childhood stays at 'Dunedin: Jean at the dining room table, working late into the night to fulfil her many writing commitments:

> There are books upon the table
> And letters for reply
> There's a tired hand still writing
> As the embers start to die.[39]

In 1947, Jean began writing regularly for a new Australian gardening magazine, *Your Garden*, edited by her FNCV friend, Ernest Lord, author of *Shrubs and Trees for Australian Gardens*. Jean's first series, 'My Friends: The Trees', was full of glowing descriptions of trees in her garden, ranging from eucalypts and wattles to Japanese maples and elms, the articles interspersed with her feelings for the trees and their contribution to the garden. A year later, a new series appeared in *Your Garden*, 'Between Women Gardeners', by Judith Green, alias Jean. Planned as a friendly talk from month to month between home makers and gardeners 'about the work we all love in our garden', this series was the closest Jean came to writing instructional gardening articles. 'No one realises so fully as the woman who plans the meals the virtue of salads made from the vegetables freshly gathered', she wrote in the first article as she discussed growing vegetables, and then moved on to describing how she used a meat saw for separating dahlias. In March, a time when Judith Green and home-makers were busy with preserving and jam-making, she also reminded them of Christmas. Now was the time to take cactus cuttings to pot for Christmas gifts.[40]

Judith Green's *Your Garden* contributions were quite different from Correa's *Garden Lover* articles, where readers felt they were receiving letters from a special friend. 'We do so enjoy reading all the doings in the garden', a couple wrote from Port Augusta in South Australia, it was like receiving a 'personal letter'. A reader from the United Sates told Jean that she read each article 'with the feeling it was especially meant for me!'[41] So when Jean described the still winter evenings in Tyers, when gum leaves were thrown on fires that had burnt low during the day, her readers could smell the tang of the leaves as the fires flared and the back logs caught in the fireplaces.[42] When Jean described a special excursion to Melbourne for children of the Tyers school, one that the Musical Cousin had helped to organise, readers could share the children's excitement when they spotted the first tram, marvelled at the size of ocean liners at the docks or walked through the gates on their first visit to the zoo.[43] Readers valued the stories Jean told of family, friends and life in Tyers, a shared warmth and intimacy.

Jean, too, conceptualised 'From Day to Day in the Garden' as letters to friends. After Amy died in September 1948, Jean told readers of her mother's death. 'There are no ends in a garden', she wrote, 'for all ends are also beginnings, and there are no ends in human lives, if they reach out in love to life, as they do who have gone from the garden, but not from our love'.[44]

Now there was one in the garden.

Chapter 9

WILDFLOWERS OF VICTORIA

Winifred Waddell was a wildflower warrior: formidable, demanding and, Jean considered, 'almost fierce' when it came to protecting Australian flora.[1] Originally from England, she came to Australia during the First World War to teach maths at a Melbourne girls' school. It was on a horse riding holiday in the Victorian high country that she developed a passion for Australian wildflowers, and she started growing them in her Toorak garden. They were difficult to establish at first, but her garden grew into one of great beauty.[2] Winifred had been appearing in *Garden Lover* articles as 'the woman who grows wildflowers', and Jean caught up with her while she was on holiday recuperating after Amy's death. She described for *Garden Lover* readers a bunch of flowers from Winifred's garden. There were twenty-five species, each with an 'exquisite yet unobtrusive beauty', and they formed one of the loveliest bunches of wildflowers Jean had seen. She found it remarkable that they had grown in a Melbourne suburban garden. They also demonstrated the potential of Australian flora as cut flowers.[3]

The difficulty Winifred Waddell experienced in growing native plants led her to become a strong advocate for wildflower protection, especially for the need to preserve native plants in their natural habitat. She founded the Native Plants Preservation Group (later Society) in 1949, dedicated to establishing wildflower sanctuaries throughout the state, enclosing them with rabbit-proof fencing and encouraging local groups to manage the reserves. By the early 1960s, there were fifty-nine sanctuaries throughout Victoria. As founder and secretary of the group, Waddell devoted her considerable energy and zeal to hunting out areas of promising bush and rallying the troops to save the plants from destruction. Jean noted Winifred's resolute commitment to the conservation of native plants in a tribute she wrote after Waddell's death. She was 'indomitable and single-minded' in her work to preserve wildflowers.[4]

It had become increasingly obvious to Waddell that wildflowers were under threat not only from bulldozers, industrial development and postwar land settlement, but also from ignorance: Victorians knew very little about their native plants and there was no popular field guide to help with identification. An accessible guide was vital because, as Jean quoted her saying, 'until they know a native plant they can't preserve it'.[5] Waddell secured funding for a field guide and found a publisher, Colorgravure, a subsidiary of *The Herald and Weekly Times*. She wanted Jean as the author.

Jean was self-deprecating about her ability to take on the task, aware that she was out of touch with botany while she had been caring for her parents. But underneath it all, she knew she could write the book. She had the botanical knowledge, writing experience and commitment to prepare a field guide that would increase knowledge of Victoria's wildflowers and help with their conservation. And now, following her mother's death, she had the time.

But she could do it only if she had access to the facilities at the National Herbarium of Victoria, and the assistance of the staff there. The Herbarium's collection was vital to Jean as it specialised in Victorian flora and contained many type specimens, the original specimens from which the descriptions of new species had been made. Jean also needed access to the Herbarium's research material and library to write the entries on plants for the field guide. And also vital to Jean was the support of the Herbarium's senior botanist, J.H. Willis, the acknowledged expert on Victorian plants, who was deeply involved with preparing a two volume Victorian flora, a work that would become the standard reference for botanists.[6] As well as his taxonomic work and collecting, Jim Willis was renowned throughout botanical circles for his tremendous enthusiasm for native plants and his great empathy with people.[7] He was a prolific correspondent, identifying specimens sent to the Herbarium and keeping in close contact with naturalists throughout the state. An active member of the FNCV and a former editor of the *Victorian Naturalist*, he valued the contribution of local knowledge and observation to the statewide botanical mosaic.

Jean and Jim Willis had begun corresponding in 1947 after Jean returned from a field trip to the Mallee and sent some of the plants she had collected to the Herbarium for identification. She appreciated his friendly letters as well as the detailed notes he sent to her. They were full of botanical information and discussion, and may have been as valuable to her as H.B. Williamson's correspondence when she was younger. Willis admired Jean's work as a field botanist, aware that her observations were extending the known range of species, and that the interesting specimens she gathered were also making a valuable addition to the Herbarium's collection. He signed his letters 'yours fraternally', acknowledging their bond through botany, and it didn't take him long to dispense with the formality of 'Miss Galbraith'. 'Dear Jean', he wrote in 1949, 'I am making bold to use the 'vernacular' mode of address, hoping that you will not be offended but will do likewise with future communications with me'.[8] Jean, who was always very correct – bordering on formal – when addressing people, was happy to reciprocate.

'I know that Miss Waddell has discussed the "popular but accurate" wildflower book with you and mentioned that she wants me to write it', Jean wrote to Willis in January 1949. 'I know quite well of course that without your assistance I can't do it but I do believe that with help from you and the facilities for study and verification of facts which visits to the Herbarium would provide, I can do it'.[9] Another major consideration for Jean was the publishers' frightening deadline. They wanted the manuscript completed by July so that the guide would be available during the spring wildflower season. This meant Jean would have only six months to plan the book, complete the research and describe with precision and accuracy up to one thousand species. She wanted Willis's opinion of the feasibility of the project before giving her answer to Waddell and the '*Herald*' people'. When Willis replied encouraging her and offering his help, she was pleased. It would be like a holiday working with plants again, she told him.[10] The book would break her botanical drought.

So there were three people with an input to *Wildflowers of Victoria*: Jean Galbraith, writer and field botanist; Jim Willis, taxonomic botanist and expert on Victorian flora; and Winifred Waddell, conservationist and wildflower warrior. During the book's preparation, Jean and Willis grew closer together as colleagues, while the Galbraith/Waddell relationship was often strained. Besides his advisory role, Willis acted as intercessor for Jean, supporting her ideas and calming Winifred's sharp reactions. 'I understand your mixed feelings about the Galbraith/Waddell literary combination', he wrote to Jean. 'You have my sympathies. "Nuf sed."'[11]

By the end of January, after Jean had told the publishers she could finish the book by early July, the race was on. Letters were flying between all three, with Winifred resorting to telegrams as Jean didn't have a telephone. There were early problems to solve such as formulating keys suitable for a popular readership and drawing up regional lists of plants. Jean was particularly concerned about her knowledge of Mallee flora – she had only spent ten days botanising there – and especially relied on Willis's help with this. Winifred took responsibility for the orchid section which Willis then revised. Jean was constantly sending queries to Willis but she also saved many for her visits to the Herbarium when she went to study the specimens, working at a bench in one of the upstairs rooms housing the collections. She fitted in easily with Herbarium staff, always eager to talk botany, and often arriving with a boiled fruit cake for staff morning teas.[12]

Back in Tyers, as she began writing the text, Jean always kept her readership in mind, aware that she was preparing a field guide for amateur naturalists. She wanted her writing to evoke 'vivid mental pictures' that would help readers with identification of the plants she was describing, but the book's pressing deadline prevented her from spending the time she would have liked to craft the plant descriptions.[13] Of the 2,200 Victorian wildflowers identified at the time, nearly half were described in the book. They were organised into one hundred sections which were then arranged in botanical sequence, beginning with ferns, the simplest forms of vascular plants, and ending with daisies, highly specialised flowers. Winifred revised each section. The olearias, she pronounced, were 'woolly' and both she and Willis worked on these. Jean was grateful for their input.

Readers of 'From Day to Day in the Garden' gained insights to the new project that was competing with Jean's gardening time. It was a 'gloriously shining day' after a frosty morning, she wrote in an article in 1949, but she couldn't go out into the garden because of her botanical work. 'By ten o'clock I had finished my housework and made the butter and set the milk, so I sat down to write. The work I was doing needed specimens and reference books, a microscope and other paraphernalia within reach'. She worked at her dining room table and ignored the tantalising view over the garden until she went out to collect kindling later in the day, a good excuse to enjoy the winter sunshine.[14]

It didn't take long for the publishers to realise that their initial deadline of six months was impossible and they extended it to early in the next year, 1950. Jean received the galley proofs in January, and began carefully correcting them. Later in the month the illustrations for the book were finalised: 175 black and white photographs, mostly provided by Jean's friend F.J. Bishop. There was panic late in February when the book was about to go to the printers and the publishers received an urgent call from Winifred to say they had the wrong index.

Willis wrote the introduction, and stressed the importance of having a popular guide to Victorian wildflowers – 'in plain language' – because so many Victorians were ignorant of their native flora. Indifference and 'the axe, fire, tillage, grazing animals, rabbit pest, noxious weeds and expanding settlement' were leading to destruction and even extinction of Australian flora. 'Miss Galbraith's work should go far in supplying a long-felt want', he wrote.[15] In her preface, Jean included heartfelt thanks for Winifred who had conceived of the project and helped in every way she could. 'She has also arranged the photographs, written the orchid section and revised every page … suggesting many improvements'. Jean's preface, like Willis's introduction, also included a plea for conservation. She wrote of the beauty of Victorian plants – 'the robe of the countryside' – there for all Victorians to enjoy and hoped her book would 'help to preserve this fast vanishing robe'.[16]

But there was no elation when Jean, Winifred and Jim received their copies in August. They were devastated to see that the publishers had ignored all of Jean's corrections on the galley proofs, and to know that 4,000 books had been printed with errors in them. Jim wrote to the manager of Colorgravure to protest about this, claiming the mistakes detracted from the reliability of 'an otherwise excellent work'. He knew they were not the fault of the author and demanded a corrigendum.[17] Corrigenda slips were printed but they only covered part of Jean's original corrections.

In a letter to Jim, Jean expressed how she felt about the book. She was trying not to waste energy 'fretting about the unavoidable'. Her pragmatism and acceptance of the inevitable prevented her from being consumed by anger and disappointment. Ultimately, she knew she had done the best she could in the time allowed, but she could not feel proud of the book. She told Jim, too, how sorry she felt for Winifred, who was extremely angry. 'She uses so much vitality "kicking against the pricks". My own feeling', she continued, 'is that you must be heartily sick of the book in which – as I said before – the Galbraith-Waddell combination is not always a happy one, though that remark is not meant to detract at all from my feeling of indebtedness to Winifred'.[18]

Despite the errors, *Wildflowers of Victoria* was a great success. As the first popular field guide to Victorian wildflowers, it was snapped up by readers who wanted to identify native plants and learn more about them. Jean received many letters from people who told her how useful the book was and how accessible they found the text.[19] 'Perhaps you will be interested to know of our splendid holiday at Wilsons Promontory with "Wildflowers of Victoria"', wrote one reader, Mollie Elder, soon after the book was published. Thanks to the book, she was able to identify nearly every flower she found, and took it everywhere in her pack. Miss Currie from Lardner near Warragul, a field naturalist and daughter of selectors who had cleared mountain ash forest from their land, wrote to congratulate Jean on the book and tell her how 'grateful' she was that it had been published. 'It would seem as if it was still in time to help some of our Flora', she wrote, although she worried that 'New Australians' could pose a threat to their survival.[20]

Through the book, Jean became an unseen presence on countless wildflower excursions throughout the state. 'We'll take Jean Galbraith,' naturalists would say as they set off on a drive into the bush and put the wildflower guide in the car.[21] Eric Webb Ware from the FNCV described the constant cry he heard on club botany excursions. 'Where's my Jean Galbraith? What does she say?'[22] Botanical artist Betty Conabere described *Wildflowers of Victoria* as the 'glovebox Bible'. Its 'lucidity', she considered, made the book essential equipment for naturalists' field trips.[23]

Jean's window of opportunity for extended botanical writing, field work and research at the Herbarium, so necessary for preparing the field guide, was short-lived as she became a full-time carer again, this time caring for her uncle and aunt, Fred and Fan Galbraith. They had become increasingly frail, with Fan beginning to suffer from dementia and in need of constant attention. They came to live at 'Dunedin' and Jean became so committed to their care that she was often unable to leave the house for long periods. 'I have an elderly very nervous invalid with me at present and cannot concentrate on anything except after she retires for the night', Jean wrote to Jim Willis in 1951 after Fan had come to stay. Her time for botanising, she told him, was 'nil … I haven't left the place here for months – and for writing – well just the minimum on which I can manage'.[24] Jean did all she could for her aunt but on medical advice, Fan was admitted to the Kew Mental Hospital in 1956, where she died a month later. Jean's gentle Uncle Fred remained at 'Dunedin' and Jean looked after him until his death in 1961.[25] For most of the 1950s, any botanical work had to be juggled with her caring responsibilities and her need to be close to the house.

After the field guide had sold out and the Victorian Education Department requested more copies, Colorgravure approached Jean in 1955 to completely revise it for a second edition. Most of this could be done at home and Jean sat down to the task with gusto, not just correcting the errors that had gone through the first time, but also improving and updating the text.[26] But she was soon devastated to find that the second edition was almost identical to the first. The only changes that had been made to the text were those printed in the original corrigendum. The corrections and revisions she had just carefully and laboriously completed at the publishers' request were not incorporated in the second edition which also had a print run of 4,000 copies. Colorgravure editor, Vera Francis, tried to justify this. The corrections had been ignored, she told Jean, because the publishers had to hurry with the publication or else the contract with the Education Department would be void. Also, there were 'practical economies' that made it impossible to do them all. But she promised to keep all of the revisions 'in case there is another reprint and time allows'.[27]

Jean's intense disappointment was evident in her letter to Willis, full of underlining. 'Colorgravure are using none of my revisions', she told him. 'It's hard to imagine wilfully reprinting errors. I had hoped this time to have an edition of which I was not ashamed'. The book's publication coincided with a family tragedy, the death of her seven-year-old niece Margaret, Angus's only child, which put her disappointment in perspective. '[O]ther happenings keep this from being too important', she told Jim. 'I refuse to fret about it and am resigned to having once again to feel apologetic about it'.[28] But this was a brave front; it was not so easy to endure the second disappointment. As she acknowledged several years later, the second edition was much more distressing than the first, after being asked to revise the book, but then having all the corrections ignored, and feeling there was nothing she could do to stop the errors being perpetuated.[29]

But once again, when the second edition appeared, Jean received appreciative responses from readers. As well as letters from many field naturalists, there were endorsements from people with a professional interest in botany. One enthusiastic user was garden designer Edna Walling, who was also a committed promoter of native flora and author of *The Australian*

Roadside, that stressed the importance of conserving roadside vegetation. She told Jean she didn't know what she would have done without the field guide to help with a new manuscript she was writing, 'On the Trail of Australian Wildflowers'. As it had been for Conabere, the field guide was a 'glovebox Bible' for Walling: her increasingly battered copy went everywhere, she told Jean.[30]

In 1958, *Wildflowers of Victoria* demanded Jean's attention again. The *Herald* was going out of book publishing, and Colorgravure was about to offload all its book stock, including the field guide. The book had been selling in shops for around sixteen shillings but the publishers were prepared to sell the remaining copies as a job lot for one and ninepence each, altogether £157. Jean's friends and colleagues in the FNCV were outraged to hear that the remaining copies would be sold cheaply to get rid of them. Knowing that Jean needed the money, they worried that the royalties would become negligible. They were also concerned that her botanical knowledge was being undervalued. E. Coghill summed it up in a letter to Jean. The club felt very strongly about the publishers' plans to 'dump your book on the market' and deprive the book of 'much of its value as a serious scientific work'.[31] The FNCV held meetings about *Wildflowers of Victoria* and an agreement was reached in consultation with Jean. The club would buy all the remaining copies from Colorgravure and give Jean, immediately, fifteen guineas in royalties. The FNCV would then take charge of marketing and distribution and Jean would receive royalties of 10% of sales. Jean refused to take any payments until the club had recovered its costs and she also stipulated that the Native Plants Preservation Society should be given a share of the profits because of Winifred Waddell's role in securing the book's publication.

Jean's negotiations over the book were a mixture of practicality and fairness. Field naturalist friends, including prominent member Arthur Swaby, urged her to buy all the remaining copies. Swaby calculated that she could get royalties of up to £800 if she sold them herself, and he urged her to be practical. 'I could shake you and all your Christian guilessness', he wrote in exasperation at her course of action.[32] But for Jean, buying the books was easier said than done. She didn't have the money for the bulk purchase, and without a telephone or car, she couldn't market or distribute the books. 'You are entirely so unmercenary that you rob yourself', was Swaby's opinion.[33]

By 1962, all the books had been sold. The FNCV had made a profit of £454, the Native Plants' Preservation Society received £226 and Jean was paid royalties of £82.[34] She had also been made an honorary life member of the FNCV in 1959 for outstanding services to the study of botany and to the club. The field guide was still in demand, and it was Jean's great wish to have a third edition printed. She wanted a book with all the inaccuracies fixed, a book she didn't need to apologise for, a book of which she could feel proud.

Jean was soon in correspondence with Nelsons about a third edition. While the Australian representatives were positive, the project had to be approved by the parent company in Edinburgh. The book was sent to a reviewer, only identified as a 'top Cambridge botanist', who produced a very discouraging report.

> [The book] seems to fall between two stools. As it only includes a selection of the species it is not going to satisfy the professional botanists for very long; on the other hand, I don't see how the non-professional flower lover is going to be able to make use of more than half of it, simply because the guides to identification are not clear enough. For a fairly large number of species the ecological guide and the black and white photographs may help the beginner to put a name to a plant with a degree of certainty. But in the larger genera, particularly the Wattles, it would be practically impossible for a beginner to find a name with certainty because of the absence of keys and because only a selection of the species are mentioned at all; there are three black and white photographs to cover this enormous group. In a case like this and with the Myrtaceae as well, it would be better to leave them out as too difficult, or not be afraid to produce some dichotomous keys.
>
> I do not believe there is a satisfactory halfway house between popular wild flowers and a good scientific flora.[35]

Jean sent a spirited defence of her book to Nelsons. Modest and unassuming as she was, Jean knew the value of her work and the extent to which it had helped people identify Victorian flora. She was not backward in defending her work. 'Either the book is condemned out of hand on the word of a botanist who knows the plants and not the conditions', she told the publishers, 'or you get in touch with people in Australia who have used it, and act on their opinions'.[36]

Nelsons were also concerned that Angus & Robertson were publishing a competing book, *Wild Flowers of Australia*, and asked Jean for comment. The book was a reprint of a guide written by New South Wales botanist and lecturer Thistle Harris in 1938, and illustrated with wildflower paintings of Adam Forster. In the defence she wrote to Nelsons, Jean was relatively dismissive of the book's text and scope. It only described 400 species for the whole of Australia, of which less than 100 were Victorian, while *Wildflowers of Victoria*, she pointed out, covered 1000 species. 'The descriptions are of little help in identification but all are illustrated in colour and are good'.[37]

Jean's suggestion of contacting an Australian reviewer bore fruit. She received a letter from Dr Ethel McLennan, formerly an associate professor in the botany school at Melbourne University. Nelsons had approached McLennan for her opinion on reprinting the book. 'To put it in a nutshell I feel emphatically that it should be', she wrote to Jean. The book needed extensive updating, revising and some new keys, but she also told Jean how useful she found it herself when she was out in the field.[38] McLennan's opinion was influential and Jean was given the go-ahead from Edinburgh to start preparing a new edition with substantial revisions and new keys. 'We'll get those corrections at last', she wrote exultantly to Jim Willis.[39] Winifred Waddell was delighted too.

It was May 1962 when Jean received the go-ahead from Nelsons. The news came at an inconvenient time: not long after Fred Galbraith's death, and just as Jean was preparing to leave on a three month trip to Queensland. Nelsons wanted the book completed quickly, which meant she had to start the revisions immediately, including a fortnight's research in the Herbarium. She wrote to Jim Willis for his opinion of a highly unconventional request.

Would it be possible to sleep at the Herbarium, so that she could work at night and make the most of her time? Would this contravene public service rules? 'I'd have a sleeping bag and would go out for meals except breakfast which is easy to prepare and would not be there for the weekend'.[40] It was fortuitous for Jean that Willis was acting director of the Botanic Gardens and Herbarium when he received her letter, and was able to give his permission. She would be there in early June, she replied, 'complete with sleeping bag – cup, saucer and plate – I shall put my belongings as unostentatiously as possible … keep doors locked and lights not on too late, have my morning meal over and be ready for work before the normal hour for opening the doors'.[41]

It was an unforgettable fortnight at the Herbarium for Jean, living, working, eating and sleeping with botany. Her bed was a couch upstairs in the 'foreign room', where the overseas collections were housed. Known as 'the baron's couch', it had belonged to Ferdinand von Mueller.[42] For two weeks, a strong smell of burnt toast greeted staff when they arrived for work in the morning. Then it was time for Jean to prepare for Queensland.

Most of Jean's botanising had been restricted to Victoria, but this trip to Queensland gave her the opportunity to see flora from new bioregions. Her friends Anne Burnet, now Hawkins, and her husband Charles, invited Jean to join them on a trip to Mooloolaba. Anne and Charles were bird and flower enthusiasts and Charles was a keen flower photographer. With the station wagon packed and Charles at the wheel, they headed north. They crossed the great Clarence River in northern New South Wales, and Jean experienced the dense rich green vegetation of the region with its sugar cane farms and 'flame trees burning against the green'.[43] When they stopped to botanise, she encountered iconic flora – a golden guinea flower twining in coastal vegetation with flowers eight centimetres in diameter, giant river she-oaks that arched overhead. It rained as they drove further north. Surfers Paradise was drenched and dismal, and the Glasshouse Mountains were obscured by mist, until Jean was rewarded with sudden views of high peaks.

They reached Mooloolaba and settled into a house with views of the sea and river, and the prospect of leisurely exploration of rainforest, heathlands, mountains and coast. 'Here I am surrounded by wildflowers and nesting birds and sunlit seas and glorious landscapes and hardly able to realise it is cold and wet in Victoria', Jean wrote to Jim Willis in August. She reported on the specimens she had collected, the experience of keying out strange plants, and of her correspondence with Nelsons who had written to say they wanted the copy of the field guide as soon as possible.[44] Life was very comfortable at Mooloolaba, playing scrabble in the evenings, feasting on tropical fruit bought from local farms. Memorable for Jean was the taste of her first avocado. But there was no escape from the monthly *Garden Lover* articles. She wrote them on the sunny verandah, describing for readers the landscapes, gardens and native vegetation of south east Queensland. It was a new experience not being able to name all the plants she saw in gardens, she told them, but there was much in the bush that helped her to feel at home.[45] She also wrote a detailed diary in exercise books to circulate among family and friends, and then keep as a permanent record of her trip. On Sundays she had quiet times by herself, reading exhortations in lieu of going to meetings.

Jean became well-versed in Queensland's temperate and subtropical vegetation. She also visited the herbarium in Brisbane and received considerable help with identification from the staff. After her time in Brisbane, she set off on a solo excursion, catching the train to Toowoomba and then changing to a smaller one travelling to Glenmorgan on the western Darling Downs. It arrived in the dark, but Jean was immediately spotted by the station master. "You for Myall Park?" he asked. Jean was going to visit David and Dorothy Gordon and see their renowned native garden.[46] Dave Gordon had started the garden on his grazing property in the early 1940s, filling it with seeds and plants collected from all around Australia. Many of the plants were not in cultivation elsewhere. Sheltered by local wattles and native pine, the garden was so extensive and overwhelming that Jean had difficulty describing what she saw. She spent two days exploring and taking cuttings, helped at times by Dave, the gardener, and an assistant. There were so many highlights: the banksia section she found breathtaking, especially the glowing orange cones of *Banksia burdettii*. The wattles and eucalypts were beyond counting and she was surrounded by spectacular grevilleas and hakeas. She described a wonderful *Homoranthus* and its mass of tiny yellow citron flowers, but with one disadvantage. "'It smells of mice", says Dot, "strong mice" and so it does, only mice mixed with honey which makes it rather worse'.[47]

Jean worked on one of the verandahs, sorting her cuttings at a large table and pressing specimens. She became friendly with the Gordons' three daughters, and spent time in the combined herbarium/studio upstairs, where Dave's specimens were housed and Dorothy painted wildflowers. On her last day, they went out in the Land Rover for Jean to see the country and its vegetation, much of it new to her: mulga, brigalow, myalls, wilga, sandalwood. 'And then we came to the Condamine! It symbolised all the far-off inland I had never expected to see. All its associations with shearing and droving, songs etc', Jean wrote in her diary, quoting lines from the folksong 'Banks of the Condamine'. They passed a group of eucalypts with grey fibrous bark and top branches that were smooth and white.

"What are they?" I asked

"Coolabahs", answered Dave.

Of course! What else but Coolabahs should be growing on the banks of the Condamine?[48]

The Gordons had become firm friends by the time Jean left Myall Park and returned to Toowoomba to meet up with Anne and Charles. They headed for home through New South Wales, enjoying more wildflower encounters. When they reached Melbourne, Jean was dropped off at Angus and Ella's in Clayton. The Queensland journey had left her with 'years of memory'.[49]

Jean didn't return to 'Dunedin' but immediately resumed her revision of *Wildflowers of Victoria*. She worked for the next ten days in the Herbarium, updating nomenclature, incorporating new discoveries, adding more species.

Once she was home, she continued with her meticulous line by line corrections and also devised new keys, as Ethel McLennan suggested these would make the book suitable for first year botany students. She approached artist Ruth Iggsten about new line drawings for a glossary and three pages of orchid illustrations.

But then, as she wrote to her friend Norman Wakefield, editor of the *Victorian Naturalist*, the 'bombshell' arrived.[50] It was a letter from Nelsons saying they would no longer be publishing the book. New policies were being introduced after a change in management, including publishing fewer technical books. The meticulously revised field guide, on which Jean had expended so much energy, was stalled. She hated telling Winifred, she told Jim Willis. 'You can imagine her'.[51]

Fortunately, Wakefield was aware that Longmans had expressed an interest in publishing the field guide and he successfully approached them to take over the project in 1964. Jean's commitment to getting the revised book into circulation was so strong that she offered to take a lower royalty. She firmly believed the book had value in 'helping people to protect plants through being able to recognise them', and a reduced royalty would keep the cost of the book down.[52] Norman Wakefield edited the revised manuscript. Although this was a great help for Jean, it further delayed publication. A lecturer at the Monash Teachers' College, Wakefield was also completing his Master of Science thesis and had to devote any spare time to this. The long-awaited proofs finally arrived in Tyers just when Jean was suffering a bad attack of bronchitis. She struggled on with checking them to avoid any further delay.

The third edition of *Wildflowers of Victoria* appeared in 1967. A new dust jacket featured an elegant Margaret Stones illustration of grass trees, which distinguished it from the earlier editions. Significantly, reviews endorsed the importance of an accessible field guide and the success of the author in bridging the gap between the popular and the scientific, something the 'top Cambridge botanist' had thought neither possible nor desirable. 'The special value of this book lies in the fact that it is an authoritative botanical work, yet one which is fashioned in a style to fill the requirements of the amateur botanist or plantsman', wrote a reviewer in *The Age*. The review in the *Tasmanian Naturalist* pointed out its usefulness for Tasmanians as there was no comparable field guide to Tasmania's wildflowers. 'The book is not intended to replace a Flora for the botanist', the reviewer continued, 'but is excellent as a field guide for the plant lover or naturalist'. Prominent naturalist J. Ros Garnet reviewed the book for the Victorian National Parks Association newsletter with a ringing endorsement of Jean's commitment to conservation:

> Jean Galbraith's book must be recognised as an important contribution to the conservation of the flora in this State. To know the plants is to value them and to value them is to wish to preserve them.[53]

Wildflowers of Victoria had first appeared in 1950 when it was welcomed by field naturalists and wildflower lovers as an accessible guide for identifying native flora. The subsequent editions were published to acclaim and the book had become an essential reference for naturalists. But for Jean, it had taken seventeen years before she had a book of which she could finally feel proud.

Chapter 10

FREELANCING

Throughout the highs and lows of *Wildflowers of Victoria*, Jean had to maintain her other writing commitments, necessary for her income. As she told Jim Willis in 1956, she was successful as a freelance writer through having developed an area of expertise, 'but you must have a lot of work published to make a living'.[1] Ironically though, when her growing reputation led to more commissions in the 1950s, her time for writing was again limited by caring responsibilities and she was cut off from field work and new experiences that would extend her botanical knowledge and provide content for articles and stories. She continued to rely on her home, garden, landscapes and memories for material, often recycling themes for new readerships. But the parochial nature of her writing did not diminish her influence. From the dining room table where she worked by the window, momentarily distracted by a flash of wings at the bird table or the colour of a flower in sunlight, Jean's writing spread around Australia and reached a diverse readership. Crosbie Morrison realised the national significance of her work. 'Not only have I a profound respect for your knowledge of field botany', he wrote to Jean, 'but I regard the work you have been doing through the schools and elsewhere to broaden the interest in, and knowledge of our flora (and especially our humbler flora) as of prime importance for this country'.[2] The 'prime importance' of Jean's work was more than increasing knowledge of Australian flora. Through her freelance writing in its many modes – her articles, stories, books, broadcasts, botanical writing and field guides – she helped countless Australians to see, understand and value their own landscapes, to delight in the beauty surrounding them and to realise the importance of protecting Australian plants.

When she was working on the first edition of *Wildflowers of Victoria*, Jean started a long association with the *Educational Magazine*, a teachers' journal published by the Victorian Education Department. The editor commissioned Jean as a 'field naturalist of some distinction' to write articles that would help teachers to identify Victorian trees.[3] Her first series, 'Know Your Trees', appeared among articles such as 'Speech Therapy for Victorian Children' and 'Is Your Science Room Safe?', and was written in her accessible, informative yet evocative style. It was followed by more series on Australian flora and she continued writing articles for the journal well into the 1960s. Jean was now writing for children in the *Victorian School Paper*, and for their teachers in the *Educational Magazine*.

She branched into broadcasting after being asked by the Australian Broadcasting Commission (ABC) to write nature study scripts for primary school children. The scripts were 'not to be fanciful', she was instructed, but 'factual accounts of interesting things in nature'. Each program lasted for thirteen and a half minutes. Her challenge was to write for a spoken medium, using simple language and short sentences. Jean sent off a draft script and was told she had the right 'spirit and atmosphere'.[4] Payment for each script with accompanying teachers' notes and activities was three guineas, and the programs were broadcast in the early 1950s. Her topics ranged from programs on butterflies and daisies to yabbies and freshwater crayfish. Inspired by Squirl or Little Chap, the orphaned sugar glider who had first appeared in a *Wild Life* article, she wrote one script called 'Feathertail, a Tiny Acrobat of the Gum Tree', which drew children's attention to these tiny marsupials and their remarkable tails. After her first bird program went to air, she received enthusiastic feedback from a teacher in Melbourne who was also a bird enthusiast. All the pupils and teachers at his school were thrilled by the program about the pardalote, he told her. 'Hoping you will thrill us with many more of your wonderful stories'.[5]

More scripts covered ferns, grasses, how leaves adapt to their environments, wattles, aphis and fish, but there was some criticism of her writing. 'While your work has been excellent, it has in some instances been rather too abstract and scientific for the age range', Janet Mitchell of the ABC wrote. 'We would like a more imaginative approach, more along the lines of the nature stories you have written for the School Paper'. Jean had avoided using her trademark story style because of the ABC's emphasis on 'the factual', but told Mitchell she was very happy to adopt an imaginative approach as it was 'more natural' to her.[6] In 1953, however, the program's orientation changed to simulating nature study excursions, and Jean was no longer required as a scriptwriter.

But this was not the end of her involvement in radio broadcasts for children. Ever since her nephew Peter had come to stay at 'Dunedin', Jean had been a devoted listener to the ABC's 'Kindergarten of the Air', a program that had begun as a wartime expediency for Western Australian children whose kindergartens had been closed for fear of Japanese invasion. The program became so popular that it was broadcast nationally. In kitchens, dining rooms and lounge rooms around the country, children joined in with songs and activities presented by a kindergarten teacher and pianist, before scrambling to sit as close as possible to the wireless, breathlessly waiting for the program's highlight, 'Story Time'. Early in 1955, Jean sent off a sheaf of stories for the much loved 'Story Time'. They were all about Grandma Honeypot, a mixture of Jean and her mother, who lived in a small cottage surrounded by a garden, bush and a stream. Her grandchildren, John and Marigold, were regular visitors and shared her adventures with birds, wildflowers, possums, orphaned feathertail gliders, honeypots [*Acotriche serrulata*], bush picnics and river pebbles.

'It was a pleasure to read stories which are excellently written', 'Kindergarten of the Air' presenter Ann Roberts wrote to Jean. She also provided advice on making some of the stories more accessible for pre-school children. 'Grandma Honeypot and the Blue Wrens', which included poetry, was more appropriate for an older age group, but as it was a 'gorgeous story', Roberts suggested Jean revise it. The story of Grandma Honeypot and the feathertail glider – more recycling of Little Chap – needed revising to get straight to the point to capture the children's attention. But Roberts also emphasised how outstanding and original the stories were:

> Please believe me when I say that your stories have a freshness and vitality that I haven't come across for many a day, so that I hope you haven't minded my comments, and I also hope you will send them back to me <u>as soon as you can</u>. I'm looking forward to telling them very much indeed.[7]

Jean worked quickly on the revisions and returned them to Roberts at the ABC. The alterations to the stories were just right, Roberts told her: 'I only hope I can do them justice'.[8] When they went to air in winter that year, the nature adventures of Grandma Honeypot and her grandchildren were heard in homes around the country.

As broadcasting the *Honeypot* stories didn't prevent publication elsewhere, Jean offered them to the *New South Wales School Magazine* where they were published for young readers during 1956. There were new stories as well, such as Grandma Honeypot – in detective mode with her offsider John – solving the mystery of the vandalised blue pansies after discovering a bowerbird's bower that was littered with blue items in the garden. The stories were illustrated by Noela Young, the *School Magazine*'s artist. Soon after 'Grandma Honeypot's Possums' was published, the editor received a letter from class prefect Judith Parker, on behalf of grade three girls at the Stockton Public School. Judith reported on how much all the girls loved the story of Grandma Honeypot and the possums, and also asked for information on the artist. 'Could you let us know who NV or NY is?'[9] Noela Young would soon become well-known to thousands of children as the illustrator of Ruth Park's *Muddle-Headed Wombat* books, portraying the 'terribubble' muddles Wombat found himself in with his friends practical Mouse and the vain Tabby Cat.

After the *Honeypot* stories had appeared in broadcasts and *School Magazine* serials, Angus & Robertson published them as a book in 1962, with Noela Young as illustrator. The book was an immediate success. 'The children have simply gone mad about Grandma Honeypot this year', a Sydney school

'Feathertail' in *Grandma Honeypot*, illustrated by Noela Young.
Reproduced with permission from Noela Young

librarian told Noela Young when she issued an invitation for author and illustrator to visit her school during Children's Book Week.[10] Had Jean been able to attend, the children could have been excused for thinking Grandma Honeypot herself was visiting, a kindly spectacled woman in her late fifties wearing sensible shoes, her hair coiled around in a plait, and a storyteller with an inexhaustible supply of nature stories who had a great rapport with children.

Drawing on her own experience in children's publishing, Noela Young told Jean she should be 'badgering A&R' to publish a follow-up *Honeypot* book. She compared Jean's writing with that of the enormously successful Leslie Rees who was the winner of the inaugural Children's Book Council

Award, and author of multiple nature stories, including the 'Digit Dick' series. 'It is a pity not to have someone writing for children who really knows and loves animals and nature', Noela Young wrote to Jean. 'People like Leslie Rees have produced successful nature stories but they have been coldly and scientifically written from second hand knowledge to a certain formula'.[11] However the charm of the *Honeypot* stories secured their own momentum. The New South Wales Education Department chose *Grandma Honeypot* as a supplementary reader for grade two pupils and a new edition of 25,000 copies was printed in 1964. A braille edition was published for visually impaired children. Nature adventures with Grandma Honeypot continued to appear in the *New South Wales School Magazine* in the 1960s, a mixture of reprints of earlier stories, as well as new ones.

Through correspondence, Jean became a great friend of the editor of the *School Magazine*, Doris Chadwick, who was also a children's writer, especially of historical fiction set in colonial New South Wales. The *School Magazine* played a major role in promoting Australian literature during Chadwick's editorship, serialising novels by Australia's leading children's authors such as Nan Chauncey, Ruth Park, Patricia Wrightson and Joan Phipson. Patricia Wrightson worked on the editorial staff, later becoming editor of the *School Magazine*, and developed a friendly correspondence with Jean. Wrightson's books, drawing on Aboriginal mythology, received wide international acclaim, and Jean greatly admired them. Wrightson always sent Jean copies when new books were published. Besides the regular income that educational publishing provided, Jean was also grateful for the contact it brought her with other writers.

Jean was also commissioned to write nature study text books. In 1963, Thistle Stead (also known as Thistle Harris before her marriage to marine biologist David Stead) asked Jean to contribute to a series of nature study texts for primary schools that she was editing for Longmans. Stead was a botanist and author who lectured in biology at the Sydney Teachers' College. She had a reputation for being forthright and dogmatic.[12] Jean knew and admired Stead as an ardent conservationist and a stalwart of the Wild Life Preservation Society, even though she had been dismissive of Stead's book, *Wildflowers of Australia*. Stead asked Jean to write a booklet about seed production, suitable for seven to nine-year-olds.[13] A very simple approach was needed, as well as plenty of suggestions for activities, and the publication would be well illustrated.

Jean was faced with a dilemma on how to write a book explaining seed production for young readers, especially after her experience with the ABC when she had followed instructions to write factual nature study scripts, but had been criticised for not adopting the story style she used so effectively elsewhere. She decided on narrative and drafted a story about a small boy, Jim, who discovered why bees were so necessary to flowers, and then followed his process of learning about pollination and seed production. The publishers rejected the story format, so she re-wrote the booklet as an instructional text, with short sections on nectar, pollen, petals, pistils and the making and scattering of seeds. She was sorry Longmans didn't like the story approach, she told Stead. 'I know if I were a seven year old I would remember it better that way, and also it is easier to infuse the atmosphere of continuous life and interest that way.'[14] For the illustrations, Jean approached Moira Pye, a friend of Lillias Lothian, Grandfather's daughter, with whom Jean was still in touch. Moira Pye was immersed in writing and illustrating a series of infant school nature study readers for use in both Australia and New Zealand, but she took on the task.[15] Thistle Stead, however, was not as easy to work with, as Jean's correspondence revealed. *From Flower to Fruit* appeared in 1965, an informative and attractive publication with brightly coloured illustrations. The last chapter, 'How Can We Help?', focused on the message of not picking wildflowers but leaving them to make seeds and reproduce.

Jean continued working with Stead and wrote another booklet, *Fruits*, for senior primary school children, published in 1966. Stead was more interventionist with this book and rewrote a chapter, 'Why Plants have Fruit', which Jean considered 'obscure' and 'not satisfactory for children'. She sent it to Longman's production manager, Lionel Godfrey, and asked him to imagine that he was a child of ten when he read it. 'Does it convey a clear mental picture?' she asked.[16]

After the success of *Grandma Honeypot*, Angus & Robertson commissioned Jean to write a natural history book for children. 'The subject I have in mind', explained the editor Barbara Ker Wilson, who was also a children's author, 'is "animals that change their form" (caterpillar to butterfly, tadpole to frog etc). I think children are particularly fascinated by changing forms of insects and animals'. It was also a book that would need 'quite lavish illustrations'.[17] Jean, whose promptness and attention to deadlines were an editor's dream, quickly sent ideas for the book, provisionally titled 'Changing Shapes'. They were 'exactly what I hoped for', Ker Wilson replied, pleased that Jean was developing the project in a much more unusual and interesting way. As well as the dramatic transformations of caterpillars to butterflies and tadpoles to frogs, Jean proposed chapters on blue gums, albatross, dragonflies, kangaroos and pitcher plants. Finding photographs to illustrate the chapters was difficult and time consuming. Jean appealed to wildlife photographers, field naturalists and the CSIRO for images such as fish eggs hatching, a lacewing cocoon, ant-lion eggs and the digestive juice of a pitcher plant. Locating a photograph of a new-born kangaroo beginning its arduous climb to the pouch was particularly challenging. With the book's emphasis on growth, Ker Wilson suggested a new title, *The Wonderful Butterfly: The Magic of Growth in Nature*.

The Wonderful Butterfly appeared in 1968 and received enthusiastic reviews commending the way the author engaged young readers in experiencing nature. A review in the English journal *Books and Bookmen* especially praised Jean's writing style. 'Mrs Galbraith beautifully and simply conveys [the wonders of nature] with a naturalist's exactness of knowledge and a poet's sensitiveness to language and imagery, always to render it more real for the child'.[18] Chapters of *The Wonderful Butterfly* were also published in the *New South Wales School Magazine*. 'We know you like books about true things', editor Patricia Wrightson wrote in her introduction to the first instalment, 'but good ones by good writers are hard to find'.[19] She warmly recommended Jean Galbraith as a good writer about true things. In a letter to Jean, Wrightson praised the way the book was infused with a sense of wonder and asked her to write about the seashore for an anthology she was preparing for Collins, *Beneath the Sun: An Australian Collection for Children*.[20]

Jean was also writing a demanding series on wattles for the *Victorian Naturalist*, beginning in 1959. The series was Norman Wakefield's idea, part of his plan as editor to make the *Victorian Naturalist* a successor to Crosbie Morrison's *Wild Life* which had ceased publication. Jean was just the person to write articles that would help with lay identification of such an abundant genus. She conveyed the wattles' differing characteristics through choice adjectives and description, laced with botanical authority. They were lively articles that also expressed her feelings for wattle, as her article on the blackwood wattle, *Acacia melanoxylon*, shows. First came an evocative opening: '… blackwood for the sheltered valleys and kinder soils. Blackwood is a king amongst wattles, a forest tree of the higher rainfall areas, where its dark green phyllodes are foil for creamy white or primrose bloom in clusters of large heads'. Then the article continued with an accessible botanical description of the phyllodes, bark, pods and wood.[21] Norman Wakefield provided photographs when he could, or the ever-reliable F.J. Bishop photographic collection was mined. Jean wrote forty-three articles on wattles for the *Victorian Naturalist*, a series that fellow botanists Jim Willis and Helen Aston considered outstanding.[22] The articles prompted Professor John Turner, head of the Melbourne University botany school and a leading ecologist, to consider writing a similar book for a general readership on eucalypts. He asked Jean if she would contribute but, unfortunately, they were both too busy to pursue the idea in the early 1960s.[23] The wattle series also inspired up-and-coming botanists to write for general readers, including Leon Costermans, who wrote books on Australian trees and shrubs. He acknowledged his debt to Jean: 'I was inspired … by your series on Victorian wattles in the Vic Nat many years ago when there was very little available on Victorian flora', he wrote to Jean in the early 1980s. 'So thankyou again Jean!'[24]

During the 1960s, Jean became involved in several educational projects that were welcome additions to her freelancing income. At Professor Turner's suggestion, Joan Law-Smith, an aspiring botanical artist who lived in western Victoria, asked Jean if she could give her lessons on botany, necessary for her to progress with her art. For several years, Jean sent customised lessons to Law-Smith, who responded with completed exercises and drawings. A warm friendship developed. Joan Law-Smith later became a distinguished botanical artist, writer and gardener. The botanical correspondence between the two women, as well the story of their lives and friendship, was later published in a book beautifully illustrated by Joan Law-Smith's art.[25]

In 1963, Jean was invited to lecture on botany at the Council of Adult Education's Spring Schools at Mount Beauty in the Victorian alps, a commitment she fulfilled for the rest of the 1960s. The weeklong schools included courses in geology, botany, birds, painting and photography, and were taught by lecturers mostly drawn from Victorian universities and teachers' colleges. In promotional material, Jean was described as an expert botanist, writer and explorer of new botanical areas: 'Her book "Wildflowers of Victoria" is a "must" for people interested in their surroundings'.[26] Jean threw herself energetically into the schools, 'climbing flowery slopes … tasting the cool mountain wind in high places … following rocky streams below the last snowdrifts, finding rock gardens in various crevices … and sharing all these with a happy company, all eager to learn'.[27] One of the students at the 1965 school was artist Betty Conabere, who had been commissioned by the Maud Gibson Trust to paint Victoria's alpine plants for the Herbarium. She remembered Jean's 'elemental delight' in the high country, and admired the way she shared her knowledge and engaged with students. Leaping over watercourses or clambering on rocky outcrops – and always wearing a skirt, Jean was not known to wear trousers – her enthusiasm for the plants was infectious.[28]

Of course garden writing remained an important staple of her freelancing as she continued with her monthly 'From Day to Day in the Garden' series. December 1965 was a milestone and she reflected on forty years of contributing to the *Garden Lover*: 480 months and 480 articles.

> There are still things new and old to write about in the garden … but I always come back to the same valley, the same comfortable shabby old house, the same garden, the same interests and pleasures, and through all, the same self who loves and lives in the garden, that has, one hopes, developed with the years, but in no radical sense changed. The things that I thought of first importance forty years ago still come first. The things that delighted me then delight me still.[29]

But Jean was only too aware that parts of the 'Dunedin' garden were turning into a wilderness and many of her articles from the late 1950s described extreme measures of slashing and burning to bring it under control. Features of the garden that had enchanted her 'Garden in a Valley' readers in the 1930s had collapsed, been smothered by weeds or were beyond repair. The hedge, Walter Thornby's nostalgic evocation of England, had grown into an impenetrable thicket that could only be removed by burning. The bush house had collapsed under the weight of its creepers and fruit trees in the orchard had grown beyond Jean's capacity to prune them. Other parts of the garden were invaded by tradescantia, smilax, monbretia and honeysuckle. A new term crept into her *Garden Lover* articles: 'ungardening'. She lit fires to 'ungarden' the bush house and the hedge while neighbours stood by with hoses. It took a week of strenuous work and she was left with smoking ruins, but she was soon planning new gardens to replace them. This slash and burn policy was the beginning of a concerted campaign that continued for several years to try to restore order. Lance paid for professional help to bring the fruit trees under control, and Jean wondered if the nurseryman who took on the task had ever been asked to prune such an overgrown orchard.

As a garden writer, she reflected wryly on what people must think of the garden: '[W]hile my garden and I live happily together', she wrote in the *Garden Lover*, 'it is an example in many ways of how **not** to garden'.[30]

Readers didn't fail to notice that although Jean was writing about rampant weed invasion and large areas of neglect, her articles were illustrated by photographs of immaculate gardens with perfect lawns and impossibly neat beds. 'I sometimes wonder as to the criteria of choice of the incidental photographs with which your pages are interrupted', was one reader's comment.[31] Fortunately, the relationship Jean had with her readers was not affected by her frank confessions of garden chaos and letters continued to stream in, showing the rapport that existed between writer and readers. A letter from Mrs J. Armitage of Swan Hill on the River Murray, illustrates this. She was about to move to the Dandenong Ranges and start a new garden, and wanted to know if Correa could look after her water lilies while a new pond was being built. The plants could be shared when her garden was ready for them.[32] Jean was only too happy to oblige.

Even with her specialty areas of natural history, botany, garden and children's nature writing, there were times when Jean found it hard to make ends meet as a freelance writer, despite her simple and frugal lifestyle and producing much of her own food. In the mid-1950s she told Jim Willis that her writing was bringing in only two pounds a week, as her caring commitments limited time for earning. Notably, the new technology and household appliances that were finding their way into Australian homes at the time were unknown at 'Dunedin'. Jean didn't have a telephone until the 1960s, and even after it was connected, her preferred means of communication continued to be letters. She did not learn to drive and never owned a car and, in spite of her great love of classical music and her delight in concerts broadcast on the radio, it was some years before she had a record player. She never owned a television. She recycled, writing articles on unused pages of school exercise books and using blank pages of a 1940s financial ledger (donated by Eva West) to draft 'From Day to Day in the Garden' articles. Folders were made from the cardboard backing of used writing pads. She used the sleeves of old shirts to make drawstring bags.[33]

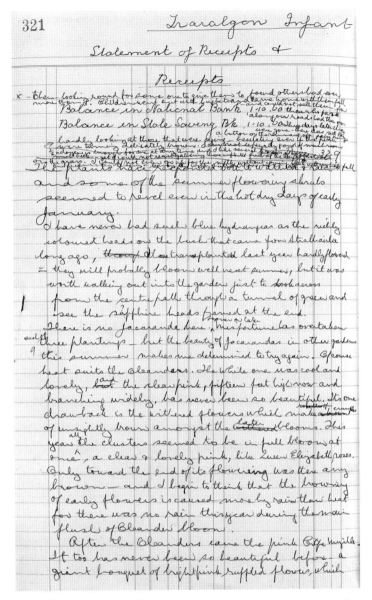

A page from a Traralgon Infant Welfare Centre ledger that Jean used for drafting articles for her long-running series, 'From Day to Day in the Garden'. Balances in bank accounts were minor interruptions to recycling.

Jean Galbraith Papers, Box 4094, MS 12637, Australian Manuscripts Collection, State Library of Victoria

Jean received support from the family. Angus carried out repairs when he came to visit. 'Doors that had stuck now open easily, gates that were rickety are satisfyingly firm, windows that had to be propped open now have their cords renewed, the possum that made its home in the wall, nibbling through the paper in two rooms, comes in no more', she informed readers after one visit.[34] In the mid-1950s, Lance and May and their family came to live in Traralgon when Lance was appointed to the staff of the primary school. It was a boon for Jean to have them so close, and especially welcome when Verna and her family moved back to Melbourne several years later. Jean was relieved when the family gave her a new tank after her water supply was threatened. Mending the leaking tank was beyond her and she couldn't afford a new one. Her nephews, now living close by, gave her hours of 'hard labour' in the garden as Christmas presents.

Garden Lover readers had some idea of her simple lifestyle when she told them the hot water service had been out of action for three months and she wrote of lighting a fire outside every morning, heating water in kettles and saucepans, and cooking breakfast at the same time.

> It is very lovely in the golden light between six and seven when the air is cool and still and I kneel before my little fire with a light-hearted feeling of holiday, making toast with a long handled wire fork, while the birds come around for crumbs. I enjoy the breakfast hour as I used to in our camping days ... Scrub wrens, blue smoke, mauve Rhododendron, Air from Handel's Water Music.[35]

Her delight in the flowers, birds, scents and sounds of the early morning was compensation for not having instant hot water. It gave her new access to beauty. She was happy to make do with the basic necessities. More important than material possessions were activities in the garden and the bush that gave her special experiences and memories. Her financial position improved in the 1960s when she had more time available for writing and was also eligible for the aged pension. The pension gave her a rise in salary.[36]

Soon after Fred Galbraith's death, Jean did something she had wanted to do for years. She caught the bus into Traralgon – it only ran on Fridays – and then boarded another travelling west along the Princes Highway, parallel to the railway line. She was keeping a look out for wildflowers growing along the line and left the bus at the next spot after spotting them. It was a spring day of sunshine and cloud, 'a perfect day for wildflowering', and she ate lunch in a sheltered hollow, surrounded by the flowers she loved the most.[37] According to Crosbie Morrison, they were 'our humbler flora' while to Jean they were 'the little flowers' or 'the flowers of the wayside', not showy or ostentatious and often overlooked. For Jean, though, they were full of wonder – the tinier the flower, the more wonderful it seemed.[38] Through her freelance writing in its many modes, her nature stories for school children and her field guides, she had worked hard to draw attention to these flowers and convey their beauty, and also to highlight their vulnerable status. Now she finally had the time to sit among the flowers she loved the most and enjoy their beauty. It was a simple thing to do, and it filled her with contentment.

Chapter 11

CHANGES

Jean's valley was changing irrevocably. For years, all that the Galbraiths could see of the State Electricity Commission's brown coal mining and power generating complex at Yallourn had been a 'city of lights long and low in the west', visible at night when they stood on a rise behind the house. But that changed after the war when the SEC was faced with meeting the spiralling demands for electricity in an energy-hungry Victoria. Operations at Yallourn expanded with the building of new power stations and extensions to the open cut mine, while the nearby dairying and railway centre of Moe was transformed into a dormitory town for SEC workers. The SEC began its inexorable march eastward to develop a new open cut mine and briquette factory at Morwell in the 1950s and build the Hazelwood power station in the 1960s. A massive development of an open cut mine and two power stations was completed thirty years later at Loy Yang, south of Traralgon. From Moe in the west to Traralgon in the east, a new region was created. The Latrobe Valley no longer meant the wide expanse of river flats between the foothills of the Great Dividing Range and the Strzelecki Ranges, but an industrial region dominated by the SEC. In an era of town planning, numerous schemes were devised to try to regulate the new developments, but there was little interest in protecting bush land or creating wildflower reserves. Great swathes of the Haunted Hills – widely known for their spectacular flora – were bulldozed to make way for extensions to the Yallourn open cut and for fire breaks. Local tracks notable for the carpets of wildflowers growing along them were widened to become roads. Flower-filled bush was cleared for housing estates and overburden dumps. The Latrobe River became polluted and began transporting industrial waste to the Gippsland Lakes. Australian Paper Manufacturers (APM) increased operations at their pulp mill to the south of Tyers and began clearing native forest on the slopes of Jean's valley for pine plantations to supply the mill. Much of the floriferous sandy country near Rosedale was cleared by APM for pine plantations too. During a time of housing shortage, the SEC's flagship, its garden city of Yallourn, noted for its avenues of deciduous trees and beautiful gardens, was systematically destroyed to mine the coal lying underneath.[1]

Although Jean was housebound in the 1950s, she was more than an observer on the hill as her valley became caught up in the whirlpool of postwar development. She continued her close association with Winifred Waddell and became the Gippsland representative of the Native Plants Preservation Society. The society's efforts to preserve small areas of bush mirrored her own ideas and actions on conservation, going back to the 1930s when she bought her small patch of bush to save it from being cleared and created her own wildflower sanctuary. Now, in the face of rapid development, preserving small areas of bush was increasingly urgent. Jean negotiated to establish wildflower sanctuaries and bush reserves with the SEC, APM, the Lands Department, the Country Roads Board, the Tourist Commission, the Town and Country Planning Board, local councils and even the Victorian premier, Henry Bolte.[2]

In a talk to a community group in Gippsland, Jean explained that her conservation stance was based on ecological and preservation reasons.[3] Reserves were needed where living things could be studied in relation to their environment, and also where species could be preserved. But she also passionately believed that people needed nature: 'unspoilt places', where people could 'watch the life of nature' and where beauty could be preserved and available to all. She argued especially that children should have access to nature to 'revel' in the unexpectedness of the bush and delight in the flowers. 'Any generation growing up without the opportunity to know the countryside in its full variety and beauty suffers irreparable loss'.[4] In her many community talks promoting wildflower sanctuaries, she often told audiences about a wildflower reserve at Traralgon South and its value to local children and the community, not knowing that the reserve – and the original township of Traralgon South – would soon disappear in the massive Loy Yang power station development.

As well as her ecological and preservation arguments, Jean's commitment to conservation was also fuelled by her faith: she deplored the destruction of God-given beauty. In her talks, she quoted from Genesis, that God had planted a garden and put man there to dress it and keep it:

> In all reverence I can say The Lord God planted a garden eastward in Gippsland but when man entered the garden he did not dress it and keep it. He bulldozed it and chopped it and slashed it and burned it and he built all sorts of unsightly buildings which are certainly useful but rarely beautiful.[5]

Jean was a descendant of selectors who had cleared virgin forest to create a productive farm, and was not against development and land clearing. Instead, she argued for what she called balanced development, explaining to the premier, Henry Bolte, that any future land clearing for farms in Victoria should always be accompanied by reserves where native bush could be preserved.[6] The reserves had benefits for farming. Remnant bush minimised erosion, created windbreaks for stock and provided shelter for native birds that kept insect pests in check.

Jean adopted a very measured, reasonable approach in her campaigning. She explained this to a group of field naturalists from the Mornington Peninsula:

> Nothing good is ever achieved by antagonising people. Be reasonable. Put yourself in other people's places. Men have to live. They have to have food and that means farms. Unfortunately they have to have cities and factories – and most people want some luxuries as well as necessities.[7]

Her methods of campaigning were shaped by her lifestyle and commitments. During the 1950s when she was caring for her aunt and uncle, there were many times when it was impossible to leave Tyers, even for a few hours, to attend meetings with government, municipal or company officials. Also, she didn't have a car, which made it difficult to attend site meetings in the bush, as they were often in isolated places. There was a certain irony when her now elderly friend, Eva West, suggested the only way Jean could travel to inspect a remote section of forest she wanted to protect from logging was by hitching a ride with a timber truck. Jean didn't have a telephone, making it difficult to discuss conservation issues with representatives from local councils, the SEC or APM. So instead, Jean fell back on her *métier* as a writer, and this became her most valuable asset in campaigns.

The popularity of *Wildflowers of Victoria* and her growing reputation as an expert on Victorian flora gave added authority to her writing and conservation arguments. She could also draw on her intimate knowledge of the area – her environmental memory – that was based on more than thirty years of detailed botanical observations. In her letters, she used lyricism to convey the beauty and significance of areas under threat. These elements are evident in a letter discussing the status of a once beautiful site near the Latrobe River with a local official.

> You probably remember a delightful 'avenue' of milk white manna gums that used to be there. Between the trees were pleasant grassy glades surrounded by wattles, eucalypts, purple berried turnip wood trees with shiny leaves, amber fruited and waxy flowered White Elderberry bushes, Elderberry Panax with its decorative leaves and berries, fragrant Violet bush, the Twining Silkpod with its curious long fruit, white clematis, wonga vine, hemp bush. Now the wattles remain and some thickets of tea tree but little else.
>
> Once we may have said "These plants grow everywhere". Now I don't know any place in the district where several of the plants I mentioned grow wild, and every patch of bush I know is disappearing. We must save something – and here is an opportunity to do so.[8]

Jean's particular concern for the spectacular flora of the Haunted Hills, where the Yallourn complex was located, led to a long association with the SEC. In her years of tireless negotiating, she often had the sympathetic ear of senior management, including the chairman of the SEC, Ralph Hunt, and the senior administrator at Yallourn, Brigadier Field. Yet as much as they wanted to preserve areas of flora, ultimately, as Field told Jean, their mandate to generate electricity and meet the ever increasing demands were of 'paramount importance to the State of Victoria'. Field tried to suggest other ways of preserving wildflowers than reserves. In response to one of Jean's letters about an area of native flora 'of unusual interest' that was earmarked for future SEC development, he suggested moving the plants or the possibility of 'reproducing' some of the species. Jean had to explain that cultivating wildflowers couldn't replace them in their natural habitat and it was the Native Plants Preservation Society's aim to preserve native vegetation in situ for future generations. This was particularly urgent in the Latrobe Valley where native plants were disappearing rapidly.[9] She did manage to secure an 'informal agreement' with the SEC forestry officer to leave a line of vegetation between the main transmission line, the railway and the Princes Highway, but she knew this would only be a temporary measure.[10]

So the breath-taking display of flowers in the Haunted Hills was soon erased. In 1955, after returning from an ANZAAS conference in Melbourne, Jean wrote in the *Garden Lover* of the disappearing 'garden' of the Haunted Hills where thousands of wildflowers had once bloomed from April to November. 'If here ... a strip of bush and wildflowers could have been preserved ...'[11]

Another powerful entity changing the face of the valley was APM. Jean's negotiations with the paper-making company began with trying to preserve a rare group of snow gums close to Tyers where APM was buying up land for plantations. But she was also concerned about the fate of land further afield near Rosedale and Longford, where APM was acquiring vast acreages for pine plantations in places where rare wildflowers grew. Jean also had extensive correspondence with the Victorian Forests Commission, especially after the Commission began logging alpine ash in the mountains to the north east of Tyers, to compensate for the loss of timber from forests closer to Melbourne after the catastrophic 1939 fires. She had sympathetic hearings from Country Roads Board officials who helped with protection of rare flora growing on roadsides.

There were some small successes, as Jean reported in her *Garden Lover* articles. She wrote of accompanying a group of shire councillors to inspect bush suitable for a reserve south of Traralgon. To the councillors it was unproductive land: "'It's nearly pure sand", they said. "It will never be any use for cultivation or pasture, but it is a good place for wildflowers and it would be a pity to let it be spoiled.'" As Jean told her readers, '[i]f everyone who had power to save and protect some small colony of wildflowers would do it as these Gippsland councillors are doing, our vanishing wildflowers could yet be saved'.[12] She wrote about going to a site near the Gippsland Lakes to help select land for a wildflower sanctuary at the new Dutson Downs sewerage farm that was being established to treat waste from the Latrobe Valley and prevent it from flowing into the Gippsland Lakes. Four thousand hectares were being cleared for the sewerage farm 'with the speed made possible by large modern machines'. Jean knew of the plants that grew there – tea tree, fringe myrtle, dampiera, boronia, kennedya, heath, hardenbergia, brown and golden peas – and found it a comfort to know that from the 4,000 hectares, fifteen or so hectares of wildflowers would be saved.[13]

Her solo campaigning changed in 1960 when an enthusiastic group of people, including Jean, met at the Morwell Fire Brigade Hall to discuss forming a local field naturalists club. People who joined the new society which became known as the Latrobe Valley Field Naturalists' Club (LVFNC) ranged from those with specialist interests – geologists, ornithologists and entomologists – to those with a love of 'natural beauty'. They began studying, documenting and protecting the local environment through working to conserve areas of bushland and roadside vegetation, compiling plant lists and bird lists throughout their region, writing submissions and spreading knowledge through nature displays and public events. The LVFNC also became involved in issues related to brown coal mining and electricity generation, such as overburden disposal, river diversion and water quality studies. The club's formation was significant for Jean because she was now collaborating with knowledgeable and energetic members who shared her commitment to studying and protecting the region and who became valued friends and colleagues. The club soon became a central focus for knowledge of the area's natural history. Its motto was 'Protect and Enjoy'.

An early LVFNC project, in which Jean's friends Ellen Lyndon and Jim Peterson played leading roles, was reserving a section of forest in the Jeeralangs, south of Morwell, as a national park. The extremely rare epiphytic orchid, *Sarcochilus australis*, the butterfly orchid, could still be found there. Establishing the Morwell National Park was a particularly difficult task as the forest was not Crown land and required the extra expense of land acquisition.[14] But this was achieved and the club was off and running.

After Fred Galbraith's death in 1961, Jean was able to throw herself into the new club's activities. She relished going to the annual campouts on Australia Day weekends and exploring new places on the many club field trips. Jean led botany excursions, always transmitting her enthusiasm for native plants to club members. While Jean's writing and botanical knowledge made her a 'star' within the club – members set off on botany excursions carrying copies of her field guide – she blended in easily with her fellow naturalists and was able to learn about their areas of expertise. According to the club's conservation coordinator, Bon Thompson, there can be a tendency for field naturalists to be competitive, but their club had a reputation as a 'very sharing club'. She thought much of this was due to Jean's influence: her personality and philosophy greatly contributed to the atmosphere at the club.[15]

During these years of rapid change in the Latrobe Valley, Jean's writing, in all its forms, served as a platform for conservation and protection of the fast disappearing wildflowers. Her conservation message permeated her writing for children, evident in her stories in the *New South Wales School Magazine* on combating erosion; discovering but not picking wildflowers; on the important role of trees as windbreaks and stabilising river banks; on revegetation and improving denuded landscapes. Her strong stance on wildflower protection was evident in the text books she wrote for the Longmans series edited by Thistle Stead, while redoubtable Grandma Honeypot's messages on respecting the natural world filtered through to readers. The three editions of *Wildflowers of Victoria* that occupied her for seventeen years were prepared with the firm conviction that spreading knowledge of native flora could help with its protection. Protecting wildflowers was a running thread in her garden writing.

Jean was also commissioned to write on conservation themes. The editor of the teachers' journal, the *Educational Magazine*, who was also a keen field naturalist, asked Jean to write a series he called 'Beauty in Distress' that stressed the urgency of preserving native plants, with the hope that a heightened awareness of conservation among teachers could be passed on to children. Published in the mid-1960s, the articles Jean wrote were direct and sober as she described the loss of heathlands, disappearance of orchids or vulnerability of ferns. She didn't absolve herself from the part she had played as a child in irresponsible picking, remembering especially the tree ferns she had gathered to decorate the hall for school Christmas concerts, 'their fronds nailed pitifully to the walls'.[16] She urged teachers to instil in pupils an interest and enthusiasm for wildflowers, to encourage them to admire the flowers' beauty without taking it.

For teachers, the articles may have become repetitive as she fulfilled her brief with a monthly description of former beauty and abundance that ended, inevitably, in a litany of loss.

> Do you know any heathlands with acres of rose and white far-spread; dense crimson on scarlet spikes along the roads; hills where dwarf wattles and peas seem to be set on a coloured mantle that dips and crumples with every hollow, and lies smooth on the rounded hills? No? Nor do I.[17]

But there was a particularly arresting article she wrote about the Tyers school ground, a cross between a story for teachers and an environmental history. Her article illustrated the importance of reserving bush for children and also the experiences the bush could offer. Based on her father's stories, her own school experiences and the impact of an increasing postwar population in Tyers, it was a history of changing landscapes and of how children had interacted with nature over time. Her account began with the earliest days of the school, when it was surrounded by dense tea tree and children played in its mysterious underworld. As settlement spread, the tea tree was cleared for a horse paddock, where children riding in from the hills tethered their horses during the day. The paddock was soon covered with wildflowers as plants shot up in the clearings, and children explored among chocolate lilies, billy buttons, milkmaids, yellow stars, triggers and buttercups. When bicycles and bus travel replaced horses, trees started growing in the horse paddock and it became a park with groves of blackwood, scattered peppermints and red box. Children climbed the trees and made cubbies when they wanted something more adventurous and creative than the school playground could offer. The paddock became too shady for the former abundance of wildflowers, but they still grew in sunny spaces. Eventually, though, as more families began settling in Tyers and enrolments increased, a progressive school committee bulldozed all the trees and levelled the horse paddock to form an oval with a cricket pitch. Organised games replaced child-centred adventures and discovery in the bush; blackwood, eucalypts and wildflowers were gone.[18]

Jean's *Garden Lover* series, 'From Day to Day in the Garden', was also steeped in calls for wildflower protection. It might be there in a passing reference to travelling on the train to Melbourne to visit the Herbarium, with readers learning how, for Jean, these journeys were now filled with trepidation. Once the railway line between Traralgon and Melbourne had been a 'pageant of flowers', she wrote, but now there were only three places where that abundance had survived. Each time she travelled on the train she was 'living in dread' that the wildflowers might be gone.[19]

The masthead for 'From Day to Day in the Garden' showed a well-tended garden, but Jean's articles ranged from life in the garden to accounts of her travel, botanical work and pleas for conservation.

Australian Garden Lover, September 1974, State Library of Victoria

Sometimes whole articles were devoted to conservation issues. In an article published at the end of 1965, Jean/Correa told her gardening readers of one attempt to save remnant bush from pine plantations. The bush was especially precious to her because of the correa still growing there. 'It is many years since red correa (known as var cardinalis) was abundant in the heathlands south of our valley', she wrote. 'We used to go out to see it every year, then during the years I could do little travelling about was an era of much clearing, and later I discovered that correa had become rare in every place where we used to see it'. Members of the LVFNC had been alerted to an area where the correa grew at Traralgon South on a hill of wildflowers above a farm, and went out to inspect the area. Jean had a special role among the field naturalists.

> I was the only one who knew those hills before they were despoiled and could tell if this was a fair sample of what they had been. It was and I shall not soon forget it.

> Already we could see various kinds of peas and riceflowers and a shower of correa bells on the high cutting. That was only the beginning. Pink bells and orchids, correa and wattles, sundews and trigger plants and coral pea. There were more bushes of correa var cardinalis than I had seen for twenty years … As we walked down the hill I found myself

thinking, "It can't be lost, not when we have found it at last". But of course it can be, as so much else has been.

She used this opportunity to outline her ideas on balanced development, of how saving this strip of wildflowers could benefit the future pine plantation as well as the local community.

> As we went towards the house above the creek flats it seemed to me that this could be a perfect example of land usage in balance. Six miles away was the town [Traralgon], encircled by farms and forest, and here were rich pastures, with their stock contented and well fed. The white house stood on a level headland jutting out from the hill, with the wildflower strip edged with manna gums behind it, while, above the wildflowers will soon be forests, well managed, and protected by the birds that will go into it from the strip of bush. Very few native birds will live in a pine forest, but they will make an excursion into it for insects if they have a strip of native bush to which they can retreat … [The company] can reserve the strip along the fence for the good of the community as well as their forests.[20]

With more time for botanising and greater mobility thanks to her Latrobe Valley field naturalist colleagues who helped with transport, Jean could resume writing articles based on her field activities for the *Victorian Naturalist* and keep readers informed of threatened areas and species. In one article on the heathlands near Rosedale – the subject of much correspondence between Jean and APM – she had to report that only fragments of the once flower-filled bush remained. 'Thousands of acres of pines have blotted out the wildflowers'. There was only one significant area left, and the best part of this was also under threat. The breath-taking species list that she included in her article would have made many a naturalist salivate.[21] With other members of the Latrobe Valley Field Naturalists' Club, Jean kept campaigning for this spectacular flowerland and tried hard to save the precious remaining section from the pines.

Although wildflowers were disappearing at a rapid rate in the bush, attitudes to native plants in the garden were changing in the 1950s as more people became interested in growing native flora. When Jean had begun writing about growing wildflowers thirty years before, few nurseries stocked native plants, and cultivating them required the dedication that Jean had shown in collecting seed, propagating cuttings, experimentation, trial and error and the questionable activity of digging up seedlings in the bush. This began to change in the postwar years. Drawing on the pioneering work of nurserymen such as George Althofer, Bernhardt Schubert and Morton Boddy, more nurseries began selling natives and stocking new cultivars and selected hybrids. Regular articles on natives were also appearing in popular gardening magazines in the 1950s, among them Arthur Swaby's series 'Know Your Natives' in *Your Garden*. Landscape designers such as Edna Walling, Eric Nicholls and Ellis Stones were promoting native plants and using them in their designs. In the 1960s, Gordon Ford, Glen Wilson and others were designing native gardens that were influenced by the natural landscape.[22] In Sydney, Betty Maloney started her pioneering bush garden, where she combined the remnant vegetation on her suburban block with native plants that provided ground cover, undergrowth and canopy, design concepts she would soon be implementing in other people's gardens.

Close to Jean in Gippsland, the genius native plant propagator Bill Cane had established his nursery, 'Clearview', on the outskirts of the dairying town of Maffra. Jean had her first visit there with native plant-growing friends Grace and Bob Auchterlonie on New Year's Eve in 1954. As soon as the car turned into the 'Clearview' driveway, she could see wonderful things: glass houses, shade houses and big sand beds filled with native plants, many of them new to her. The visit was the beginning of a close plant association with Bill Cane and provided added stimulus to her long held passion for growing native plants. 'I came home with one determination', she told *Garden Lover* readers:

> I could not spare the precious bed northeast of the garden door for Dahlias any longer. After this flowering they must go to the front garden

to make room for the treasures from Maffra – Boronias pink, white and red, and the Fan flowers promised later. What a year it will be with such a beginning![23]

Jim Willis was a great admirer of Bill Cane's botanical skills, describing him as an 'enthusiastic, tough, nuggetty, lovable plantsman'. To this, Jean added the additional qualities of humour, endless kindness and generosity, and the abilities of a 'born researcher'.[24] Like Willis, she applauded Bill's outstanding achievements in native plant cultivation and his acute observations in the bush. Bill's interest in native plants had grown from beekeeping. He set out to learn about honey flora, but was soon experimenting with growing wildflowers, collecting seed and propagating cuttings. He worked out means of cultivating notoriously difficult species, including the wild cherry, and had a 'spectacular achievement' when he was able to strike eucalypt cuttings.[25] He was always searching in the bush for varieties with unique colour forms or variegated foliage that he could propagate and introduce to the nursery trade. Bill regularly sent species not previously described to Jim Willis at the Herbarium, including a banksia that he found in the Mount Tamboritha area. Eventually convinced it was a new species, Jim Willis named it *Banksia canei*, the mountain banksia, adding a sixth banksia to the five that were then described for Victoria.[26] Bill gained much of his botanical knowledge from *Wildflowers of Victoria*. It was 'the only book of its kind', he wrote to Jean.[27]

Bill Cane and Jean formed a deep friendship and botanical partnership, corresponding regularly. When she was housebound looking after Fred and Fan, Jean appreciated Bill's letters full of interesting observations on his many trips into the bush. She was 'Auntie Jean' to the Cane children, and it became a tradition for Bill and Norah Cane and their children to visit 'Dunedin' on New Year's Day, always arriving with plants. One year they came with a blandfordia, the giant Christmas bell, and when it flowered for the first time two Christmases later, vibrant with yellow-tipped red bells, nothing, she decided, 'could look more Christmas-like'.[28] With encouragement from Bill,

Jean entered a children's story competition run by the Honey Council in 1956. Bill patiently answered all her questions about honey production and hive management, and then read through her story. He was complimentary, but decided that a story for the Honey Council needed more of a 'plug' for using honey. She took his advice and won the prize of £10, a handy sum.

Bill mailed her a steady stream of plants for the garden, wonderful packages waiting at the Tyers post office for Jean to collect. He also called in regularly with plants for her to identify that he had found on his forays into the bush. Any dilemmas she had with his specimens were passed on to Jim Willis to resolve. Jean learnt – and practised – his methods of propagating and asked Bill, who appeared in 'From Day to Day in the Garden' articles as the 'wildflower man from Clearview', if she could use his information in her articles. Generosity and humour were evident in his reply. 'Although I want to make a living propagating "natives", I also want as many species as possible grown, and I can't do it all myself'.[29]

In March 1957, Jean and Bill set off for Melbourne to attend the inaugural meeting of the Society for Growing Australian Plants (first known as Australian Growers of Australians). The meeting had been convened by Arthur Swaby, who had a vision of native plant growers throughout Australia cooperating and sharing information as they experimented with seed-raising and propagation. Through systematic recording of results and collaboration with professional botanists, more native plants could be brought into cultivation. He used his 'Know Your Natives' column in *Your Garden* to discuss his ideas and publicise nationally the formation of the new group. That evening Jean and Bill joined with movers and shakers of the native plant world who were crowding into the Horticultural Hall in Victoria Street.[30] During the meeting, life memberships were awarded to people with a track record of promoting or growing native flora and sharing their knowledge with others. They included George Althofer who had established a native plant nursery in New South Wales in 1938; David Gordon for the outstanding arboretum of Australian plants he had developed on his Queensland property;

Thistle Stead, author of gardening books on native plants and field guides to Australian wildflowers; and Jean Galbraith in recognition of thirty years of sharing her knowledge on Australian flora, from her first articles on native flowers in the *Garden Lover* in 1926, through to her field guide, *Wildflowers of Victoria*. Jean wrote to her sister-in-law May about the pleasure of receiving the life membership – and also of her relief at not having to pay membership fees.[31]

The first years of the society were not easy ones. Swaby withdrew in 1962, uncompromising in his original vision for the society and concerned that members were not seriously engaged with research or growing new species.[32] But over the years, the society became a spearhead for encouraging cultivation of native plants in home gardens and in public spaces, promoting the study of Australian plants and supporting the nursery industry in developing better forms of native plants. It also played an active role in protecting native plants in their habitat and encouraged growing endangered species in botanical gardens. Jean remained a strong supporter and was an early contributor to the society's quarterly journal, *Australian Plants*, notable for its enticing cover photographs of wildflowers and its valuable notes on botany and cultivation. Soon after the journal started in 1960, an issue carried a double act by Bill Cane and Jean Galbraith: an article on propagating eriostemons by Bill Cane and the first of five botanical articles by Jean on the genus *Eriostemon*.[33] Her research for these articles had been extensive and she made key contacts with botanists at universities and herbaria in other states. She continued to write detailed but accessible botanical articles for *Australian Plants* on other genera.

But although Jean had been a passionate grower of native plants since girlhood and had constantly promoted their place in the garden, she knew that cultivated wildflowers could never supplant the wonder of seeing them in the bush. She reminded her readers of this. One of her earliest memories of spring, she wrote in the *Garden Lover* in 1959, had been seeing a hardenbergia 'throwing a purple mantle over sunlit rocks'. Now, when hardenbergia no longer grew wild near her, she could look out of her window and admire the beautiful purple of one she had planted in her garden. But, as she explained, the 'loveliest bush flowers, grown in the garden, lose something because of their changed setting'. Her garden plant could never have the same magic as the wild hardenbergia blossoming over the sun warmed rocks.[34] That was one of the many reasons why wildflower gardens could never supplant wildflowers in the bush and she continued with her mission of preserving native flora by campaigning for wildflower sanctuaries.

Jean's reputation for writing about wildflowers and her passion for their conservation led to a collaboration and friendship with landscape designer and fellow garden writer, Edna Walling. They had first met at the Herbarium, introduced by Jim Willis, but their close friendship began when Walling sent a copy of her manuscript 'On the Trail of Australian Wildflowers' for Jean to look over, adding how useful *Wildflowers of Victoria* had been when she was writing it.[35] As a landscape gardener, Walling was known for her beautiful garden designs, for the harmony she created between garden and house, for her stone work and for the mastery of her plantings. She was also a photographer and writer: a long-time contributor to *Home Beautiful* and author of three garden books published in the 1940s. She developed a passion for Australian plants and sometimes used her articles to champion their beauty in the garden and the bush. An article published in 1947 showed the depth of her feeling for wildflowers when she described a visit to the Grampians. The sight of thousands of baeckia and boronia forming a soft pink cloud on a sandstone plateau filled her with wonder. 'To have seen anything so exquisitely beautiful before one died seemed to be all that mattered!' she wrote in the article.[36] Like Jean, she observed with anguish the rate of disappearing native vegetation, especially from roadsides, and this led to her book *The Australian Roadside*. Published in 1952, the book was filled with her photographs that showcased and celebrated the roadside vegetation that she loved, and the importance of preserving it. The book impressed Jean, who had drawn people's attention to the beauty and vulnerability of roadside flowers and trees a decade before in her *Wild Life* series, 'Flowers of the Wayside' and 'The Bush Road'. Jean and Edna began collaborating in the 1960s and their friendship continued until Edna's death in 1973.

They were drawn together by a love of beauty. Very different people, Edna was self-promoting and demanding. She travelled extensively throughout Victoria and interstate completing landscaping commissions, many of them on a grand scale. She was a risk-taker. As a young woman she bought land east of Melbourne in Mooroolbark where she built her own cottage and then oversaw the development of a village of rustic cottages that she called Bickleigh Vale. When she was in her seventies, she left the places that had been significant to her – the village she had created and her retreat on the Great Ocean Road – and moved to Queensland. By contrast, Jean was rooted in one place, with no desire to live anywhere else. Her work had been on a small canvas, inspired by her garden and landscapes. She was self-effacing and avoided telling gardeners what to do. But there was also much that she and Edna shared. Their writing contained the same passion for plants and celebration of beauty. They both knew what it was like to experience transcending joy at the sight or sound of beauty. 'Oh! I'm lucky - & grateful', Edna wrote to Jean in the 1960s, 'my prayer is "make me worthy Lord" ... and as I write I'm listening to some divine Mozart'.[37] Above all, they shared a profound love of Australian flora, and a determination to try to protect it in the bush.

It was Edna who initiated their collaboration. She had set up a dark room at the Barn, her home in Bickleigh Vale, and once her printing technique improved, she began pursuing new ideas for publishing. 'I am optimistically thinking of sending a small selection of my photographs to Thames and Hudson in London (this is just between ourselves) under the title "The Australian Bush"', she wrote to Jean in 1963, 'and am wondering if you would feel inclined to do the captions?' She wanted to combine their skills of photography and writing. When Jean agreed to collaborate, Edna sent an enthusiastic reply: 'Even the <u>thought</u> that you may agree to collaborate in the compiling of this book ... makes me happier than I have been for a long time'.[38]

Inspired by the ABC's 'devotional session this morning', Edna came up with a title for the new project, 'Australia: the Harvest of a Quiet Eye', that incorporated a quote from Wordsworth's 'A Poet's Epitaph'.[39] She began sending a steady stream of photographs to 'Dunedin'. Jean jotted down captions. 'Old Man's Beard, Clematis, Travellers Joy – Whatever you call it the name recalls a fleece of cream stars in spring and in summer a robe of thistledown as the curled and feathered seeds cascade over shrub and tree'... 'In the north-west the pale Chamomile Sunray (*Helipterum anthemoides*) runs up to the trees like the foam patterned shallows of a wave'.[40] Soon Jean had piles of photographs to admire and describe. It was an absorbing project to pick up whenever she had the time. Edna was the driving force, always exploring ideas and possibilities: 'Do you think flowers are more appealing to the general public than trees? ... I adored your caption for the yellow box. How you bring out the main beauty of a photograph'.[41]

But the 1960s were lean years for Walling when it came to publishing. She had enjoyed great success with her first gardening books but her book on the conservation of roadside vegetation was not as popular and her next manuscript, 'On the Trail of Australian Wildflowers', didn't arouse the interest of publishers. With her customary energy, she sent 'The Harvest' to a succession of publishers: Cassells, Landsdowne Press, Melbourne University Press, Jacaranda Press, Sun books, Nelsons and Reeds. She experimented with different ways of presenting the photographs and text and even suggested that Jean approach the publishers, thinking Jean Galbraith had a better chance of being successful than Edna Walling. 'I don't want you to think I've got a chip on my shoulder when I say that in Melbourne my chances of getting anything accepted are very slender', she told Jean. 'I am so completely happy to be the illustrator of your valuable prose'.[42] But there was no interest for a book that represented Australian flora in words and images. The black and white photographs were out-of-step with the colour publications of the 1960s.[43] In spite of the rejections, Edna was always positive about the project. 'Even if we don't succeed in getting it printed we can make it OUR BOOK and get someone to bind it'.[44]

Edna appreciated Jean's letters in this lean time. 'Jean dear', she wrote from the Barn, 'how your letters warm the heart'. She discussed with Jean her plans to move to Queensland, and ideas of transferring her property near Lorne to the Bird Observers' Club as a bird sanctuary and turning the Barn at Bickleigh Vale into a rest home. So many of her friends had found it restful and she felt this could prevent the land from being subdivided by rapidly encroaching suburbia. 'I appreciate your opinion, your wise reactions', she told Jean.[45]

Their correspondence continued after Edna moved to Buderim in Queensland in 1967. Not long before her death six years later, she was still thinking about 'The Harvest', but was resigned to their work remaining unpublished. She sent Jean more photographs to add to the many she already had. 'I'd so much rather think that the prints may be used, even if only to show *your* friends than left with a publisher who would hardly be expected to value them', she wrote from Buderim. Knowing Jean's frugal ways of scrimping, saving and recycling, she continued: 'I can even picture you lacing them together covering them with brown paper and putting them in your book-case. Far better than in some cellar door dear. Anyway it's yours you don't have to use them, you just enjoy them'.[46]

Within ten years of Walling's death, her work came to prominence again. Surviving Edna Walling gardens were sought out, her exquisite garden plans were collected and new assessments of her work and life were published. Her position as one of Australia's greatest landscape gardeners was restored. There was praise, too, for her photography. Suddenly her writing was in demand. Her books were reprinted and many of her articles were collected and published in book form. 'On the Trail of Australian Wildflowers', the manuscript that had been stored at 'Dunedin', was also published. But the 'Harvest of a Quiet Eye', the collaboration between Galbraith and Walling, remained in folders and yellowing typescript. This interplay of words and images by two women who could evoke the beauty of the Australian bush in painterly photographs and words was not made available for others to enjoy.

Jean's extraordinary environmental knowledge based on years of close observation of her valley and surrounding hills, made 'Dunedin' a port of call for scientists and botanists from a range of government departments such as the Soil Conservation Authority, the Victorian Forests Commission and the National Parks Authority. They came with queries relating to plants, mammals, birds, rivers and forests. Even though Jean was highly critical of the Forest Commission's alpine logging operations, her relations with forestry officials were always friendly, reflecting the reasonable approach she endorsed for conservation campaigns. 'Though we may differ in opinion concerning some forest operations', a senior official wrote to Jean, 'your views are respected and integrity unquestioned'. [47] He also thanked her for helping his staff with their study of local flora, an acknowledgement of the significant role that Jean was now playing in mentoring a new generation of botanists.

Young botanists came to Jean for information and left as friends. Josephine Piggin, a Forest Commission botanist who was appointed to Gippsland, wrote of how she learnt from Jean's 'great first-hand knowledge of her environment' and how Jean fostered her understanding of 'the whole forest, of the whole catchment and the whole ecosystem'. But more than a mentor, Jean also became a friend, and with her zest for life, there were some memorable times at 'Dunedin':

> feasting on a platter of orange spongy fungi gathered under her pine trees, lightly fried in butter, a squeeze of lemon, a grind of pepper … whilst watching the honeyeaters and bowerbirds, and listening to a Beethoven string quartet on her old gramophone.[48]

Evan Chesterfield, a young forester undertaking a masters degree in botany at Melbourne University in the 1970s, remembered nervously pushing open Jean's picket gate on his first visit to 'Dunedin'. He was concerned about imposing on her. His thesis topic involved mapping species in the mountainous Macalister River catchment to the north-east of Tyers, but his training as a forester hadn't prepared him for the detailed knowledge of smaller plants that the study required. A friend working at APM had suggested he come to see Jean. Evan was warmly welcomed and Jean relished helping with identifications. He was soon visiting fortnightly, arriving with bundles of specimens collected from the mountains. He found it better to bring specimens to 'Dunedin' than send them to the Herbarium as Jean could identify from leaves, whereas Herbarium staff required flowers or fruit. Her knowledge, energy and intuitive approach amazed him. Working at her table in the dining room, the kettle boiling on the fire, Jean was indefatigable and determined as she examined the specimens, leaping up to consult references or her own herbarium specimens. 'There was a glint in her eye like a blue wren'.[49]

Soon Evan began arriving with plants that were new to Victoria, and Jean shared her excitement with Jim Willis. Evan had arrived with another batch of 'spoils', she wrote to Willis on a winter's day in 1973, and she had sat up until two o'clock in the morning dissecting and examining two unusual *Hibbertia*. She was frank about her conclusions: 'I'm absolutely stumped'.[50] Working with Jean, whom Evan Chesterfield considered to be 'one of the best', along with Victorian botanists Jim Willis and Cliff Beauglehole, his knowledge and expertise rapidly increased. Their friendship endured.[51]

While Jean was mentoring younger botanists, the battle for the Little Desert was being waged in Victoria. It was a battle that reflected changing attitudes to the use of public land and revealed that widespread support existed for conserving the state's flora and fauna on Crown land.[52] Public outrage had erupted over the Bolte government's plans to open up thousands of hectares of sandy land for farming in the west of the state, an area known as the Little Desert, and home to rich and diverse flora and fauna, including the mallee fowl. The strength of opposition to farming the Little Desert convinced the government that a review of all Victoria's public land was needed to avoid an electoral backlash. The Land Conservation Council (LCC) was established in 1971 with the task of surveying Victoria's public land and making recommendations to government on the fair and balanced use of this land based on extensive scientific reviews, public comment and consultation.[53] The state was divided into seventeen regional study areas and the process of reviewing, receiving submissions and community consultation began.

Preparing submissions for the LCC became an important part of Jean's conservation writing. She diligently prepared submissions relating to public land in regions from the Mallee to East Gippsland. Evan Chesterfield observed her exhaustive scholarly work first hand as she prepared the submissions. When it came to preparing her submission on the Alpine Study Area, she was 'almost overwhelmed', she told horticulturalist Daphne Pearson in 1977. It was the 'the hardest and the most important study so far'.[54] Historians of the LCC endorse the Alpine Study Area as the most contentious because of the competing land-uses in alpine areas – logging, cattle grazing, ski resorts and bushwalking. Campaigning for alpine national parks had been a major activity since the 1930s.

In her own region of Central Gippsland, Jean 'fought hard' for reserving land in the heathlands at Rosedale, her colleagues from the Latrobe Valley Field Naturalists' Club remember. Her submission to the LCC contributed to the formation of the Holey Plains State Park and capped off a campaign she had been waging since the 1950s to save the amazing diversity of wildflowers growing on the low sandy ridges near Merrimans Creek from being cleared for pine plantations.[55] Although she could only save a small pocket of this floristically rich sandy heathland from the pines, one fifth of the plants recorded for Victoria can be found there, with some species endemic to the park. Holey Plains State Park is now recognised as a site of national botanical significance.[56]

Jean's submissions to the LCC reveal another aspect of the writer whose love of her landscapes had fostered a deep conservation commitment. Jean had been campaigning with pen and lyricism but her submissions to the LCC required a different form of writing. In these, Jean's deep knowledge of native flora and her thoughts on the future use of public land were transmitted by clear, well-reasoned prose. Professor John Turner, a long-serving member of the LCC, recorded just how influential her submissions were. Regarded by council members as scholarly and balanced, many of her submissions, he claimed, formed the basis 'for some of our most important recommendations to the State Government'.[57]

In mid June 1980 an article in *The Age* on the State Electricity Commission of Victoria's 'huge power plan' sent shockwaves around the Latrobe Valley. Revealed were plans to build ten gigantic power stations – each described as Loy Yang-sized – and increase the current Latrobe Valley generating capacity by eight times.[58] The following day an article headed 'How Green Was Her Valley' appeared in *The Age*, and featured a large photograph of Jean. Sitting at her dining table strewn with papers, and with a view of tangled garden through the window, a sombre Jean explained that even one more Loy Yang would be unbearable: 'All the things that make this place valuable to me would not exist – could not exist – with another Loy Yang'.[59] As planning historian David Langmore has written, the financial costs of this new SEC development would be astronomical, while the social and environmental implications would be 'absolutely extraordinary ... The magnitude of the proposals was truly mind boggling'. Living in the region could even become intolerable.[60] The plans were scaled back to building seven new power stations.[61] Two would be located just south of Tyers on the Latrobe River flood plain.

Jean's environmental memory stretched back to a valley before indus-trialisation. She was 15 when the SEC began exploiting the vast brown coal reserves along the Latrobe River. The power station and briquette factory were no more than lights she could see at night in the distance. For years she wrote about her perfect valley and its beauty. But the beauty had been steadily disappearing with the encroaching power generation. Jean was also aware of the implications of industrialisation for people of the region as well as for the environment. The beautiful garden city of Yallourn had disappeared. The township of Traralgon South would soon be submerged in the Loy Yang open cut. And if the SEC's latest plans were implemented, Tyers and the garden in a valley would no longer exist.

The SEC's astounding projection for a forest of new power stations was eventually abandoned and Tyers was saved. But by the mid-1980s, with the SEC's relentless expansion to the east, Jean could see distant smokestacks and cooling towers of the Loy Yang power stations from her front gate.

Chapter 12

A COMMISSION FROM COLLINS

Western Australia has one of the most diverse floras in the world. More than 12,000 species grow there, mostly in the south west, and many endemic to the state. The age of the land and its stability – in contrast to volcanic eruptions and glaciation in the eastern states – has been responsible for the slow accumulation of species over time. Bordered by sea and desert, the plants have evolved in isolation. From July to December, they erupt into flower as they compete for water and nutrients, many with large showy blooms to attract bird and mammal pollinators. Western Australia has long been a botanist and flower lover's paradise and in 1964, Jean, Anne and Charles were planning their own pilgrimage to the west. Jean's anticipation was obvious in her letter to Jim Willis: 'The prospect of the four months botanizing is almost overwhelming – so much to see – to learn – to enjoy! I feel it will be necessary to stay home for years after this to absorb it all'.[1]

They planned to drive from Victoria to Port Lincoln, staying along the way with a string of friends, many of them *Garden Lover* readers, and then camp on the trip across the Nullarbor, Jean pitching her small green tent, and Anne and Charles sleeping in the back of the station wagon. They had selected wildflower hotspots from Geraldton to Esperance as bases where they would either camp or stay in cottages. There were careful preparations before they set off: gaining permits to pick wildflowers for botanical study, herbarium specimens and propagation; making contact with Western Australian botanists and herbarium staff; and writing to local naturalists for advice on places to visit. Jean also contacted the Perth ecclesia and was given names of Christadelphians who lived in the areas they hoped to visit. They set off in July but all three became ill on the Eyre Peninsula and they had to rest up in Port Lincoln. They were 'a shaky lot' as they drove towards Ceduna, especially Anne who had developed bad bronchitis. At Penong, Jean had to go into the hotel – an unfamiliar venue – to buy lemonade, and was pleasantly surprised, she told her family, by a 'large spotless friendly man behind a very clean counter covered with a white towel (presumably the bar counter) and a general atmosphere of good housekeeping and cheerful friendliness'.[2] Their first base was Geraldton where they planned to stay for a month and as they drove closer, their plans were rewarded: 'we all had to exclaim over the wildflowers. Hovea, eucalypts, grass trees, among flowers thick as they used to be at Gormandale, snow white hakea – fleeces of it …'[3]

At Geraldton they were welcomed by the local branch of the Tree Society, a conservation group dedicated to tree planting, reserving native vegetation and campaigning for national parks. The society provided the best of local knowledge, as members took them to their favourite flower places. Jean was asked to give a talk at the Tree Society meeting, which was reported in the local paper. She was described as 'one of the leading botanists in the Commonwealth and author of books on this subject'. Jean told members of the great interest taken by the eastern states in Western Australian wildflowers and of their importance as a major tourist attraction. 'The necessity of guarding such assets had been realised the world over'.[4] Jean collected 200 species from within a few kilometres of the town. She also met with Christadelphians while she was in Geraldton and attended their meetings.

It was at a Tree Society meeting in early August that they heard of the spectacular display of flowers at Carnarvon to the north. Anne and Charles knew of people with a station near Shark Bay, the most westerly point in Australia and close to Carnarvon, and asked if they could camp on the property. Their drive north was magical, through what Jean described as the 'country of everlastings', a double rainbow that stretched along the road as far as the eye could see. They were welcomed at the homestead, 'Yaringa', where camping was not considered for a moment. Jean was given a room opening onto a verandah, where a large table for sorting specimens had been placed, along with a pile of newspapers for plant pressing. On a tour of the station, they noted that the sheep grazed on native vegetation and also that the property was deliberately kept understocked. The flowers were in the millions: sheets of everlastings, buttons, purple daisies, stackhousia, goodenias and swainsonias. Six different eremophila were in flower. There were fan flowers, flannel bush, fragrant native tobacco and cotton bush. Mulla mullas were everywhere, as were quandongs and sandalwood. They looked on in amazement, dazzled by the colour and abundance of the flora. The property, Charles pronounced, was 'simply 330,000 acres of flower garden'.[5]

Jean recorded the trip in her *Garden Lover* articles, telling readers that she was writing on the other side of the country 'amongst those western wildflowers ... which I had never expected to see growing wild'. She gave readers a taste of the thrills she was experiencing.

"Look at *that*!" Jane would exclaim.

"Did you see *that*?" George would say stopping the car and I would jump out, eager to make new discoveries.[6]

She shared with readers their drive to the Murchison River estuary; her descriptions helped them to imagine the brilliant colour and variety of the plants.

I will never forget the drive to the mouth of the Murchison River where a 335,000 acre national park has lately been reserved [now part of the Kalbarri National Park]. For miles the varied colours of the roadside bordered acres of undulating gold and pink and white: gold of guinea flower, Synaphea and many Wattles, pink of Isopogon and Myrtles, white of Smoke bush and Lamb tails and Grevillea; while every space between the taller flowers was carpeted with blue of Dampeira and royal purple of Fanflowers, deep pink of Calytrix and pale pink of Baeckia, the white embroidery of Sundews and Trigger plants, Beard-heath and lilies, the tufted gold of Conostylus, the regal red and green of Kangaroo Paw.

They camped near the estuary and left with the greatest reluctance. It was, Jean wrote, 'a flowerscape that every botanist and wildflower enthusiast could ever hope to see'.[7] Her article with its lyrical descriptions of the wildflowers caught the attention of staff in the national parks service who asked if they could print extracts in promotional material they were planning for the new park.

The variety of the Western Australian plants filled Jean with awe. Examining the leaves of pea flowering plants was like discovering a musical theme with endless inventive variations. Some had fat leaves like sausages, some were thin and dry and triangular. One species was horned on one side and not on the other while another was thin and V shaped. Some were strap-like, some intricately divided, some bent upward like a butterfly's wings. Their diversity was 'almost overwhelming and I remember the feeling of awe with which I looked at them, finding more and more variety'. She found herself continually quoting from 'The Scribe', by Water de la Mare.

> What lovely things
> Thy Hand hath made.[8]

But there were disturbing scenes to describe for readers as well. 'I have seen many beautiful flowers – thousands of beautiful flowers already – in this western country, but greater than the surviving beauty is the evidence of destruction.' Land was being cleared at an alarming rate. 'We in Victoria have learnt through loss and tragedy the danger of too much clearing in marginal lands. Must every state learn with equal pain?'[9] She described cleared roadsides, once the haunt of banksias, and now invaded by weeds. She wrote of the failure to leave windbreaks of native vegetation, resulting in denuded paddocks and erosion. Further south, the native flora along the roadside had been replaced by capeweed. 'The infinite varied and colourful wildflowers they have replaced along the narrow roads can be seen in no part of the world except this wonderland of south western Western Australia', Jean wrote.[10] Now the wildflowers were gone. The expedition brought new treasures but it also brought new regrets.

They stayed in Perth in a flat belonging to the 'Yaringa' people but Jean couldn't enjoy her visit to the full as she had come down with bronchitis.

She was still able to spend time in the Western Australia Herbarium working on identifications, meet with wildflower growers and go to the King's Park wildflower show, where one of the organisers was a *Garden Lover* reader. Soon they were on the road again, driving south to their next base, Augusta, where the cottage they had booked had a surprise waiting for them. Wildflowers were growing through the lawn, invading garden beds, clustering under the clothesline: kennedya, hardenbergia, dampiera, pimelia, hibbertia, leucopogon, and many others. 'We had not before had a house actually in the middle of wildflowers. It was wonderful', Jean wrote of their two week stay.[11] She counted fifty different varieties of wildflowers just on her short walk to the post office. There was time to catch up with her microscope work, update notes and press and label plants.

They reached Albany in early October and stayed in a Country Women's Association flat looking over King George Sound, where famed botanist Robert Brown and botanical artist Ferdinand Bauer had landed from Matthew Flinders' *Investigator* in the early nineteenth century to collect and illustrate native plants from the south west. They collected over 500 species, even though it was summer.[12] For Jean, Albany became as much 'a place of friends as of flowers', as they met up with members of the Albany Wildflower Society who took them out on excursions. The secretary had been particularly keen to meet Jean as she had been reading her *Garden Lover* articles for sixteen years, and was now following the Western Australian trip in the magazine's pages. She took them to iconic plants such as scarlet banksias and the insectivorous Albany pitcher plants, organised a memorable trip to the Stirling Ranges and drove them on back roads to wonderful displays of local flowers. But the bush, Jean noted, was being cleared at a disturbing rate. Albany's police sergeant was president of the Wildflower Society, and also keen to show them the local flora. Jean accepted his invitation to speak at the next meeting. Their visit coincided with the resiting of a First World War memorial to Albany, the port where the first Anzacs had departed for Gallipoli, fifty years before. The unveiling ceremony was attended by large crowds, including the prime minister, Robert Menzies. Jean, Anne and Charles were willingly press-ganged into helping with a special wildflower show planned as part of the town's celebrations. It was all familiar to Jean – fresh bushy smells and the task of imposing order on a jumble of flowers. She revelled in it. But she was distressed when she saw the number of flowers that had been picked, particularly orchids. There were enough white spider orchids to fill a bucket, she told her family.[13]

On their way to Esperance, they met up with their Albany friend Sergeant Daniel at Ravensthorpe, and he showed them rare banksias, vivid flowers and, 'best of all, a low thicket of Bell Fruited Mallee and Red Moort, both in flower, one bright yellow and the other crimson'.[14] Esperance was a time of seascapes, flowers and birds, and then it was time to drive to Kalgoorlie to catch the train back across the Nullarbor. Jean had time to meet with a local botanist who was writing a book on the goldfields flora, before she boarded the train.

In Adelaide she spent time at the Herbarium, meeting botanists she had been corresponding with about tetratheca for an *Australian Plants* article and catching up with Noel Lothian who was now director of the Adelaide Botanic Gardens. She stayed with a *Garden Lover* reader who had contacted Jean twenty years before to express how *Garden in a Valley* had helped her after her son's death in the war. They had been corresponding ever since.[15] She rendezvoused with Anne and Charles and they set off for home, returning via the Coorong and Portland. Jean had been immersed in wildflowers for four months. Her knowledge of Australian flora had been greatly extended, she had seen species that dazzled and the endless variety had filled her with awe. But her memories were coloured by sadness at the vulnerability of such botanical riches, unique in the world, yet at risk from land clearing and weed invasion. The trip continued to give her a fund of material for articles. She wrote of the progress of the Western Australian bed she started at 'Dunedin', filled with plants that Bill Cane had propagated from cuttings she had sent to him from the west.

She arrived back in Tyers at the end of October, with the garden to make ready for her niece Marjory's wedding. 'This green land was home'.[16]

There wasn't much time for Jean to absorb all the new botanical information from Western Australia. She received a telephone call early in 1965 from John Cody of Collins Publishers, inviting her to write a field guide to Australian wildflowers as part of Collins' international series of pocket field guides. Cody sent her a copy of their British wildflower guide which described 1,300 species. He realised, of course, that there were many more species in Australia and wanted Jean's ideas on how to approach an Australian edition.[17] With her usual promptness and excitement at the prospect of a new project, Jean drafted a reply. She told him of her commitment to Longmans who were publishing a third edition of *Wildflowers of Victoria* and her concerns that a book such as Collins proposed with coloured illustrations could affect their sales. She also set out her most pressing problem: finance. As a freelance writer she couldn't live – even with the most stringent economy – while working on a project that would take several years to complete. 'Unless I can solve this problem I can't undertake the work though I certainly want to do it'.[18]

In her hunt for a solution, Jean contacted the Commonwealth Literary Fund that administered grants for writers and publishers, to ask if 'informative writing' was supported by the fund, and explained the nature of her project. The response she received made it clear that a field guide was outside the scope of the fund, which existed to assist Australian imaginative and creative writing. History, biography and literary criticism were included, but books such as Jean's were not, although she was welcome to apply. She sent a feisty response and defended the writing of a field guide as a creative and literary work. '[S]uch a book can – and, to serve its purpose well, should – be a work of art as well as a reference. Because it is to be for general readers who wish to identify plants, not for trained botanists, it should give them a series of vivid mental pictures of flowers described, not a mere list of characters, and this is what I wish to do'. She drafted a description of the alpine marsh-marigold to illustrate the vivid mental pictures that were so important to her botanical writing: flowers overhung by melting snow, their long white sepals stained red at the base, their stamens prune-red, short stalks that lengthened after flowering to hold a burr-like cluster of pointed fruits. Whatever staff at the Commonwealth Literary Fund made of her reply, it was an important manifesto of Jean's approach to botanical writing for a lay readership: the importance of using a poet's sensibility to create word pictures and capture the essence of the species – its colour, texture and shape – to help the reader identify the plant and learn about its characteristics.[19]

Collins solved the problem of finances by offering an advance on royalties. Now firmer ideas for the book could take shape. Jean suggested restricting it to plants growing in Australia's eastern temperate region, which included about 4,000 species and encompassed all of New South Wales, Victoria and Tasmania, as well as south east Queensland and eastern South Australia to the Eyre Peninsula. Preparing the book would be an immense task. Jean was committed to observing plants in their natural habitat, but she didn't drive. She lived in a small country town and was isolated from colleagues and specialist botanical libraries. She would have to visit herbaria in five capital cities: Brisbane, Sydney, Melbourne, Hobart and Adelaide. And publishing a field guide was a complex business, as she knew from her experiences with *Wildflowers of Victoria* where she was still hoping that a third edition would get it right. This much larger project had the added complication of dealing with publishers based in both Sydney and London.

It was Jim Willis who had recommended her to Collins and Jean told him how she felt about undertaking the book.

> One thing after another has happened to open the way to do it and I feel now I should be a coward to refuse it … It isn't the work I mind (though it does cause a few tremors). After all, it's the kind of work I love. The main trouble, now I think the finance is sorted out, is fear of my own incompetence, but I shall just have to do the best I can'.[20]

She had decided not to include grasses, sedges, ferns and subtropical rain-forest, and asked Jim if it would be 'atrocious' to leave out eucalypts.

Another major task associated with the book would be organising the illustrations. Collins had told her that sourcing and paying for them was her responsibility and recommended she use slides or transparencies. She was pleased, as she told Jim, that she had already received offers of help. One came from H.J. King, a noted wildflower photographer and naturalist from Launceston in Tasmania, whom Jean knew well as he was a Christadelphian and she had visited him when she was on field trips in Tasmania. Bill Payne, editor of the SGAP journal *Australian Plants*, was custodian of a large slide collection and offered any of them for reproduction without charge. Members of the Latrobe Valley Field Naturalists' Club were ready and waiting to put their cars at her disposal and drive her on field trips.

Jean's editor in Sydney was Stephen Dearnley, who soon became a good friend. Her first task was to prepare a detailed synopsis and she was relieved when Dearnley agreed that eucalypts could be left out; he felt that general readers wouldn't think of eucalypts as wildflowers. Jean also started work on sourcing the illustrations. She had a quick trip to Tasmania to look at King's photograph collection and began corresponding with other photographer naturalists scattered around Australia's temperate zone. She also approached a local artist, Camilla Jakobson, to do the black and white line drawings that were required. Camilla Jakobson had worked as a botanical artist at the University of Riga in Latvia before war broke out and had come to Australia from a displaced persons camp in the postwar years. She settled at Yallourn, where her husband worked for the SEC, and quickly became an enthusiastic grower of native flowers at her new home. She had appeared as 'Calla' in *Garden Lover* articles. Pleased to be drawing again, Calla told Jean she didn't want any payment for illustrating over 300 species, but Jean ignored this. Costs for the photographs were already mounting. When Jean's first advance for £102 arrived from Collins, £62 went to H.J. King.[21]

There had been very little contact with the general editor of the pocket guide series, Michael Walter in London. He had not commented on the synopsis or discussed the contract with Jean. Dearnley was 'appalled' by this silence.[22] When Walter eventually sent his feedback in May 1966, the appraisal was not what Jean wanted to hear. Although he strongly endorsed the project, he didn't want to use photographs and argued instead that the book should be illustrated by a botanical artist who could bridge the gap between art and science by producing illustrations that were botanically correct, but that also captured the essence of a flower. With artwork, Walter argued, there was greater control over botanical detail, the colours were more accurate and a higher standard of reproduction could be achieved. But Jean was firm in her response. While she was a great supporter of botanical art and its combination of art and science, she could not afford to pay an artist and would only continue with the book if photographs were used.[23] Dearnley helped by sending some of the photographs to London to show Walter 'the high standard'. Walter backed down and told Jean to proceed with the book. Her contract arrived in September. It was a relief to know where she stood, Jean wrote to Dearnley. She had been planning a field trip to South Australia that included botanising in the south east, working at the herbarium in Adelaide and then driving with friends who knew the flora of the Eyre Peninsula to see as many flowers as possible and fill in her gaps. Now that the contract was signed, she could set off on what would be an 'expensive trip'.[24]

After her return from South Australia, writing became a priority. Jean overcame her self-doubt as she immersed herself in the plant descriptions.[25] She planned to have the text finished by mid-1968 and was now dealing more closely with Michael Walter in London, who was becoming aware of the difficulties of distance when editing a manuscript as 'complex and original as this'. Frustratingly for Jean, who was a conscientious correspondent, he was not always prompt with his replies.

Another extensive field trip was necessary. Jean wanted to examine wildflowers in New South Wales and southern Queensland. Her recently retired friend Jill Rossiter, a member of the Latrobe Valley Field Naturalists Club, offered to drive her to Queensland. They set off in Jill's four wheel drive on a two month trip at the end of July, 1967. Her time limited, Jean tapped into local knowledge and liaised with naturalists who could guide her to flowers in their districts. *Garden Lover* readers were kept up-to-date with the trip.

> Grafton gave us sunshine, warm hearted orchid lovers who showed us the northern orchids in bloom and a naturalist who took us to the mountainside all flecked and veiled with flowers beneath towering Gymea lilies coming into bloom. They shared their flowers with us and welcomed us to their meetings.[26]

They went as far north as Mooloolaba and also visited the Gordons at Myall Park where Jean was again amazed by the 'indescribable variety' of David Gordon's native garden. At Stanthorpe near the New South Wales border, a local naturalist drove them around the granite hills and located most of the flowers Jean wanted to see. South in the Blue Mountains, they were without a naturalist contact until Jean enquired at the tourist bureau and was given the name of a woman who 'knows about the mountain flowers'. The naturalist was only too pleased to help; she had been reading Jean's articles for years. Jean was able to spend several days studying the Blue Mountains flora and see many plants that were new to her.[27]

They stayed for a week with a friend near Woy Woy, close to a national park. Here, the Gymea lilies reminded her of masts on ships and the waratahs were 'in their glory'. Jean spent a week in the Sydney Herbarium and then drove with Jill to Canberra to visit the newly opened Australian National Botanic Gardens.[28] Her mission was accomplished, she wrote to Stephen Dearnley when she returned to Tyers in October, as far as 'travelling, note taking, general studies etc. of the northern temperate plants are concerned'. She now had 'a large heap of notes, a larger heap of specimens (at present being checked at the Sydney Herbarium) and largest of all a heap of unsorted happy memories … while the CAE Spring School looms in the near future'.[29]

By 1968, Jean was able to send completed sections of manuscript to Michael Walter in London, but she was running behind in her schedule and wouldn't have all the text finished by the middle of the year, as she had originally hoped. Over Easter, she told Walter, she would be 'putting aside my work long enough to listen to the whole of the St Matthew Passion without interruption', and would then plunge back into writing.[30] She had to revise her finishing date to April the following year. She keenly felt her isolation from research libraries and there were frequent trips to Melbourne to work at the Herbarium, as well as detailed correspondence with the herbaria in other states. She queried plant distributions and nomenclature and sent specimens for identification. She may have tried the patience of the Sydney Herbarium as she received a stiff note telling her to consult botanists at the Melbourne Herbarium because it was in her state. There were also long letters to Michael Walter in London, answering queries, explaining, justifying. Walter was trying to simplify the book's arrangement and make it easier for readers to navigate and find illustrations. Jean was dubious. But in October 1969, with a manuscript of 150,000 words and 3000 species described, Jean had finished writing. 'TIME TO DO MORE GARDENING SEEMS TO BE APPROACHING', she wrote in the *Garden Lover*. 'The manuscript that has been my chief occupation for nearly five years is complete, and the remaining work shall only take part of next year'.[31] Camilla Jakobson, Jill Rossiter and Jean made a ceremony of posting the manuscript to Collins, each carrying a parcel to the Tyers post office. 'A thousand pages of MS are a terrifying thought … What a work you must have produced', Patricia Wrightson commented.[32]

During this respite while Jean waited for the proofs, she turned her attention to the garden and admitted that it was out of hand again. She was in the middle of slashing and burning in autumn when she received a parcel from Bill Cane at 'Clearview' and found two glowing red sprays that resembled *Grevillea banksii* but were 'larger, richer, redder, somewhat "jucier"'. They were flowers of a hybrid grevillea that had grown at Myall Park. Dave Gordon called it after his daughter, Robyn, who died from leukaemia in 1969. He had sent cuttings of the grevillea to Bill Cane and other nurseries for propagation. 'Because I loved Robyn and her family, Bill sent me flowers',

Jean told her *Garden Lover* readers, and she reflected on the plant's beauty and significance. 'When it is available from the nursery it will carry her name into countless gardens, so that even those who did not know her will treasure her flower, and her name will always mean to them something beautiful'.[33] Jean's prediction was right. Grevillea "Robyn Gordon" became one of the most popular of all Australian plant cultivars, loved for the beauty of its deep red flowers and for its long flowering season.[34]

If Jean had felt self-doubt about her ability to undertake the Collins book, a telegram she received at the end of July in 1970 telling her she was the recipient of the Australian Natural History Medallion, should have convinced her of how highly her work was regarded by her peers. The medallion was awarded annually to the person judged to have made the most outstanding contribution to the understanding of Australian natural history. Jean received the award for promoting interest in natural history and conservation in the general community and for promoting 'a greater awareness of our natural heritage'.[35] The citation endorsed the national impact of her writing. Jim Willis and Arthur Swaby wrote of the award and Jean's achievements in an article in the *Victorian Naturalist*, illustrated with what Jean described as her 'unphotogenic face'. Among her achievements, they praised her contributions to the *Victorian Naturalist*, altogether 81 papers, with special mention of her outstanding series on wattles. They endorsed her gift for imparting nature information to children in the many stories and articles she had written. 'For quality of work and impact on the public, no-one could be a more worthy recipient', Willis and Swaby claimed. And they also celebrated Jean:

> To those of us who have experienced the hospitality of her happy home, the warm friendliness yet innate modesty of her personality and her big-hearted capacity to see only the better side of everyone else's nature, this present honour seems long overdue.[36]

Accolades poured in from those who knew Jean well, and those who knew her only through her writing. Lottie Banfield, a field naturalist from Bairnsdale, was familiar with Jean's activities: 'When I think of all the people you have helped, scientists, botanists, field naturalists, teachers, students and children, I am amazed that one person can reach out to so many'.[37] A headmaster from a primary school in New South Wales who wrote to congratulate Jean, told her how familiar she was to him, although they had never met, from her articles in *Wild Life* and stories in the *New South Wales School Magazine*. The common sentiment of field naturalist clubs from Toowoomba to Tasmania was that no-one deserved the medallion more than Jean for her services to natural history. Friends were delighted that her work was recognised. Edna Walling sent a telegram from Buderim, while another friend told Jean she could hardly stop cheering: 'It's the best, happiest decision the medallion selectors have made for years and I want to cheer and cheer and cheer…'[38]

Jean began drafting an acceptance speech.

> I still can't quite believe it's real … Jean Galbraith who has obstinately lived in the country all her life – picking up bits and pieces of knowledge as they come to hand, and enjoying every one of them – but knowing so little compared with all there is to know! … I feel I'm a kind of patchwork of other people's gifts and all the bits and pieces they gave me make their design against a background of the countryside which is the very fabric of my being.[39]

But when it came to the November presentation, she didn't speak of the debt to her mentors or reflect on the centrality of her landscapes which were her constant source of inspiration, refreshment and beauty. Instead she spoke of the wonder of plants and how they enriched her life.

During her time in the spotlight, Jean received many queries on the progress of the Collins book by naturalists who were keenly, some impatiently, waiting for a more comprehensive guide to Australian wildflowers. At the time, Jean was in difficult conversation with Michael Walter about keys for the book, waiting for comments he kept promising he would send. But her field guide anxieties didn't stop her caring for others. Betty Conabere visited Jean in spring of 1970, in a state of exhaustion from painting wildflowers for a book commissioned by Nelsons. While at 'Dunedin', she slept and worked in her kombi van that she parked under the oak and continued painting at a furious pace, up before dawn to make the most of the light. She joined Jean for lunch just as the first shimmering notes announced the start of the ABC radio serial, 'Blue Hills', a favourite of Jean's. In the evening, when Betty was 'almost blind with exhaustion', Jean played records until her visitor felt relaxed and was able to eat dinner. Like many other visitors to 'Dunedin', Betty Conabere felt cherished during her stay there, 'enfolded in Jean's care'.[40] Jean's Christmas that year was shared with Lance and May, who were moving to Beechworth after seventeen years in Traralgon. Jean tried to keep Christmas 'unshadowed' by their imminent departure.[41]

There was a field guide crisis brewing – another 'bombshell', as Jean described it. It came from Michael Walter in January and it shook Jean to the core. The text, he assured her in his effusive style, was now in 'apple-pie order' and he thought the book was 'an absolute boon', but he couldn't help having 'neurotic worries' about the illustrations being inferior to the text, and reminded her that back in 1966 he had 'groaned' at using transparencies to illustrate a wildflower book. Just recently he had been working on a field guide to wildflowers of Britain and northern Europe, with a 'superlative artist', Marjorie Blamey, who was responsible for the illustrations. 'I couldn't help wondering whether she couldn't do a marvellous set of plates for you'. In fact she was 'absolutely thrilled' when he asked her. He recommended Marjorie Blamey as a fast worker. Walter also reminded Jean that the transparencies were of mixed quality and would present 'some awful problems' at the production stage. He was aware of the disadvantages of employing an illustrator – the artist would share twenty-five per cent of the royalties – and of the problems of finding specimens to paint, especially as the Australian flowering season was over. These 'snags' might seem overwhelming 'but a guide like this is a really important publication and we ought to think of ways of making it just as good as possible to start with'.[42]

Jean waited a day before replying so that she could respond more calmly. She agreed that the book must be as good as possible but maintained that she couldn't change the illustrations. At least two of the five years she had devoted to the manuscript were spent on the illustrations, she told him. 'If you knew my labours and near despair in this field in the 5 years between beginning the work and posting the illustrations to you! The writing and research associated with it were pure pleasure – the labours associated with the illustrations were almost more than I could cope with. I couldn't do it again even if my heart were in it'. And how could she face the photographers who had given so much help? She couldn't say to them "thankyou very much but I've something better now so all your work is wasted." She could 'never think of the book without feeling ashamed'. Also, she had also spent over 100 pounds on the photographs, 'not a large amount but enough to keep me as I normally live for three months'.

She was completely overwhelmed when she considered how the specimens could be collected and sent to England. Michael Walter, she was sure, had no concept of Australian climate and distances. It had been impossible for her to get specimens in a usable condition from Queensland to Victoria, she told him. They had to be photographed where they grew or not at all. And she didn't think herbarium specimens would be suitable for an English artist unfamiliar with Australian flora, either. '[I]f an artist has never seen a grevillea or *Adenanthos* she has no mental picture to breathe life into the dry bones and though a photograph may help she can't improve on it without the risk of the "improvement" being wrong'. Jean was adamant. She couldn't face the work, expense or the difficulties of getting specimens to the artist, Marjorie Blamey, whose work she greatly admired.[43]

Jean had a precedent that showed the difficulties and expense of sending Australian flowers for illustrating in the UK. This was the on-going project of painting and describing the endemic flora of Tasmania, financed by Lord Talbot de Malahide who, with estates in Tasmania and Ireland, had become a lover and grower of Tasmanian plants. He had commissioned the distinguished Australian botanical artist, London-based Margaret Stones, to paint the wildflowers and then decided the illustrations should be published as a series of books, with the botanical text written by Tasmania's foremost native plant expert, Dr Winifred Curtis. There were 254 flowers to illustrate. Stones worked from fresh flowering and fruiting specimens flown over from Tasmania in Tupperware containers, as well as using herbarium material from the Royal Botanic Gardens at Kew. Talbot, Curtis and H.J. King were the main plant collectors, but other naturalists helped, and even bushwalkers setting off for remote areas of Tasmania returned carrying specimens for the project. Curtis examined the specimens in Hobart before they were flown to England, and Stones sent her completed artwork to Curtis for checking.[44] When Jean described the Tasmanian project to Walter in 1971, it had been in progress for four years, with much left to do. In fact, it wasn't completed until 1978. Jean pointed out that Talbot's agent in Tasmania dealt with all the problems of despatching specimens to London.

The decision on illustrations was left to Sir William Collins, who was on his way to visit the company's Australian offices, and could discuss the dilemma with the Sydney staff. He agreed that the problems of collecting and sending specimens to the UK were far too great and that they should stick to the original plan of using photographs and line drawings.[45] Jean could now breathe easily. Sir William was an enthusiastic bird watcher and came to see Jean and her usually bird-filled garden at Tyers, but unfortunately there were more mosquitoes than birds at the time of his visit.

Correspondence with London now focused around lists, checks and production notes. The 368 transparencies were organised by colour, making identification easier for users, and placed in the middle of the book. Up to eight photographs were arranged on each page. The colour proofs were sent to Jean for checking, with instructions to mark in such comments as 'too blue', 'too yellow', 'too red'.[46] Gippsland artist and naturalist Charles McCubbin was commissioned to draw wildflowers for the cover, which, like the other books in the field guide series, was hardback with a white background and the title in green and black. The cover was washable.

While she was waiting for the galley proofs to arrive from Collins, Jean worked on another project, a tribute to Winifred Waddell who had died in 1972. She had been asked by the Native Plants Preservation Society to edit the wildflower articles Winifred had written in the *Junior Age* during the early 1960s, so they could be published as a memorial volume. Jean condensed five years of Winifred's articles into a year's flowering guide to Victorian wildflowers, with an entry for each month. Published as *A Wildflower Diary*, she thought Elizabeth Cochrane's flower illustrations made it 'a very attractive book indeed'.[47]

Arriving home from a restful stay with Jim and Mavis Willis in Melbourne in July 1973, Jean went straight to the Tyers post office to collect the galley proofs that were waiting for her. She began preparing for a period of intense proof reading by making a big stew and dealing with a saucepan full of apples. 'I shall be working on proofs so long as concentration allows – no more botany, no more letters – and necessary housework by way of relaxation!'[48] She survived the three careful readings 'pretty well', she reported to Willis in September. She was also locked in discussion with Michael Walter defending her dedication to the book which he considered too long and in danger of looking 'typographically inelegant'. It was 91 words long, with 19 commas in the first sentence. Although Jean considered the dedication 'simple justice' and her way of thanking all the people who had assisted with the book, she pruned it to a simple statement: 'For the Latrobe Valley Naturalists and all who helped'. Her acknowledgements to individuals were placed in the preface, which she ended with words that had been in her mind during the years she worked on the book, a verse from Robert Browning.

God is seen God

In the star, in the stone, in the flesh, in the plant and the clod,

And thus looking within and around me I ever renew

(With that stoop of the soul which in bending upraises it too)

The submission of man's nothing-perfect to God's all-complete.[49]

Jean expected the page proofs early in 1974, but they didn't arrive until mid-1975. She bunkered down for six weeks, proof reading and compiling the index, which spread out to 35 pages. She had 'all the help I could use': six members of the Latrobe Valley Field Naturalists' Club and Jill Rossiter who was now living in north east Victoria. With 3000 species described in the manuscript, there were 6000 names (common and scientific) to index, as well as nearly 700 photographs and line drawings. Again she felt her confidence was shaken: her spelling was poor, her eyesight not good for reading italics and she seemed to have forgotten all her Latin.[50] When the proofs were completed, a friend drove her to Melbourne and she hand-delivered them to the Collins office for air freighting to London. A packed day followed – a visit to the Herbarium, a quick viewing of a botanical art exhibition, visits to two different suburbs and dinner with Angus and Ella – and then she was collected by her driver who was returning to Gippsland that night. They drove through the dark punctuated by on-coming headlights.

Jean had first thought the Collins field guide would be out in 1971, but the delays in production meant it didn't appear until winter in 1977. She was 59 when she started working on the project and 71 when she had the book in her hand. There were two launches to celebrate its arrival: one in Melbourne at the Collins showroom in St Kilda Road, and one in Gippsland at the art gallery in Sale, organised by gallery director Gwen Webb. Camilla Jakobson's line drawings were on display at the gallery. Jean was distressed that the drawings had been acknowledged only in small print in the preface, and the display would give the artist greater prominence. The print-run of 15,000 books sold briskly.

Like many reviewers, Graham Pizzey, in his Melbourne *Herald* review, marvelled at the scale of the book and how Jean had compressed information on plants from such an extensive region into one volume. 'Over 3000 of the region's almost 4000 plants are described – an immense task indeed'. He had reservations, though, on whether readers would persevere with the keys, even though he considered them 'marvels of simplicity'.[51] There were grand pronouncements on Jean's contribution to Australia and Australians, while others praised the book's layout that made it so easy to use. Some readers suffered from divided loyalties. Sheila Ridland from Beaumaris described the book as 'excellent' and 'invaluable', and especially commended the layout, but, she concluded, 'your new book will in no way take the place of my well-thumbed, much-annotated and greatly treasured copy of "Wildflowers of Victoria"'.[52]

Importantly, many of the comments Jean received paid tribute to her as a writer, especially for her accessible language and for writing with love. 'Into the publication, the author has poured all the dedication and love for the Australian flora which is her hallmark', wrote a reviewer in the *Canberra Times*.[53] 'Your introductions and notes sound just like you and not a bit like the more ordinary guides', Patricia Wrightson commented, 'a gentle relaxing of the scientific complexities down to the novice's level'.[54] Expert naturalist Keith Rogers, writing from his remote mountain station at Wulgulmerang in East Gippsland, expressed his appreciation for her 'gift' of 'putting everything in ordinary simple language'.[55] As Betty Conabere wrote, 'I now know what an enormous burden you have been carrying and yet you emerge from almost every page with delight! It imparts information in your particular manner of sharing knowledge – with love'.[56]

There was no-one whose opinion Jean valued more than that of Jim Willis, and it was Willis who wrote the review for the *Victorian Naturalist*. He left readers in no doubt of the book's significance and value to people around the country. With the new field guide, he wrote, native flowers could be identified 'whether on an excursion to Kangaroo Is, the Grampians, Hobart, Mount Kosciusko, the Blue Mountains or Lamington National Park'. He couldn't 'speak too highly of this excellent, very readable and easily understandable volume'. He noted that recent changes in nomenclature were missing, but acknowledged that this was due to the book's long time in production, and he also wondered why some common species had been omitted. But these were 'minor blemishes'. They in no way detracted from 'the value of a splendid production that, one believes, will be in constant demand by many inquirers for years if not generations'.[57]

Chapter 13

FAME

'It is time to say goodbye, and how can I say it?' Jean wrote in 1975, as she sat at her table with its view of late spring flowers and frenetic activity at the bird table, soon after delivering the completed page proofs to Collins.[1] It was almost fifty years since the eager young woman had written her first article for the *Garden Lover*, and now she felt it was time to stop. She wanted to finish on the fiftieth anniversary of her first series, 'Australian Native Flowers', and before she turned seventy.[2] She could savour the pleasure of knowing that native plants were now widely grown in Australian home gardens, and that many gardeners knew what a correa was. Her final article, published in December 1975, began with descriptions of gardens in the Dandenongs and the pleasures of late October and early November days, and ended with this valediction:

> I have become so used to sharing day to day in the garden with you all that I have hardly begun to realise yet how I shall miss it … You can, if you think of me in the future, think of me gardening still, enjoying sunshine and rain, birds and flowers, and above all, my great richness of friends. At Christmas, there will be the Christmas Tree alight, and at New Year, a whole year of beauty before us, still shared in one sense. Perhaps I shall still share a little of it with you from time to time, but so far the Editor has not suggested that, so if this is a complete goodbye, please remember how large a part your friendship plays in my life, friendship of those whom I have never met as well as those whom I know.[3]

She didn't receive any reply from the editor acknowledging her retirement and could only assume he approved. There was no recognition for her fifty years of contributions. As she told Jim Willis, 'it seems strange to have left what was (to me) quite an important part of my life, without even a ripple'.[4] Her loyal readers responded, though, explaining what her writing had meant to them. 'It was not until after the war that I was introduced to your garden in GL [*Garden Lover*]', a reader, George, wrote in a card he sent to Jean. 'Then you introduced me to the Wildflowers of Victoria in that splendid book published by the Herald. Soon after that a friend gave me "Garden in a Valley", a delightful book that spends more time off the bookshelf than on it. So you and your garden are indeed old and valued friends'. A reader from Hawthorn expressed heartfelt regret. 'I can't bear that you should stop writing! Dear Correa it has been so wonderful all these years, the way you have been able to share the things that surrounded you'. As a reader from Strathbogie in country Victoria wrote, 'it just won't be the same Garden Lover without you. I have enjoyed travelling around the country with you via your pen, reading about your garden and the way your plants behave or misbehave … thankyou for the years of reading pleasure you have given me and others'.[5]

In spite of her sadness at the break with her readers, there was also a wonderful sense of freedom from the constant commitment of producing monthly articles, writing while she was ill with high temperatures, scribbling in foyers before concerts started. In all that time, she missed only one deadline.[6] Jean was still busy with her botanical work: detailed reports for the Land Conservation Council; regular correspondence with the Herbarium and botanical friends and colleagues over puzzling specimens; mentoring younger botanists and identifying the numerous specimens that were sent to her. There was plenty of time now for travel and field trips. She continued to write hymns with her cousin Ian Hyndman, Jean providing the words and Ian setting them to music, and there were new commissions, too. She began a series of natural history articles for the *Christadelphian*, in response to a request from the editor for contributions on 'the wonders and beauty of God's work in flowers'.[7] For a lover of alpine flowers, a particularly enjoyable commission that came her way was writing the botanical notes for a folio of limited edition prints of alpine flowers, published by the SEC in 1977.[8] There was also the shock of her brother Lance's sudden death that year.

Her botanical work was put on hold for several months in 1978, when her brother Angus gave her the generous gift of a trip to the UK, all expenses paid. This was a significant event for Jean, both culturally and botanically. As a child of the Empire, her education had been dominated by British influences, and the writers and poets she turned to again and again were English. Quotes from their work peppered her writing: Francis Thompson, Richard Jeffries, Robert Bridges, John Masefield, Mary Webb, Shakespeare, Browning, the seventeenth century theologian, Jeremy Taylor, to name a few. She had also spent a lifetime reading English botanists, gardeners and nature writers. Now, in her early seventies, she would be able to see the plants, gardens and landscapes she had been imagining since childhood.

Jean spent time in London, visiting historic buildings and gardens. Her companions on an excursion to the Kew Gardens were Jim and Mavis Willis, who were staying in London at the same time. She visited the Royal Horticultural Society's gardens at Wisley, especially delighting in the rock gardens and alpine house. She also visited Christopher Dearnley, brother of her Collins publisher, Stephen Dearnley, and organist at St Paul's Cathedral. She spent time in Devon, Surrey and St Albans. Staying in a cottage in Wales, she saw coastal cliffs that were 'pink with thyme and sea drift, purple with Cranesbill and orchids … gold with trefoil and potentilla and spires of Lady's Bedstraw'.[9] She met her cousin Edith Ladson for the first time, after corresponding with her for forty years. She travelled to Stirling in Scotland where her nephew Peter and his family were based while he was on sabbatical leave, and she also visited 'Culcreuch', once the castle of the Galbraith clan. She travelled through the highlands as far north as Thurso where she looked over the North Sea to the Orkney Islands.

Jean extended her holiday with a visit to Switzerland to see the alpine flowers that had fascinated her since childhood. Switzerland surpassed all expectations, and she delighted in the alpine flower meadows: 'flowers and flowers and flowers – meadows full of gentians and Pyramid Orchids, white and gold anemones and ranunculi, yellow Tollus and countless others'.[10] She saw snowbells at St Gotthard Pass. As with all her holidays, she returned to Tyers with carefully stored memories to unpack and enjoy, but this time they were not shared in articles with *Garden Lover* readers.

After a lengthy break from garden writing, Jean received an invitation from Collins in 1983 to write a book about a year in her garden. Collins wanted something 'warm and caring but with information sound and accurate', she told her friend John Turner, now retired from Melbourne University and living in Castlemaine in central Victoria.[11] She immediately set to work, liaising with her former field guide editor, Stephen Dearnley, and sending him a rough outline of ideas and sample text. She began jotting down observations and ideas as she walked through the garden early in the morning, to be woven into text later in the day or evening.

The Collins' commission reflected the revival of cottage gardening that was becoming prevalent in Australia in the 1980s, at the expense of Australian plants and native gardens which had been popular a decade before. Garden historian Richard Aitken has written of a 'collective longing' in the 1980s for European plants and gardens, and how this spawned the sudden appearance of specialist nurseries stocked with perennials and 'long cherished annuals', as well as new garden books that would help gardeners manage this style of garden, especially the difficult task of maintaining herbaceous borders.[12] There was a new appreciation for old gardens, much of this due to the work of the Australian Garden History Society, which had formed in 1980 and promoted historic gardens as a significant part of Australia's heritage. After publishing articles about a garden she had tended for sixty years, Jean was well known as the custodian of an old garden.

This growing interest in historic gardens was accompanied by a revival of interest in old houses. Australians were rediscovering Victorian and federation cottages in inner suburbs of capital cities and country towns. Many were in poor repair and the new owners became renovators, careful to retain the historic street frontages but adding open plan extensions suited to late twentieth century living. The new cottage dwellers embraced English-style cottage gardens, filling their small frontages with a profusion of flowers: roses, foxgloves, delphiniums, cosmos, aquilegia, daisies, poppies. They sought out varieties of old roses, planted heritage fruit trees, lined their paths with lavender hedges and edged garden beds with catmint. As 'second wave' cottage gardeners, they were not perpetuating memories of English gardens, as their nineteenth century predecessors had. They wanted to achieve harmony between house and garden.

As a garden writer for more than fifty years, Jean had seen flowers and gardening styles come in and out of fashion, something that amazed and often amused her.[13] She wrote about the plants she loved, whether native or exotic, fashionable or homely, and this was how she approached writing *A Gardener's Year* for Collins. She had wanted the book to begin with a chapter on her grandparents' move from Beechworth to Tyers in the 1870s, another indication that for Jean, garden, family and place were intertwined, but Dearnley found her family chapter too detailed as an opening for the book.[14] She rewrote the introduction and reflected instead on the important contribution of gardeners. 'We who plant gardens give the earth something that may outlast generations, a continuing beauty'.[15] Writing about a year in the garden, her text moved between past and present, drawing on memories of sixty years in the garden. The rock garden that had been Jean's passion in the 1930s was still her passion fifty years later. Her love of trees had not diminished and she admitted to having a shaded garden with limited places to grow flowers. Collins wanted the manuscript by the end of 1983, a deadline Jean met with her usual professionalism, writing the last entry on New Year's Eve.

The year she was documenting has become etched in Australian bushfire history as the year of the Ash Wednesday fires. On a day of searing heat and low humidity in February, after a long period of drought, fires broke out in Victoria and South Australia, killing 75 people. This event formed an undercurrent in the book. Jean's year had begun with drought and a struggle to keep plants alive. She put vegetable-growing on hold to save water for trees and shrubs. The day of the fires, 16 February, was spent by the radio, listening to the calm voices of presenters on ABC radio, as the full horror of the day unfolded. Her account of the day's events concentrated on the offers of help that flooded in, rather than the suffering.

In Tyers, the drought broke in March, with a day and night of steady rain. As the rain continued through autumn, she wrote of birds returning to the garden, of smelling the tang of wet gum leaves again and seeing a wash of pale green spread through the brown valley. Now was the time for planting and resurrecting the vegetable garden. While her own garden greened and revived, she included in the book letters that had been written by friends from Millicent in South Australia, whose home, farm and stock had been destroyed in the fires, along with their renowned native garden. They wrote to Jean of signs of regeneration in the garden: lignotubers shooting, seeds germinating in their thousands, blackened eucalypts turning green, carpets of lilies flowering in the spring, grass trees 'like armies' with their tall white flowers.

Weeds grew apace in Tyers as the rain continued throughout winter. Jean wrote of correas, camellias and jonquils, and described wildflower excursions in the bush. Spring brought birdsong and roses, buddleias, three species of mock orange, bottlebrushes and the blue and purple flowers of November. The book ended with December and Jean feasting on berries she had grown. She described lilies and flowering vines, the gold filigree from the silky oak scattered on the grass and Christmas celebrations in her house and garden. It rained on New Year's Eve.

While she was writing *A Gardener's Year*, Jean received a letter from Peter Cuffley – artist, author, gardener and graphic designer – asking if he could visit the garden. While he had been researching a book on cottage gardens in Australia, he'd been lent a copy of the extremely rare *Garden in a Valley*. He was entranced by the book, a 'testament to a sense of family and place', as well as its story of garden-making.[16] Cuffley had grown up in the Dandenong Ranges among cottage gardens tended by his family and other dedicated gardeners, and it was memories of family and place, and a love of old gardens, that had inspired him to research cottage gardens. When he and a gardener friend visited 'Dunedin' in spring that year, 1983, pushing open the old picket gate into the garden, Cuffley felt they were entering a gardener's paradise. They wandered up a path leading to the house, exclaiming at the plants, stooping under flower-laden archways, and caught a glimpse of Jean, now 77, in a brown dress and thick stockings, deftly weeding the rock garden. She ushered them into a room filled with books and flowers. The kettle was boiling on the fire, birds flashed past the window: 'the afternoon took off and soared'. But soon he was back in the garden, passing through tunnels of growth and areas of sunlight, exploring paths and bending over flowers. As Jean led him to the front fence to see the bower bird's bower, she had stories for every tree and flower they passed.[17]

A week later, at the launch of his enormously successful *Cottage Gardens in Australia*, Peter Cuffley, with Helen Vellacott and Jean's friend John Turner, hatched a plan to republish *Garden in a Valley* and make this story of an Australian garden available to new readers.[18]

When Turner contacted her about the plan, Jean's reaction was cautious. Back in 1970, encouraged by Betty Conabere, she had sent *Garden in a Valley* to Collins but was told it was too dated to reprint. Jean felt that decision still held, even though she was aware that books such as hers were becoming popular again. 'Of course I should <u>like</u> an edition … especially as I think it is my best work', she told Turner.[19] Jean hadn't looked at the book for forty years, and it took some courage to reread it. She started with the concluding chapters first – reflective chapters on landscape, change and the garden's healing propensities – and read them approvingly. Then she forced herself –'almost shrinking' – to start at the beginning and read it right through. But once the ice was broken, she was enthusiastic about the project and agreed the text was suitable for reproducing in its entirety, except for the references to digging up ferns and wildflowers in the bush. 'It was harmless when it was done … but it's not harmless now'.[20] Five Mile Press agreed to publish the book.

Peter Cuffley and John Turner had clear ideas on how the new edition should look. They were influenced by a recent illustrated edition of Flora Thompson's rural memoir, *Lark Rise to Candleford*, filled with flower vignettes and illustrations of rural life: thatched cottages, farm scenes and flower-filled gardens.[21] Although aware that the pictures romanticised rural life, Cuffley and Turner wanted a similar quality of production for Jean's book, with illustrations of plants and favourite flowers that were mentioned in the text, complemented by family photographs, paintings and botanical art.[22] As the project developed, it became obvious that the new edition of *Garden in a Valley* would be as much a tribute to Jean herself as a desire to have an important book back in circulation. This was evident in a letter John Turner sent to botanical artists, asking them to contribute to the book. Republishing *Garden in a Valley* was merited because of the value of the story, he told them, but also 'as a memorial to Jean Galbraith, whose work in field botany, natural history and gardening publications – and her two floras – has given so much help and pleasure to thousands of Australians'.[23]

Cuffley and Turner sought out paintings of gardens, flowers, people and landscapes in collections at the National Gallery of Victoria and regional art galleries, to capture time, place, rural life and the beauty of flowers. Jean's botanical artist friends prepared to paint specific plants mentioned in the text, but some of their plans came to grief. Rain ruined the maiden blush rose that Joan Law-Smith was poised to paint, so she contributed daffodils instead. Betty Conabere had to resort to work she'd completed several years before, an Irish peach apple in Jean's orchard, after she was seriously injured in a car accident. Celia Rosser sent graceful fuchsias and Latrobe Valley field naturalist, Bart Sterkenburg, painted a collection of Gippsland wildflowers. John Turner, also a keen artist and printmaker, contributed several prints, including the picket gate at 'Dunedin', the evocative entry to the garden.

Peter Cuffley set to work on the cover illustration, a painting of the garden at the time the text had been written. His research was thorough, based on the garden plan published in the 1939 edition of *Garden in a Valley*, photographs of the garden from the 1920s and 1930s, discussions with Jean, and studying plants from the period still growing in the garden. He painted it as a bird's eye view, looking down on the garden. There was the bush house, pond, fountain and seat, with a young Jean working nearby; behind the house were the artist's sleepout and the vegetable garden; rose bowers stretched over the Via Rosarius on an orderly path to the front door; the second rock garden was in front of the study and fruit trees were dotted in the orchard to the east. Hay-making was in progress in the paddock behind the house, adding to the picture's golden glow. There were glimpses of Jean's bush sanctuary through the trees lining the Top Road. 'Yes, that is exactly how it was', Cuffley remembered Jean saying when she saw the completed work. 'It makes me want to write a story about someone who stepped into a painting'. [24]

While Peter Cuffley was designing the book, John Turner became a hands-on editor, advising Jean while she wrote a new foreword. Much of it was recycled from the rejected *Gardener's Year* introduction. Now she had the opportunity – and encouragement from Turner, who endorsed a 'historical and geographical' introduction – to write about family and place. [25] She began with her grandfather's migration from Scotland; wrote of the family's life on the goldfields at Beechworth; recounted the move to a selection overlooking the Latrobe River valley; and told the story of the Galbraiths establishing a farm and new home in Gippsland. Except for a reference to the view of distant power stations from her gate – 'our legacy of past forests' – the foreword ended where the garden story began, with her family's move into 'Dunedin' when she was eight. 'It was here, in 1914, that we began to build the Garden in a Valley. It still survives under my care'. [26]

Her initial reluctance aside, Jean was soon keen to have the book out quickly: 'the present nostalgia for old things, especially old gardens, won't last forever, though some of us will continue to love them', she told Turner. [27] And things were moving quickly. She signed the contract at the end of 1984 and finished correcting the galley proofs the following April. She was also involved with reissuing work written by Edna Walling, whose reputation had risen with the appreciation for old gardens. When Victor Crittenden of Mulini Press asked Jean if she had a neglected manuscript lying in a bottom drawer, she told him she didn't have one of her own, but she did have a manuscript that Walling had sent her, 'On the Trail of Australian Wildflowers'. Crittenden took on the task of editing Walling's haphazard manuscript, and Jean worked on updating botanical nomenclature and preparing an index of botanical names.[28] She also launched the book at the iconic Melbourne bookshop, Margareta Webber's. Included in *On the Trail of Australian Wildflowers* was discussion of how natural bush settings act as a guide for the design of native gardens and it became an influential book for landscape architects designing Australian gardens.[29] It was soon out of print. Jean contributed a foreword to another book of Walling's, first published in 1952 as *The Australian Roadside*, and reissued in 1985 as *Country Roads: The Australian Roadside*. Jean emphasised how this book was 'Edna Walling's effort to share with us the beauty she has seen and ask us to protect what we could so easily lose'.[30] Jean's friendship with the now legendary Walling was further highlighted when the ABC's 'A Big Country' came to film part of a documentary on Walling at 'Dunedin'. Jean's friends completed a big clean-up of the garden for the occasion. 'It was marvellous'.[31]

But now it was time for Jean's work to come under the spotlight. The handsome new edition of *Garden in a Valley* appeared towards the end of 1985, ten years after Jean had farewelled her *Garden Lover* readers. There was no launch but the book was celebrated by those whose efforts had brought it back into print. Peter Cuffley collected Jean from Tyers and drove her to Castlemaine for a celebratory dinner hosted by John and Kaye Turner. The book was an immediate success. In January, Jean's editor from Five Mile Press wrote about plans for reprinting and asked if there was any chance of another Jean Galbraith/Five Mile Press publication.[32]

Why was a set of gardening articles written in the 1930s so popular fifty years later, and in an increasingly secular society? Certainly influential was the timing of the book's appearance, at a time of enormous enthusiasm for older style gardens. But *Zeitgeist* was only part of the explanation for the book's popularity, as the letters Jean received from readers revealed. In telling the story of her garden, Jean had written about what it meant to garden. She had captured the wonder of gardening, its excitement and significance. These experiences resonated with her readers and the book provided evidence that garden writing as a literary genre was eagerly sought by Australian readers.

Readers – and most who wrote to Jean were women – told her of the immense pleasure they received from the book. A reader in outer suburban Melbourne described the 'beautiful self indulgent day' she had spent on Boxing Day, staying in bed all day to read her Christmas present, *Garden in a Valley*. 'Your garden is already a garden of significance to me'. Like Jean, she was grateful to her parents who had taught her to love gardens and rejoice in flowers. 'I loved it – I eat it up like fruit salad', was one reader's way of praising the book, while another reader described how *Garden in a Valley* put her in a 'happy kind of daze'. It was now on her bedside table so that she could reread her favourite chapters. Yet another wrote of rationing her reading to two pages a day to make the experience last, the book resting on a table in the front room between sessions. A reader from New South Wales told Jean that she had read *Garden in a Valley* twice but didn't expect to finish it in her lifetime. She wished other garden writers could write like Jean Galbraith. Jean's approach to garden writing– full of story, reflection and philosophy, rather than as a venue for instruction – delighted readers and they wrote to tell her of the joy her writing brought.[33]

In *Garden in a Valley*, Jean had written about her own life in the garden but readers found that she was writing about their lives too. Some responded with intensely personal letters, telling her of the flood of memories the book released, while others wrote detailed garden biographies that described the significant gardens in their lives, a combination of family history and plants. A reader from northern Victoria found that 'every chapter had parts of me in it' and she described for Jean her mother's garden and her childhood garden, and of the impact the book had on her.[34] A reader from England mused on what she liked best about the book. Was it the development of the garden, descriptions of the Victorian countryside and its wildflowers, or glimpses of family life in the early part of the century? Ultimately, she decided that *Garden in a Valley* resonated with her own life, and she wrote of the memories it revived of the garden her mother had tended for fifty years.[35] Other readers told Jean that she expressed what many gardeners felt, but couldn't write themselves. 'You have put many of my thoughts and feelings into words for me', wrote one reader from the ACT.[36] For a reader from Queensland, *Garden in a Valley* was an echo of her feelings which, she told Jean, she could never express herself.[37] 'Garden-making, like gardening itself', wrote the great English twentieth century garden designer, Russell Page, 'concerns the relationship of the human being to his natural surroundings'.[38] Jean Galbraith had expressed this for her readers.

Responses did not come just from readers who shared similar gardening memories of the 1920s and 1930s. The book's appeal spanned generations as younger gardeners, too, wrote to tell Jean of their gardening experiences after reading the book. A young mother from the Dandenongs was so inspired by the stories in *Garden in a Valley* that she sent Jean six pages describing her own childhood and garden on an orchard near Healesville. She had read *Garden in a Valley* twice in the past few weeks and felt that she had been walking with Jean in the garden and had shared in the gardening adventures. 'Never have I enjoyed a book so much'.[39] The book also appealed to non-gardeners. When a woman in New South Wales, with no interest in gardening, was given *Garden in a Valley* to read while she was convalescing, she felt daunted by what looked to be a 'deadly dull' read. Her favourite books were spy stories and thrillers. But she was enthralled. 'The garden is a story of adventure, achievement, shared experiences, mystery and true love', she wrote to Jean. 'What reader could wish for more?'[40]

In her review of *Garden in a Valley* published in *Landscape Australia*, Joan Law-Smith wanted to convey to readers the book's many layers and depth, a difficult task within the limited space she had been allocated. 'It is impossible to sum up in a few paragraphs the philosophy and richness of thought and experiences … that are within the pages of this book', she wrote. 'It is inspiring to read a book written by one who cares so deeply for the cultivation and perpetuation of all that is beautiful in the world of nature'.[41]

When the book was reprinted in 1986, John Turner told Jean to enjoy the royalties that were flooding in. 'Well, I am', she replied, and detailed how she was spending the money. It was 'restful' not to have to worry about the cost of groceries and she now had an investment account put away for emergencies. She had bought a new hearthrug, a copy of *Close to Nature* by John Landy – and she was planning to go on a trip to Kangaroo Island with the Field Naturalists' Club of Victoria.[42]

Jean had always had a steady stream of visitors to her garden but now readers started flocking to 'Dunedin' – up to nine at a time – and sometimes without warning.[43] They came looking for the garden of the 1920s and 1930s, so beautifully portrayed by both the text and Peter Cuffley's cover. Where was the Way of Roses? Where was the bush house? Where was the hedge, the artist's sleepout? Instead, visitors found a wild and magical garden of great beauty. Pools of sunlight alternated with dark shady places; tunnels and paths led to secret gardens; archways sagged under waterfalls of flowers. Visitors delighted in meeting Jean and being shown around the garden. She led the way in her thick stockings and sensible shoes, often wearing a dress and cardigan of brown or green, a brooch at her throat, and her eyes flashing behind old fashioned glasses as she pointed out loved plants and told their stories. 'To be led around an old garden by someone who has planned it and worked in it for a lifetime is a very special privilege', Isobel Tipping wrote in *The Age* after her visit to 'Dunedin'. 'For here every tree and plant is known and, yes, loved for its own significance'.[44]

The magic of these visits often extended inside to Jean's dining room, erudite with books, journals, papers and notes; homely with family photographs and worn furniture; nature-filled with flowers and specimens covering every flat surface; hospitable with the kettle boiling on the open fire and chairs drawn close to the warmth. Elisabeth Murdoch of the famed 'Cruden Farm' garden expressed her pleasure at visiting 'Dunedin' and meeting Jean. 'The beautiful simplicity and charm of your writing is matched by your character and personality … It was a joy to go around your garden with you, and being introduced to your special treasures'.[45] Another visitor, Julie Langford, turned to poetry to capture her experience of a visit to 'Dunedin'. It was an experience that many visitors shared:

To Jean Galbraith

Enveloped
By the scent
Of native mint
I stepped into fantasy's reality –
A garden of love and lingering
Where beauty and wildness tangle,
Through a gate where time bends
  Is it now or then?
…an hour or a year?
The air dripped with green and silver
But the blossoms burst over it all.

A mirror of the garden's sparkle
Were her eyes
Surrounded by fading walls and books
She, too, is growing worn
But warm!
Warm as the fire's welcome
With its black kettle steaming.[46]

Jean turned 80 in March 1986. Her garden writing career was entering a late flowering. Not only was *Garden in a Valley* a great success, but new writing projects were in the pipeline. Anne Latreille, gardening editor of *The Age*, came to visit 'Dunedin' after being sent a review copy of *Garden in a Valley*. She had found the book so 'compelling and different' that she drove to Tyers to interview Jean, arriving on a day of soft spring rain, and pushing open the old picket gate to a drift of pink petals – crab apples, roses, camellias. It was, she remembered, a magical morning.[47] Several months later, when she was planning a revamp of *The Age*'s gardening pages, she invited Jean to write 'cuttings', short contributions of around 500 words. At first, Jean was concerned about having the time. Her already voluminous correspondence had increased with the publication of *Garden in a Valley* and she was committed to answering readers' letters. She was also inundated with visitors to the garden: unlike Gertrude Jekyll, she didn't tell readers to stay away. But she felt 'honoured' to write for *The Age*, and devised ways to fit in the new commitment. She would have to handwrite the cuttings, she told Anne Latreille. It had been her practice throughout her writing career to draft articles longhand – she couldn't think at a typewriter – and then type them for submission, but typing had become too painful now that she had arthritis in her back. She didn't mind being paid less for her contributions and sent some neatly written cuttings for perusal. Latreille had suggested that Jean look at Vita Sackville-West's *Garden Book*, a selection of the enormously popular gardening articles that the chatelaine of Sissinghurst had written for the *Observer*. Jean was familiar with the book – she had a copy – but her cuttings were quite different. 'One has to write in one's own way', she told Latreille.[48]

Jean's cuttings appeared regularly in the gardening pages in Tuesday's *Age*. The format suited her, enough words for a short meditation on a plant, sharing a thought she had in the garden that morning, describing delicate patterns of petals and stamens, wildflowers in the bush, birds in the garden, flowers sitting in front of her in a vase or memories that her plants evoked. Anne Latreille remembered her own eagerness to see what had been written, opening Jean's envelopes while she was still at the letter box.[49] Interspersed with the cuttings were longer articles too, such as Jean's memories of the wildflower shows in the Melbourne Town Hall, the beauty of wattles in early spring, or the wild cyclamen that returned each year in her orchard. One article featured the Irish strawberry tree in her garden and recorded her childhood memories of one that she had loved in the Beechworth public gardens. Her detailed description of the tree in her garden conveyed its beauty: the white clustering flowers resembling lily of the valley, abundant berries turning from yellow to red in autumn, the birds that feasted there. Soon after, an article by John Turner on the genus *Arbutus* appeared in the gardening pages of *The Age*, stimulated by Jean's article. Interweaving botany and memory, Turner wrote of first seeing the Kilkenny Irish strawberry tree on a student research trip to Ireland in the early 1930s. His article concentrated on the history and distribution of the *Arbutus* and what it revealed of the vegetation history of the British Isles.[50] The two articles were elegantly complementary: Jean's a personal story of a tree and its beauty; Turner's a foray into botanical history.

Anne Latreille typed Jean's contributions herself so that Jean could be paid in full for her articles. Jean was amazed at the payment she received – it seemed 'outrageously high' – and she was now able to employ someone to work occasionally in the garden and do the jobs she couldn't manage.[51]

Although Jean had met Collins' deadline and finished writing *A Gardener's Year* at the end of 1983, the book didn't appear until 1987. Reviewers not familiar with her writing were struck by its originality. In Wagga's *Daily Advertiser*, for example, the reviewer explained how *A Gardener's Year* differed from other gardening books, written in story form and not full of gardening advice, and pronounced it 'an unending delight'.[52] T.R. Garnett, developer of a large country garden, the 'Garden of St Erth', reviewed the book for *The Age*. The text reminded him of Gilbert White, the eighteenth century naturalist and ecologist, whose masterpiece, *The Natural History of Selborne*, recorded White's observations of birds, plants and animals in his parish. 'The combination of acute scientific observation (and an exact sense of colour) with a lyrical Christianity-based simplicity (nothing cloying about it) makes one think of Gilbert White', Garnett wrote.[53]

As a follow up to *Garden in a Valley*, Five Mile Press decided to publish the first few years of Jean's long-running series, 'From Day to Day in the Garden'.

The articles from 1943 to 1946 were chosen, with the backdrop of war adding historical interest. These were the years when Peter was living at 'Dunedin' and when her father, Matt, died. Jean was caring for a young child and her increasingly frail parents; producing food for the family from the vegetable garden and orchard with all the planting, manuring, weeding, harvesting, bottling and preserving that that involved; and also writing a stream of articles for *Wild Life* and *Walkabout*, the *Victorian School Paper*, the *New South Wales School Magazine*, *My Garden* and the *Garden Lover*. There were hints that she felt overwhelmed at times.

Jean tentatively titled the new book 'Letters to My Friends', which reflected how she had regarded her 'Day to Day in the Garden' articles. In 1975, when she had ended the series and farewelled *Garden Lover* readers, she had emphasised how garden writing had brought her so many friends. She expressed these sentiments when writing the introduction to 'Letters to My Friends' in 1989: 'when you write books, garden books anyway, you find friends everywhere. So the title of this book is literally true … Through these monthly articles I have made many friends'.[54] But as the publishers wanted 'garden' in the title, it was changed to *A Garden Lover's Journal* – 'which if not distinguished is at least harmless', Jean wrote to John Turner.[55] A new introduction was required. Published in 1989, *A Garden Lover's Journal* was another attractive production, with garden photographs from Jean's collection, covers from the *Garden Lover* and many flower and vegetable illustrations.

A Garden Lover's Journal did not have the same success as *Garden in a Valley* and was eventually remaindered, a new experience for Jean who was used to her books selling out. While it did not have the strong storyline of *Garden in a Valley*, it is notable for its fine garden writing. The beauty of the writing was celebrated by Betty Conabere who commented on the book with an artist's eye. Through the book's 'word pictures', Betty felt Jean shared her perceptions of colour 'as few artists can manage to paint'. She compared reading *A Garden Lover's Journal* to listening to a Mozart concerto, both with 'many layers of delight'.[56]

The publication of new books and the regular appearance of Jean's cuttings in *The Age* led to another outpouring of letters. A couple from Queensland wrote of reading Jean's books in rotation. They had read *Garden in a Valley*, had just finished reading *A Garden Lover's Journal* and now planned to re-read *A Gardener's Year*, because they missed having something 'Jean Galbraith' to read.[57] *Age* readers wrote of turning straight to the gardening pages on Tuesdays, to see if there was anything written by her. Their praise was extravagant, one reader telling Jean that her cutting was 'the only article worth reading in the whole of *The Age* that day'. Like many other readers, she was collecting Jean's cuttings and pasting them into a scrap book so they could be read again and again.[58]

Another of Jean's *Garden Lover* series was published in 1990. Victor Crittenden, who had published Edna Walling's *On the Trail of Australian Wildflowers*, had also approached Jean about reprinting 'Two – and a Garden', which had appeared in the *Garden Lover* in the early war years. He remembered reading the articles in the 1940s.[59] This series was based on the property that Jean's former school teacher J.W. Elijah and his wife Mabel had bought in the Dandenong Ranges and their restoration of the old homestead garden. With a new title, *Doongalla Restored: The Story of a Garden*, and the cover featuring a scene at 'Doongalla' painted by Mabel Elijah in the 1940s, the book contained the first half of the series. 'Doongalla' was now incorporated into the popular Dandenong Ranges National Park, and this gave the book added historical significance, as it told the story of a garden hidden away in the mountain ash forest of a national park famous for its fern gullies and lyre birds. The once private garden was now accessible to all.

Back in 1984, John Turner had hoped the republishing of *Garden in a Valley* would be a memorial to Jean for her work in field botany, natural history and garden writing, which, he said, had brought pleasure to thousands of

Throughout her writing career, Jean received countless letters from readers, but few arrived with such an unconventional address as this one.

Jean Galbraith Papers, MS 12637, Australian Manuscripts Collection, State Library of Victoria

Australians. And this is what happened. In a form of cross fertilisation, the republication of Jean's books became a conduit for people to express appreciation not just for her garden writing but also to express how her contributions to botany, conservation and natural history had influenced their lives. 'Coincident to tracing a plant in your Guide to Wildflowers', a couple from Melbourne wrote, 'we found ourselves reading your article in the *Age* 1 October and it occurred to us that this was a good time to say "thankyou" for the pleasure and information you have given us for so many years'.[60] Writing to Jean after reading a cutting on cyclamens that had sent her running out into the garden to check her own plants, a reader from Portland told Jean she had been a fan of hers since buying *Wildflowers of Victoria* in 1950. She discussed cyclamens but she also told Jean of her mammoth revegetation activities and how she had just finished planting a thousand red gums and wattles.[61] A reader from the Wimmera who wrote to Jean of her own childhood gardening memories after reading *Garden in a Valley*, also told her of how she valued both *Wildflowers of Victoria* and the Collins field guide, and described her involvement in the conservation of roadside plants. Readers enthused about her gardening books and articles, but they also reiterated how her field guides, even the outdated *Wildflowers of Victoria*, were their constant companions. They wrote of how she had inspired them in all her modes of writing and, consequently, of how she had enriched their lives.

Chapter 14

OLD AGE

Writing to John Turner in 1989 about ageing, a subject that often cropped up in their letters, Jean maintained that discomfort was to be expected, 'but fortunately we also have much to enjoy'.[1] For Jean, aged 83, there was much to enjoy. Entry into her eighties had coincided with the republication of much of her earlier writing that brought her in close contact with readers again and eased financial concerns. She was enjoying her new commission of writing for the gardening pages of *The Age* and was continuing to make friends through the garden. She also received more recognition for her botanical work. These fulfilling experiences were added to the deep contentment she received daily from her faith, her garden, her love of nature and her continued wonder at the beauty of the natural world, even as her strength for gardening lessened and her eyesight deteriorated.

Jean had lived alone since the early 1960s, but she was never lonely. Once she adjusted to living by herself, she told John Turner, she 'positively revelled' in it.[2] Now Jean was the only Galbraith in the valley, her family widely dispersed. Angus, her only surviving brother, lived in Beechworth. As a widower, he had found love and companionship with May, Lance's widow, when they married in 1984. Lance and May's children also lived away from Gippsland with their families: Marjory near the Yarra at Warrandyte in a garden where native orchids and other wildflowers grew, Geoffrey in the old Ladson home at Beechworth, John in Bilpin near the Blue Mountains and Tim in India. Lawrie and Lin's son Peter lived with his family in Brisbane where he worked at the University of Queensland. But while most descendants of the Galbraiths and Ladsons were scattered, Jean was in close contact with her extended network of cousins and their children. She considered it her good fortune 'to be surrounded with kindness, with friends, with beloved relatives, not living near, but joined by letters and shared interests, and visits'. There were nineteen great nieces and nephews 'to keep one from feeling old', as well as 'good friends and neighbours, books and music, a garden, pleasant work to do, a steadfast faith and a sure hope'.[3] The Latrobe Valley field naturalists had become family to Jean, and it was with them that she celebrated most birthdays and Christmases.

Christmases remained a highlight on Jean's calendar. They were just as important to celebrate alone in old age as when she was young and thirty people gathered under the oak at 'Dunedin' on Christmas Day, or when Peter and his family drove down from Queensland and she created a Christmas wonderland for the children, her tree shining with 'the most mesmerising coloured lights'.[4] Jean scrupulously maintained the Christmas rituals she had developed over the years. She made all her own cards, a tradition that may have started when she sent handmade cards to patients in the Austin Hospital in the 1920s and 30s.[5] The cards were decorated with pressed flowers – often natives from her garden – and each year she wrote a Christmas poem that was printed inside. Making the cards was pleasant work, she told Esther Wettenhall, a writer and native gardener friend, in the late 1980s, 'but it takes weeks'.[6] The many cards she received from friends, readers, admirers and family were strung around the walls and the doors in her dining room – wherever the bookcases left room for them – and they held great significance. 'It is like having my friends looking out at me from the walls – so many with news – weddings, births, exams passed', she wrote.[7] Each year she placed a welcoming verse on the front door to greet all visitors to 'Dunedin'. She had heard it read on an ABC broadcast and hastily jotted down the words, with no idea of who had written the poem. Family and visitors loved reading the verse as they entered 'Dunedin'. They felt it summed up Jean's generosity and hospitality, and some adopted it for their own homes at Christmas.

If you come cheerily
Here shall be jest for you
If you come wearily
Here shall be rest for you
If you come borrowing
Gladly we'll loan to you
If you come sorrowing
Love shall be shown to you
Under our thatch friend
Peace shall abide for you
Touch but the latch friend
The door opens wide to you.[8]

On Christmas Eve, the tree was decorated and the house full of flowers. Her Christmas cake was iced and often decorated with currants from the garden to simulate holly berries. Gifts had been arriving from friends around the country, but Jean always saved opening them for Christmas morning. She rose early and unwrapped her presents while carols played in the background. Then she was ready for the stream of telephone calls from family as they rang with their greetings. Christmas dinners were often spent with Bon and Ollie Thompson, her field naturalist friends from Traralgon South, who came to Tyers to collect her and later drove her home. In the evening, with the Christmas tree alight, Jean listened to more Christmas music – carols, *The Messiah* – and reflected on the words.[9]

Her pleasure in writing was unabated and she kept *The Age* well supplied with cuttings. In 1991, when Anne Latreille commissioned her 85-year-old contributor to write an article on gardening in old age, it drew enthusiastic responses from older readers who told Jean how personal and special the article was. 'I now know gardening goes on as long as we live', a reader from Hawthorn wrote. 'Thankyou for your stimulating and thoughtful notes and make sure, please, they continue for a very long time'.[10] The next year, when Jean was asked to supply a summary of her life to the International Biographical Centre at Cambridge, she ended with a note on her current activities: 'Now at the age of 86 and not very physically active I am content to garden a little … and write little paragraphs and occasionally long ones for the Melbourne *Age*'.[11] Her nephew Tim published a book of her poems in 1990, *The Poet's Spring*.

Although they were now well out of print, Jean's field guides were still in great demand. 'Collins must be out of their minds to let it lapse', a field guide user from Phillip Island wrote to Jean in 1991, after expressing shock at finding the book was no longer available. It had been her great delight to have a book that enabled her to identify flowers and distinguish between similar plants, she told Jean. Her copy was now battered from use and she had her name down on a waiting list at a second hand bookshop.[12] Republishing the Collins field guide had been under discussion in the 1980s, and later the Latrobe Valley Field Naturalists' Club was keen to oversee a new edition, but problems with copyright proved overwhelming. People were also desperately searching for *Wildflowers of Victoria*, and hoped she could help them find copies they could give to young naturalists who kept spiriting theirs away.[13]

Jean received further botanical recognition when *Dampiera galbraithiana* was published in *Telopia*, the journal of the National Herbarium of New South Wales, in August 1988. As she explained to Jim Willis, the dampiera had been discovered by Evan Chesterfield back in the 1970s while he was working on his survey of the Macalister catchment, and he had brought it to her for determination. She had been completely stumped and took it to the Herbarium in Melbourne where she examined every species of dampiera. The closest she could find was *D. scottiana*, a New South Wales dampiera, but she was still very doubtful although Herbarium staff accepted this as the identification. 'I heard no more of it and almost forgot it – so the description and name in *Telopea* really <u>was</u> a surprise'.[14] The plant's common name was the Licola dampiera. In 1993, a rare and beautiful boronia growing in dry open forest north of Stockdale was published in the Herbarium's journal, *Muelleria*, as *Boronia galbraithiae*. It was not a new field discovery – Jean had collected it in 1956 – but it had recently been determined by Herbarium staff as a separate species, and named in honour of Jean who had recognised its distinctiveness.[15] 'Modest Lady, Dainty Flower', a feature article on Jean and the plant, appeared in *The Age*, written by native plant expert, Sue Forrester, who had driven to inspect the boronia in its isolated location near Dargo. The large coloured photograph of the flower that illustrated the article displayed its delicate beauty.[16] Recognition of her botanical work – she was described in the *Muelleria* article as the 'doyenne of Victorian botanists' – endorsed that there was much for Jean to enjoy in old age.

But her health fluctuated. Fortunately, her old demon from childhood, eczema, no longer troubled her after she consulted a new skin specialist in the 1970s, but she still had regular bouts of bronchitis. Arthritis and back pain limited her gardening and she also endured an attack of shingles. Osteoporosis began to take its toll, leaving her stooped and increasingly frail. She wrote to John Turner about a fall that had left her with severe back pain and told him how she fared during a long spell in bed at 'Dunedin'. Angus and May came to stay and after they left, field naturalists and 'quite wonderful friends' called in daily bringing food and helping in the house and garden. 'Of course that was the sort of helpfulness one shouldn't depend on', she wrote. She had the telephone, radio and books within easy reach on her bedside table. Eventually, she could hobble on two sticks, but it was some time before she could resume daily walks to the post office to collect her mail. Now she often accepted offers of a lift.[17] Her bed, she considered, was 'the very last thing in comfort and luxury', with its solid wooden base, inner spring mattress, electric blanket and *pièce de résistance*, a lambswool, a gift from Edna Walling's niece who lived on a grazing property in Queensland.[18] She went to bed early in the evenings, retreating to the comfort of electric blanket and lambswool, and read until late. With her back problems though, she was able to do less in the garden.

In March 1989, she reported that she couldn't dig, but she could still weed and water – and sometimes plant. Her friends held regular working bees in the garden. They insisted she use an electric jug and stop boiling water in the cast iron kettle on the open fire. It was too hazardous and heavy for an elderly woman with osteoporosis.[19] She began using a staff to steady herself in the garden. Her eyesight was failing. For a writer and voracious reader, this was a severe blow.

At the beginning of 1993, relatives began discussing with Jean the advantages of moving from 'Dunedin' to a retirement unit at Yallambee Village in Traralgon. She accepted their advice. A cutting illustrated by Peter Cuffley's painting of the garden in a valley appeared in *The Age* in early July. Its heading was 'Goodbye for Now'.

> I am moving very soon to a small unit with a very small garden, but in the garden on which I look out as I write, the flowers of spring are coming as ever, and each year brings greater beauty to the trees in the orchard.
>
> I shall be only ten kilometres away and intend to visit my garden often. The loveliness of all the seasons will be there, and I will pretend not to see the weeds.
>
> There are camellias flowering now, and brave clusters of nerines are still white and pink. Outside the bedroom window of my new home there is already a bird's nest in a flowering shrub.
>
> I do not say goodbye, for I hope to write again when all the moving is in the past.
>
> Goodbye – for a while.[20]

We can only imagine what Jean faced, leaving her home of nearly eighty years: the familiar rooms full of books, the 'glowing fires' in her fireplace, the cluttered table by the window where, microscope at the ready, she had studied Australian flora and had written almost daily about nature and the beauty of plants. She would be leaving the garden she had tended since 1922, the garden that was her companion, a source of wonder and spontaneous joy, the receptacle of memories and stories, a tapestry of her life in plants.

She left with great reluctance, Ian Hyndman said, 'and yet with that attitude of acceptance which was a very real part of her character'. [21] Her acceptance of the move was reflected in her letters as she described her new home. 'My nice home help comes as she did before, my friends say I am, in most cases, nearer than before … I have my own pleasant living room, bathroom, kitchen'. [22] She wrote, too, of the convenience of the unit, how warm it was – she could put the heater on in the morning before she started dressing. She wrote of the people who visited and the flowers they brought. She was especially grateful to her relative Roma Missen who called in regularly and helped in so many ways, always bringing flowers that she arranged beautifully. According to one of her visitors, Jean's main disappointment at Yallambee was seeing only exotic birds – blackbirds and starlings – but she had been delighted by the recent sighting of a magpie lark. [23]

Jean's move from 'Dunedin' was a loss also shared by her extended family. For them, 'Dunedin' had been an oasis of tranquillity. 'It was there and Jean was always there with her welcoming smile'. [24] For Jean, though, there had been some easing of the pain at leaving by not selling the property. Each weekend friends and field naturalists, or Ian and Judy Hyndman while they were based in Traralgon, drove Jean to spend a day at 'Dunedin', to see the birds and flowers and sit in the garden. She described these visits to her cousin Verna: collecting scraps of blue paper to take for the bower birds, of being able to walk around the fenceline when she could barely walk around the garden before, of lamenting the state of her poor tulips but bringing back bunches of jonquils to the unit. [25]

Her first Christmas away from 'Dunedin', 1993, Jean sent her handmade Christmas cards. They were no longer decorated with pressed flowers but they still contained her Christmas verse:

Rich the giving
Of sun and rain
As summer comes
To the earth again

Ripening harvest
Fruit on the trees
Young birds flying
Sweet of bees

New Year, Christmas
Feasts of birth,
Gifts of Heaven
Sent through Earth

But greater giving
Than sun or dew
The Christmas blessing
Come to you.

Her extensive correspondence continued. Many people wrote expressing their sympathy for her move and applauding her spirit, while letters still flowed from readers with appreciations of her field guides, articles and garden books. Gardening friends discussed the seasons and reported on what was flowering in their various gardens, be they native gardens, rock gardens, hill gardens, country gardens or suburban gardens. Joy from Marlo, at the mouth of the Snowy River, was one of many naturalists who kept her regularly supplied with observations of birds and plants in regions around the country. Regular letters from family reported on their activities, as well as those of their children and grandchildren. Her cousin Edith in England, a similar age to Jean, was still writing her acerbic letters and avidly discussing the poetry and books that they both loved. 'Don't worry about the nose', she wrote to Jean in 1994, after receiving a photograph, 'a good sized nose is said to give character … You have a fine intellectual forehead anyway'.[26] She was concerned, though, about Jean's eyesight and suggested her envelopes be addressed by someone else: she didn't know how they actually found her. Many of the letters Jean received at Yallambee contained news of the death of friends and relatives, as they had in her last years at 'Dunedin'.

It was her deteriorating eyesight that eventually forced Jean to send a resignation letter to Anne Latreille at *The Age*. 'I hate having to write this letter', she began, in an almost illegible hand, and described the impact her eyesight was having on her writing. She could no longer read her correspondence, even with a magnifying glass, and now had to wait for someone to read the letters aloud to her. 'I can't even see what I have just written'.[27] Her last publication, a cutting on purple loosestrife, was published in April 1995 when she was 89 – almost seventy years after meeting Ralph Boardman at the wildflower show and receiving her first garden writing commission.[28] Her career as Jean Galbraith, writer, had come to an end. So had her prolific letter writing. As she explained to Peter Galbraith in 1995, she was writing few letters. 'I simply can't see well enough to inflict much of it on my readers'.[29] The Christmas card she sent out that year, still with a poem, had a similar message for her friends: 'I am finding writing difficult and this will be my last Christmas card'.

Her ninetieth birthday was celebrated at Yallambee in March, 1996. Many of the cards she received were handmade by friends and featured pressed flowers from their gardens or stunning photographs of Australian flora. Not long after this milestone birthday, her family decided that she should move to 'Olivet', a Christadelphian nursing home in the Melbourne suburb of Ringwood. With her poor eyesight and general frailty, Jean could no longer live independently in her unit and needed a higher level of care. 'Olivet' was infused with a Christadelphian ethos and Jean knew most of the residents there. It was also close to her niece, Marjory.

After moving to 'Olivet', Jean gained comfort from many visitors and also from the letters and cards she received. Marjory read the letters to her and wrote replies. Bon Thompson's warm, lively letters, and those of June Lubcke, kept Jean up-to-date with field naturalist club happenings, conservation issues, field trips, bird and flower census work. The sight of glorious wattle bloom or memorable flowers in the bush moved field naturalists to write and share their joy with her. Others sent her leaves to feel and hold. They wrote of special events in their gardens, such as her old friend Ellen Lyndon, a distinguished naturalist, writing of the *Brachychiton* that had flowered for the first time in twenty-seven years.[30] Family letters released warm memories, some taking her back to her girlhood. A cousin, Shirley, described her chance meeting with a woman whose parents had bought the Tyers butter factory from the Galbraiths in 1921. When they moved into their new home in Tyers, she told Shirley, they found the table set, the stove lit and the kettle boiling, a welcoming gesture from Jean's mother and one the family had not forgotten.[31] May's letters arrived regularly from Beechworth and were comforting. Their faith, she told Jean, was a 'wonderful possession'.[32] At Christmas, when cards arrived, there were still some that addressed her as 'Correa'.

'Dunedin' was sold in 1997 to Tyers farmers, Max and Ollie Archbold. The house was now badly run down and in need of repair, the garden even more overgrown. The Archbolds renovated the house and worked on the garden, and also opened a tea room in Jean's former dining room. Ollie wrote regular letters to Jean at 'Olivet', telling her what was happening in the garden, and Jean found them cheering, as a comment from May shows. She had heard from her daughter Marjory that Jean was feeling 'desolate', May wrote in the winter of 1997, but had enjoyed a letter from Ollie about the garden.[33]

'If ever I had to live away from here I would be only half alive', Marjory Burgess remembers her aunt saying, years before she left 'Dunedin'. It was a feeling Jean had first experienced as a young girl, not wanting to leave her beloved valley to go away to school, and a sentiment that endured. Marjory feels the truth of this statement when she thinks of Jean's 'sad last years' in 'Olivet', when she became less able to see, hear or think. 'The distorted messages she received through her dimmed senses and mind led her to be lost to us ... Even loved Bible passages read or said loudly sounded wrong to her. She did not recognise her dearest old friends'.[34]

Yet more botanical recognition came her way. In 1998, *Prostanthera galbraithiae*, the Wellington mint bush, was formally described in *Telopia*, in recognition of Jean as one of the first people to recognise its distinctiveness, for her strong campaign for its protection, and also for her contribution to Victorian flora. The rare mint bush, with flowers ranging from mauve to deep purple and with maroon spots at the centre, grows on only two sites in Victoria, including land near Rosedale that, thanks to Jean's campaigning, was saved from pine plantations and eventually reserved as the Holey Plains State Park.[35] But Jean was not aware of the naming or how she had been honoured. She was not aware of her brother Angus's death in 1998, or of the publication of *Poems for Peter*, the poems she had written for her young nephew back in the 1940s.[36]

Jean said in her last years that she wished she could go to sleep and 'wake up in the Kingdom'.[37] She died on 2 January, 1999, aged 92.

In death, Jean came back to her valley and was buried at the Traralgon cemetery, where many of her family and the Artist from *Garden in a Valley* are also buried. Set on a ridge, the cemetery looks out over Jean's country: the foothills of the Great Dividing Range to the north and the blue hills of the Strzeleckis to the south. Ian Hyndman led the funeral service, speaking of her deep faith and belief in the resurrection. 'She died believing that she will rise to life again at the resurrection when Jesus returns'.[38] Later, at the graveside service, the Twenty-Third Psalm was recited, a favourite from Jean's earliest years when its words and picture had hung on the wall in her bedroom at 'Home'.

Soft rain was falling on the day of her funeral. As Evan Chesterfield remembered, it was just like the rain that Jean loved the most, the soft gentle rain of autumn, with the sound of raindrops hitting the leaves.[39]

There were many obituaries, and while they listed Jean's publications and contributions to botanical knowledge, garden writing and conservation, they also stressed her extraordinary character, selflessness and compassion. They remembered her as a good person, at home at 'Dunedin'. As Anne Latreille wrote in *The Australian*:

> Friends remember her in her book-lined living room full of fresh flowers, the bird-tables outside the window shimmering with life and movement, the worktable cluttered with papers, the kettle boiling on the open fire. A track was worn on the carpet to her bedroom, which housed her herbarium …

> For the record, her achievement was as a botanist and naturalist. But memories of her remarkable personality – sincere, devout, inquiring, cheerful, resourceful – will not fade.[40]

The obituary botanist Helen Aston wrote in the *Victorian Naturalist* ended with a ringing tribute to the person Jean was:

> I treasure the memories I have of her and feel very privileged to have known such a unique and selfless person. Warm and friendly, joyful in her Christian faith, generous, cheerful, compassionate and caring, yet ever-modest, she had a remarkable and endearing personality which will not be forgotten by all those who knew her. [41]

Josephine Piggin who had come to Gippsland as a young botanist working for the Victorian Forests Commission wrote to Marjory about her memories of times with Jean at 'Dunedin. As a botanist, Jean had been inspirational, but also inspirational was the way she lived her life:

> Her simplicity of life, wanting for nothing, coveting nothing, in thorough appreciation and enjoyment of every moment, of every happening, her great first hand knowledge of her environment and philosophy of life has become greatly meaningful to me …[W]ith age, I am appreciating it more and more.[42]

NOTES

Introduction

1. 'Exhibition of Wild-Flowers', *Victorian Naturalist*, November 1925, p. 145

2. See interviews with Jean Galbraith by John Nicholls, 1986, and Esther Wettenhall, 1992; Ralph Boardman to JG, 10 December 1925, box 3463 folder 8, Jean Galbraith Papers, MS 12637, Australian Manuscripts Collection, State Library of Victoria, cited hereafter as the Jean Galbraith Papers with box and folder numbers.

3. See E.E. Pescott, 'Foreword' in Jean Galbraith, *Garden in a Valley*, Horticultural Press, 1939, and T.R. Garnett, *The Age*, 9 July 1987.

4. Betty Conabere to Jean Galbraith (hereafter JG), 4 February 1990, Jean Galbraith Papers, 3468.7.

5. See Anne Latreille, *Kindred Spirits, a Botanical Correspondence, Letters by Jean Galbraith, Drawings by Joan Law Smith*, Australian Garden History, 1999, p. 201.

6. JG draft of acceptance speech, Australian Natural History Medallion, Jean Galbraith Papers, 4106.4.

7. Taken from JG's writing: 'Flowers of the Wayside', *Wild Life*, September 1940; 'Australian Native Flowers', *Garden Lover*, February, 1926; 'Epacris Impressa: Who Grows it Now?' *My Garden*, June 1941.

8. See Katie Holmes, Susan K. Martin and Kylie Mirmohamadi for a summary of this literature in *Reading the Garden: The Settlement of Australia*, Melbourne University Press, 2008, pp. 26–29.

9. 'Garden of Memories', *Australian Garden Lover*, February 1927, p. 434.

10. Elisabeth Murdoch to JG, 17 August 1989, Jean Galbraith Papers, 3467.7.

11. See Julie Langford's poem, 'To Jean Galbraith'; Rosemary Abbott, 'A Chance Encounter with Jean Galbraith', *Wellspring*, vol. 3, 2000; comments by Jean Galbraith's great nephew, David Galbraith, 25 February 2012; and appreciations of visits to the garden in the Jean Galbraith Papers, 3486.

12. See, for example, Morag Harrison to JG, 22 September 1990, Jean Galbraith Papers, 3468.7.

13. Peter Cuffley, 'Our First Visit to Jean Galbraith at Dunedin', Peter Cuffley Collection.

14. See newspaper articles in the *Latrobe Valley Express* and *Age*; Rosemary Abbott 'A Chance Encounter with Jean Galbraith'; JG's visitors' book, in possession of Marjory Burgess, Warrandyte, as well as descriptions of visits, Jean Galbraith Papers, 3468. See also 'Cyclamens' Return a Meeting With Friends', *The Age*, 18 March 1986.

15. 'Foreword' in JG, *Garden in a Valley*, Five Mile Press, 1985.

16. Anne Latreille, former gardening editor of *The Age*, mentioned the worn carpet in her obituary of JG in *The Australian*, 14 January 1999.

17. J.H. Willis and Arthur Swaby, 'Award of the Natural History Medallion', *Victorian Naturalist*, October 1970, pp. 297–8.

18. Josephine Piggin to Marjory Burgess, 3 March 1999.

Chapter 1. Settling in the Valley

1. JG, *Garden in a Valley*, Five Mile Press, 1986, p. 8.

2. See for example JG, 'How Andrew Became an Australian', *Victorian School Paper*, July 1948, pp. 91–92; JG, 'From Day to Day in the Garden', *Australian Garden Lover*, July 1974; JG, 'The Boys of Mount Hope Farm', July 1950, Jean Galbraith Papers, box 3472.

3.   For comprehensive research on the Galbraith family see Ian Hyndman, *Andrew and Sarah Galbraith and Family: Pioneers of Tyers and Beechworth*, Bethel Publications, 1997. See draft of JG's acceptance speech for the Australian Natural History Medal, 1970, Jean Galbraith Papers, 4106.4.

4.   Ian Hyndman, *History of Beechworth*, Bethel Publications, 1995, pp. 5–12.

5.   *Garden in a Valley*, p. 10.

6.   See *Andrew and Sarah Galbraith and Family* pp. 34–37.

7.   'The Boys of Mount Hope Farm'.

8.   See Carole Woods, *Beechworth: a Titan's Field*, Hargreen Publishing Company, 1985.

9.   *Andrew and Sarah Galbraith and Family*.

10. *Garden in a Valley*, p. 9.

11. *Andrew and Sarah Galbraith and Family*, p. 49.

12. *Andrew and Sarah Galbraith and Family*, p. 53.

13. *Garden in a Valley*, p. 9.

14. *Andrew and Sarah Galbraith and Family*, p. 55.

15. See Tyers School Correspondence Records, VPRS 640, unit 2182, Public Record Office of Victoria (PROV); *Andrew and Sarah Galbraith and Family*, p. 59; *Garden in a Valley*, p. 10.

16. *Andrew and Sarah Galbraith and Family*, p. 62.

17. JG, 'Story of a Schoolground', Jean Galbraith Papers, box 3472; see also Tyers School Correspondence Records, VPRS 640, unit 2182, PROV.

18. Greg Brinsmead, 'The Development of Butter Factories in Gippsland', *Gippsland Heritage Journal* no. 3, 1987, pp. 3–11.

19. See Department of Agriculture medal, 1902; *Andrew and Sarah Galbraith and Family*, pp. 69–71.

20. JG,' The Paddock', *Australian Garden Lover*, October 1938, p. 23.

21. *Garden in a Valley*, p. 10.

22. *Garden in a Valley*, p. 10.

23. *Andrew and Sarah Galbraith and Family*, p. 76.

24. *Andrew and Sarah Galbraith and Family*, p. 63.

25. Discussion with Jean's niece, Marjory Burgess; see also Peter Galbraith, 'Remembering Jean and Dunedin', author's collection.

26. *Garden in a Valley*, p. 10; *Andrew and Sarah Galbraith and Family*.

27. See *Andrew and Sarah Galbraith and Family*.

28. *Christendom Astray from the Bible* was first published in 1884. The magazine that Robert Roberts founded in 1864 was renamed *The Christadelphian* in 1869. See also 'Who Are the Christadelphians? and What Do They Believe?, *Herald of the Coming Age*, December 1971.

29. JG to John Lothian, 6 November 1928, Jean Galbraith Papers, 3462.3.

30. *Andrew and Sarah Galbraith and Family*, p. 75.

31. *Andrew and Sarah Galbraith and Family*, p. 164.

32. For a comprehensively researched history of the Ladson family, see Ian Hyndman, *Alfred and Jane Ladson and Family: Beechworth Pioneers*, Bethel Publications, 2006.

33. *Alfred and Jane Ladson and Family*, pp. 43–44.

34. This was the opinion of Ian Hyndman, Amy's great nephew and historian of the Ladson family. See *Alfred and Jane Ladson and Family*, pp. 125–135.

35. *Alfred and Jane Ladson and Family*, p. 64.

36. *Andrew and Sarah Galbraith and Family*, p. 80.

Chapter 2. Childhood

1. See John Nicholls, Interview with Jean Galbraith, 1986.
2. JG, 'From Day to Day in the Garden', *Australian Garden Lover*, July 1974, p. 35.
3. JG, 'A Child's Garden', Jean Galbraith Papers, PA 93/55.
4. John Nicholls, 'Two Gippsland Naturalists: Jean Galbraith and Bill Cane', *Gippsland Heritage Journal*, no. 1, 1986, p. 33.
5. JG, *Garden in a Valley*, p. 15.
6. JG to John Lothian, 9 April 1928, Jean Galbraith Papers, 3462.3.
7. John Nicholls, 'Two Gippsland Naturalists', p. 34.
8. JG to John Lothian, 24 May 1931, 3462.3, and JG, 'What Do You Keep in Your Mind?', Jean Galbraith Papers, 3469.1.
9. 'What Do You Keep in Your Mind?', Jean Galbraith Papers, box 3469.1.
10. *Garden in a Valley*, p. 46, p. 52.
11. Donald Macdonald, 'At the End of the Moonpath', in Joshua Lake (ed), *Childhood in Bud and Blossom: A Souvenir Booklet of the Children's Hospital Bazaar*, Atlas, 1900. See also JG, 'Moonpath Land', Jean Galbraith Papers, 3469.3.
12. *Andrew and Sarah Galbraith and Family*, p. 99.
13. JG to John Turner, n.d., John Turner Collection, University of Melbourne Archives, TURN00804.
14. JG, 'The Road', Jean Galbraith Papers, PA 95/146.
15. *Andrew and Sarah Galbraith and Family*, p. 131.
16. See *Garden in a Valley*, pp. 16–17 and *Alfred and Jane Ladson and Family*, p. 142.
17. Marjory Burgess, 'Notes on Jean Galbraith', 2008.
18. JG to John Lothian, 16 April 1931, Jean Galbraith Papers, 3462.3.
19. JG, 'Begonias on the Porch: Garden in a Valley', *Australian Garden Lover*, June 1939; JG, 'From Day to Day in the Garden', *Australian Garden Lover*, April 1948.
20. JG, 'The Paddock: Garden in a Valley', *Australian Garden Lover*, October 1938.
21. *Garden in a Valley*, pp. 55, 62.
22. Fragment, Jean Galbraith Papers, PA 93/95, box 2/8.
23. JG, 'From Day to Day in the Garden', *Australian Garden Lover*, July, 1974.
24. Matthew Galbraith to JG, October 1917, Ian Hyndman Collection.
25. Angus Galbraith to Esther Wettenhall, n.d. [1990].
26. JG to John Lothian, 25 June 1928, Jean Galbraith Papers, 3462.3.
27. BBC Religions Christianity – Christadelphians, www.bbc.co.uk/religions/Christianity/subdivisions/Christadelphians_1.shtml, accessed 22 June 2011.
28. This is evident in her correspondence.
29. JG, 'Flora and Fauna of Traralgon Shire', Jean Galbraith Papers, 3469.1.
30. JG, 'Blackwarry to Gormandale', *Walkabout*, September 1943, p. 7.
31. 'Notes on Plants', Jean Galbraith Papers, 3473.2.
32. *Garden in a Valley*, p. 46.
33. JG, 'From Day to Day in the Garden', *Australian Garden Lover*, January 1970.
34. R.T. Littlejohns and S.J. Lawrence, *Birds of Our Bush or Photography for Nature Lovers*, Whitcomb and Tombs, 1920; 'A List of Tyers Birds', December 1920, Jean Galbraith Papers, 3474b.
35. Tom Griffiths, 'Editorial', *Gippsland Heritage Journal*, no. 13, 1992, p. 2.

36. Hugh Anderson, 'Macdonald, Donald Alaster (1859–1932)', *Australian Dictionary of Biography*, volume 10, Melbourne University Press, 1986, p. 249.

37. JG to John Turner, 11 January 1985, John Turner Collection, University of Melbourne Archives, TURN00804.

38. JG to John Lothian, 9 April 1928, Jean Galbraith Papers, box 3462.3.

39. JG, 'Notes on Plants 1919', Jean Galbraith Papers, 3473.2.

40. Nature Study Notes, 1920, Jean Galbraith Papers, box 3473.3; Gene Stratton Porter, *Music of the Wild: With Reproductions of Performers, Their Instruments and Festival Halls*, London: Hodder and Stoughton, 1910.

41. These books are held in the Ian Hyndman Collection, Beechworth.

42. Draft of a letter to Cinderella, Ian Hyndman Collection.

43. *The Leader*, 21 August 1917.

44. *The Leader*, 13 October 1917.

45. 'The Seasons of Nature', Jean Galbraith Papers, 3472.

46. JG to Matthew Galbraith, 5 November 1917, Jean Galbraith Papers, 3461.3.

47. Professor Smyth, Teachers' Training College, 21 July 1921, Tyers School Correspondence Records, VPRS 640, Unit 2182, PROV.

48. See Andrew Spaull, 'McCrae, James (1871–1939)', *Australian Dictionary of Biography*, vol. 10, Melbourne University Press, 1986.

49. JG to John Lothian, 1 January 1928, Jean Galbraith Papers, 3462.3.

50. 'Notes on Plants', Jean Galbraith papers, 3473.2.

51. JG to John Lothian, 12 September 1927, Jean Galbraith Papers, 3462.2.

52. Mabel Elijah to JG, a series of mostly undated letters in the Jean Galbraith Papers, 3461.4 and 3463.1.

53. Poem, fragment, Jean Galbraith Papers, 3469.4.

54. JG to John Turner, 11 January 1985, University of Melbourne Archives, John Turner Collection TURN00804; see also Esther Wettenhall, Interview with Jean Galbraith, 1992.

55. See philosophy notes in the Jean Galbraith Papers, 3472 and PA 93/55, and an undated letter from Mabel Elijah, 3463.1.

56. JG to the Galbraith family, March 1921, Ian Hyndman Collection.

57. See *Garden in a Valley*, p. 111.

58. JG to the Galbraith family, March 1921, Ian Hyndman Collection.

59. Mervyn Davis, Questionnaire, Jean Galbraith Papers, PA 93/55, 2.6.

Chapter 3. Becoming a Botanist

1. JG, Fragment, Jean Galbraith Papers, PA 93/55, box 1.

2. These were the flying duck orchid (*Caleana major*) and the common bird orchid (*Chiloglottis gunnii*).

3. 'Exhibition of Wild-Flowers', *Victorian Naturalist*, November 1922, pp. 80–84.

4. *The Age*, 2 August 1988.

5. John Nicholls, 'Two Gippsland Naturalists', *Gippsland Heritage Journal*, no. 1, 1986, p. 33; Esther Wettenhall, Interview with Jean Galbraith, 1992.

6. See John Foster, 'Natives in the Nineteenth Century Garden', *Australian Garden History*, vol. 2 no. 4 1991, p.5; Meredith Fletcher, 'Exotic Natives: The Field Naturalists' Club of Victoria Wildflower Shows', *Victorian Historical Journal*, June 2008, pp. 93–106.

7. 'Exhibition of Wild-Flowers', *Victorian Naturalist*, November 1919, p. 105.

8. 'Exhibition of Wild-Flowers', *Victorian Naturalist*, November 1921, p. 61.

9. See Richard Aitken, *Gardenesque: A Celebration of Australian Gardening*, Miegunyah Press, 2004, pp. 126–145, for an overview of Australian home gardening in the 1920s.

10. Field Naturalists' Club of Victoria Minute Book, 20 August 1922, FNCV Archives, instructing that flowers on display could not be sold until 9.30 pm.

11. 'H.B. Williamson, an Appreciation', *Victorian Naturalist* March 1931, p. 172.

12. George Coghill, 'History of Wild Flower Exhibitions 1885–1929', Box AB3, 0032/045, FNCV Archives.

13. See Linden Gillbank, *From System Garden to Scientific Research: The University of Melbourne's School of Botany under its First Two Professors1906–1973*, University of Melbourne, p. 11, and correspondence with Linden Gillbank, 2012.

14. H.B. Williamson to JG, 5 December 1922, Jean Galbraith Papers, 3461.6.

15. JG, Draft Talk, 1970, Jean Galbraith Papers, 4106.4.

16. H.B. Williamson to JG, 2 August 1924; 28 March 1928, Jean Galbraith Papers, 3461.6.

17. H.B. Williamson to JG, 13 October 1922, 18 March 1924, Jean Galbraith Papers, 3461.6; Jean Galbraith, Notes on Tyers Plants, 1922, Jean Galbraith Papers, 2473.5a.

18. H.B. Williamson to JG, 1 December 1923, Jean Galbraith Papers, 3461.6.

19. H.B. Williamson to JG, 28 March 1927, Jean Galbraith Papers, 3461.6.

20. JG, 'Edith Coleman, a Personal Appreciation', *Victorian Naturalist*, July 1951, p. 47; 'First Lady Recipient of the Natural History Medallion – Mrs Edith Coleman', *Victorian Naturalist*, September 1950, p. 99.

21. Charles Barrett to JG, 18 August 1923; 17 February 1927, Jean Galbraith Papers, 3461.1.

22. JG to John Lothian 1 July 1927, Jean Galbraith Papers, 3462.2.

23. JG to John Lothian, 27 June 1927, Jean Galbraith Papers, 3462.2.

24. JG to Charles Ladson, 6 December 1932, Jean Galbraith Papers, PA 93/55.

25. H.B. Williamson to JG, 21 January 1926, Jean Galbraith Papers, 3461.6.

26. JG, 'How the Black and White Fantail Builds its Nest, *Victorian Naturalist*, September 1925, p. 126; 'Magpies as Peacemakers', *Victorian Naturalist*, December 1925, p. 211.

27. JG, 'Forest Regeneration in Gippsland', *Victorian Naturalist*, June 1926, pp. 53–56.

28. Charles Barrett to JG, 14 January 1923; 24 February 1927, Jean Galbraith Papers, 3461.1.

29. J.W. Elijah to JG, 1 August 1925, Jean Galbraith Papers, 3461.4.

30. See correspondence with Reuben Patton, Jean Galbraith Papers, 3461.4.

31. See correspondence in Jean Galbraith Papers 3461.3.

32. JG to John Lothian, 16 September 1928, Jean Galbraith Papers, 3462.3.

33. Jenny Hammett, 'Eva West: Leading the Way in Local Government', *Gippsland Heritage Journal* no. 10 1991, p. 30.

34. Eva West to JG,17 June 1926, Jean Galbraith Papers, 3461.3.

35. Eva West, 'Nature Study Diary', 25 August 1925, Jean Galbraith Papers, 3474.6.

36. Eva West, 'Nature Study Diary', entries for 1926, Jean Galbraith Papers, 3474.6.

37. JG to John Lothian, 1 January 1928, Jean Galbraith Papers, 3462.2.

38. JG to H.B. Williamson, 18 November 1929, Jean Galbraith Papers, 3461.5.

39. JG, 'Book of Our Camps', in possession of Matthew Burgess.

40. JG to John Lothian, 2 February 1930, Jean Galbraith Papers, 3462.3.

41. JG to John Lothian, 9 June 1929, Jean Galbraith Papers, 3462.3.

42. JG to John Lothian, 26 August 1928, Jean Galbraith Papers, 3462.3.

Chapter 4. Making the Garden

1. Ian Hyndman, *Andrew and Sarah Galbraith and Family*, p. 133; *Garden in a Valley*, p. 17.

2. JG, 'Garden in a Valley, Always Growing Always Changing', *Australian Garden Lover*, November 1935, p.145.

3. JG to John Lothian, 14 August 1927, Jean Galbraith Papers, 3462.2.

4. See Notes on Tyers Plants 1923–1928, Jean Galbraith Papers, 3473.5b.

5. Notes on Tyers Plants, 28 October 1927.

6. JG to HB Williamson, 8 November 1929, Jean Galbraith Papers, 3461.5; *Garden in a Valley*, p. 26.

7. *Garden in a Valley*, p. 27.

8. JG to John Lothian, 17 November 1929, Jean Galbraith Papers, 3462.3.

9. Richard Aitken, *Gardenesque: A Celebration of Australian Gardening*, Miegunyah Press, 2004, p.130.

10. *Garden in a Valley*, pp. 19–23.

11. See *Garden in a Valley*, p. 100.

12. JG, 'Dreams That Come True', *Australian Garden Lover*, April 1936, p. 11.

13. JG, 'The Daffodils Come', *Australian Garden Lover*, August 1937.

14. Vera West to JG, 21 September 1927, Jean Galbraith Papers, PA 98 75.

15. JG to John Lothian, 28 March 1928, Jean Galbraith Papers, 3462.2.

16. *Garden in a Valley*, p. 96.

17. Mabel Elijah to JG, 14 February 1927, Jean Galbraith Papers, 3461.3.

18. *Australian Garden Lover*, June 1932.

19. *Australian Garden Lover*, October 1926, p. 285.

20. HB Williamson to JG, 14 August 1929, Jean Galbraith Papers, 3461.6; JG to HB Williamson, 21 August 1929, Jean Galbraith Papers, 3461.5.

21. JG to HB Williamson, 30 August 1929, Jean Galbraith Papers, 3461.5.

22. *Australian Garden Lover*, March 1927.

23. Grace Envall to JG 13 August 1929; Grace Envall to JG, 23 September 1929, Jean Galbraith Papers, 3461.2.

24. Eric Dane to JG, 24 August 1929, Jean Galbraith Papers, 3461.2.

25. JG to family, 30 October 1929, Jean Galbraith Papers, 3461.2.

26. Walter Thornby to JG, 23 March 1931, Jean Galbraith Papers, 3463.2.

27. Walter Thornby, Diary, 24 February 1933, Jean Galbraith Papers, 3474.

28. *Garden in a Valley*, p. 56.

29. JG to John Lothian, 28 December 1928, Jean Galbraith Papers, 3462.3.

30. JG to John Lothian, 21 December 1930, Jean Galbraith Papers, 3462.3.

31. JG to John Lothian, 3 January 1930[31], Jean Galbraith Papers, 3462.3.

32. JG to John Lothian, 10 January 1932, Jean Galbraith Papers, 3462.6.

33. Fanny Hodgson to JG, Jean Galbraith Papers, 3 April 1932, 3463.1.

34. JG to John Lothian, 25 September 1932, Jean Galbraith Papers, 2462.6.

35. The steam whistle from the 'Emden' was given to John Monash as a war souvenir after the ship was sunk by HMAS 'Sydney'.

36. *Garden in a Valley*, p. 136.

37. JG to John Lothian, 2 March 1930, Jean Galbraith Papers, 3462.3.

Chapter 5. Correa

1. H.B. Williamson to JG, 13 February 1925, Jean Galbraith Papers, 3461.6.

2. Jean always referred to the magazine as the *Garden Lover*.

3. Interviews with Jean Galbraith by John Nicholls and Esther Wettenhall.

4. Ralph Boardman to JG, 10 December 1925, Jean Galbraith Papers, 3463.8.

5. Ralph Boardman to JG, 31 December 1925, Jean Galbraith Papers, 3461.1.

6. 'Australian Native Flowers', *Garden Lover*, February 1926, p. 581.

7. See May Gibbs, *Snugglepot and Cuddlepie*, Angus & Robertson, 1918; also Peter Bernhardt, *Wily Violets and Underground Orchids: The Revelations of a Botanist*, University of Chicago Press, 2003, pp. 15–28.

8. 'In a Fold of Hills', *Australian Garden Lover*, January 1927, p. 394.

9. 'In a Fold of Hills', p. 395.

10. 'As the Days of a Tree', *Australian Garden Lover*, January 1928, p. 380.

11. Mark Tredinnick, *Place on Earth, an Anthology of Nature Writing from Australia and North America*, University of New South Wales Press, 2003, pp. 31–39.

12. See Nicola Shulman, *A Rage for Rock Gardening: The Story of Reginald Farrer Gardener, Writer & Plant Collector*, David R. Godine, Boston, 2004, dust jacket and p. 40.

13. Shulman, *A Rage for Rock Gardening*, p. 40.

14. Charles Barrett to JG, 17 February 1927, Jean Galbraith Papers, 3461.1.

15. Tom Griffiths, *Hunters and Collectors: The Antiquarian Imagination in Australia*, Cambridge University Press, 1996, pp. 136–141.

16. See Donald Worster, *A Passion for Nature: the Life of John Muir*, Oxford University Press, 2008.

17. JG to John Lothian, 24 May 1931; 25 June 1928, Jean Galbraith Papers, 3462.3.

18. Donald Macdonald to JG, 26 January 1932, Jean Galbraith Papers, 3463.1.

19. See Libby Robin, 'Nationalising Nature: Wattle Days in Australia', *Journal of Australian Studies* vol. 73, 2002, pp. 13–26.

20. See 'Wattle', *Australian Garden Lover*, July 1926, pp. 148–150.

21. *Australian Garden Lover*, January 1926, p. 338.

22. See T.C. Wollaston, *Our Wattles*, Lothian Book Publishing, 1916.

23. *Australian Garden Lover*, December 1965; See fragment, Jean Galbraith Papers, PA 95/146.

24. See Katie Holmes, Susan K. Martin and Kylie Mirmohamadi for a summary of this literature in *Reading the Garden: The Settlement of Australia*, Melbourne University Press, 2008, pp. 26–29.

25. 'A Garden of Memories', *Australian Garden Lover*, February, 1927, p. 434.

26. 'Garden of Memories', p. 434.

27. These have now been combined to form the Tarra Bulga National Park.

28. Williamson to JG, 20 February 1926, Jean Galbraith Papers, 3461.6.

29. E.E. Pescott to JG, 19 April 1931, Jean Galbraith Papers, 3463.8

30. Donald Macdonald to JG, 14 January 1932, Jean Galbraith Papers, 3463.1.

31. See Jean Galbraith Papers, 3463, for readers' letters.

32. Coral Dow, 'Tatungalung Country: an Environmental History of the Gippsland Lakes', PhD thesis, Monash University, 2004 pp. 209–217.

33. Fred Barton to JG, 15 May 1927, Jean Galbraith Papers, 3461.3.

34. See letters published in the *Australian Garden Lover*.

35. Herbert Rumsey to JG, August 1929; 20 January 1930, Jean Galbraith Papers, 3463.5.

36.   Law Somner to JG, 9 May 1931, Jean Galbraith Papers, 3463.5.

37.   E.E. Pescott, 'Appreciation of "Correa"', *Australian Garden Lover*, July 1926, p.163; *Australian Garden Lover*, August 1926, p. 183.

38.   'Christmas Trees', *Australian Garden Lover*, December 1926, pp. 334–5.

39.   JG to HB Williamson, 18 July 1928, Jean Galbraith Papers, 3461.5.

40.   *Australian Garden Lover*, August 1926, pp191–2.

41.   Gilbert Wallace to JG, 14 September 1927, Jean Galbraith Papers, 3461.1.

42.   JG to John Lothian, 29 March 1931, Jean Galbraith Papers, 3462.3.

43.   JG to Williamson, 14 April 1930, Jean Galbraith Papers, 3461.5.

Chapter 6. Grandfather

1.   Editorial, *Garden Lover*, April 1925, p. 2.

2.   John Lothian to JG, 22 March 1927; 22 June 1927, Jean Galbraith Papers, 3462.1.

3.   *House of Lothian is Seventy Five*, Lothian Publishing Company, 1963.

4.   Cecily Close, 'Lothian, Elizabeth Inglis (1881–1973)', *Australian Dictionary of Biography*, vol. 15, Melbourne University Press, 2000, pp. 125–6.

5.   Richard Aitken, *Seeds of Change: An Illustrated History of Adelaide Botanic Gardens*, Bloomings Books, 2006.

6.   John Lothian to JG, 3 July 1927, Jean Galbraith Papers, 3462.1.

7.   JG to John Lothian, 1 August 1927, Jean Galbraith Papers, 3462.2.

8.   John Lothian to JG, 8 August 1927, Jean Galbraith Papers 3462.1.

9.   JG to John Lothian, 27 June 1927, Jean Galbraith Papers, 3462.2.

10.   John Lothian to JG, 3 July 1927, Jean Galbraith Papers, 3462.1.

11.   JG to John Lothian, 25 September 1932, Jean Galbraith Papers, 3462.6.

12.   JG to John Lothian, 25 November 1927, Jean Galbraith Papers, 3462.1.

13.   Ian Thompson, *The English Lakes: A History*, Bloomsbury Publishing, 2010, p. 203.

14.   John Lothian to JG, 9 May 1937, Jean Galbraith Papers, 3462.5.

15.   Gladys Cole, *Flower of Light, Biography of Mary Webb*, Duckworth, 1978.

16.   John Lothian to JG, 15 March 1931, Jean Galbraith Papers, 3462.4.

17.   Gladys Cole, Introduction to *The Spring of Joy: Nature Essays*, www3.shropshire-cc.gov.uk.

18.   JG to John Lothian, 14 June 1931, Jean Galbraith Papers, 3462.3.

19.   JG to John Lothian, 30 October 1927, Jean Galbraith Papers, 3462.2.

20.   JG to John Lothian, 18 October 1931, Jean Galbraith Papers, 3462.3.

21.   Ian Burk, 'Establishing Vocal Lineage: AE Floyd and the Voice Production', *Context Journal of Musical Research*, no. 24, 2002.

22.   JG to John Lothian, 14 August 1932, Jean Galbraith Papers, 3462.6.

23.   JG to John Lothian, 19 February 1928, Jean Galbraith Papers, 3462.3.

24.   John Lothian to JG, 10 June 1934, Jean Galbraith Papers, 3462.5.

25.   John Lothian to JG, 8 August 1927, Jean Galbraith Papers, 3462.1.

26.   John Lothian to JG, 29 December 1927; 22 January 1928, Jean Galbraith Papers, 3462.1.

27.   John Lothian to JG, 11 November 1927, Jean Galbraith Papers, 3462.1.

28.   John Lothian to JG, 11 November 1927 Jean Galbraith Papers, 3462.1.

29.   F. Bishop to JG, 12 April 1929, Jean Galbraith Papers, 3461.4.

30.   Dorothy Ebels to JG, 3 August 1929, Jean Galbraith Papers, 3461.1.

31. Correa, 'The Flower Year in Victoria', *Gardeners' Chronicle of America*, November 1929, p. 394.

32. Dorothy Ebels to JG, 29 November 1929, Jean Galbraith Papers, 3461.1.

33. H.B. Williamson to JG, 11 November 1929, Jean Galbraith Papers, 3461.6.

34. John Lothian to JG, 10 May 1931, Jean Galbraith Papers 3462.4; John Lothian to JG, 14 March 1933, 3462.5; John Lothian to JG, 27 August 1935, 3462.5.

35. JG to John Lothian, 24 May 1931, Jean Galbraith Papers, 3462.3.

36. JG to John Lothian, 29 November 1932, Jean Galbraith Papers, 3462.6.

37. JG to John Lothian, 28 November 1928, Jean Galbraith Papers, 3462.3.

38. JG to John Lothian, 7 April 1935, Jean Galbraith Papers, 3462.6.

39. JG to John Lothian, 14 June 1931, Jean Galbraith Papers, 3462.3.

40. JG to John Lothian, 3 May 1937, Jean Galbraith Papers, 3462.2.

41. JG to John Lothian, 5 February 1927 [28], Jean Galbraith Papers, 3462.2.

42. John Lothian to JG, 11 February 1928, Jean Galbraith Papers, 3462.1.

43. JG to John Lothian, 28 March 1928, Jean Galbraith Papers, 3462.2.

44. John Lothian to JG, 25 March 1928, Jean Galbraith Papers, 3462.1.

45. JG to John Lothian, 9 July 1928, Jean Galbraith Papers, 3462.3.

46. JG to John Lothian, 25 June 1928, Jean Galbraith Papers, 3462.3.

47. John Lothian to JG, 15 August 1928, Jean Galbraith Papers, 3462.1.

48. JG to John Lothian, 21 June 1931, Jean Galbraith Papers, 3462.6.

49. John Lothian to JG, 26 March 1933, Jean Galbraith Papers, 3462.5.

50. See Anne Latreille, *Kindred Spirits: A Botanical Correspondence, Letters by Jean Galbraith, Drawings by Joan Law-Smith*, Australian Garden History Society, 1999, p. 32.

51. Walter Thornby, Diary, 22 September, 28 October 1934, Jean Galbraith Papers, 3474.

52. JG to John Lothian, 31 December 1934, Jean Galbraith Papers, 3462.2.

53. Peter Galbraith, 'Remembering Jean and Dunedin', 2012.

54. Verna Clarke to Esther Wettenhall, 4 January 1990.

55. JG to Charles Ladson, 6 December 1932, Jean Galbraith Papers, PA 93 55.

56. JG to Charles Ladson, 6 December 1932, Jean Galbraith Papers, PA 93 55.

57. Donald Macdonald to JG, 12 February 1932, Jean Galbraith Papers, 3463.1.

58. JG to Charles Ladson, 6 December 1932, Jean Galbraith Papers, PA 93 55.

59. JG to John Lothian, 7 July 1929, Jean Galbraith Papers, 3462.3.

60. JG to John Lothian, 5 March 1937, Jean Galbraith Papers, 3462.2.

61. John Lothian to JG, 22 November 1931, Jean Galbraith Papers, 3462.4.

62. John Lothian to JG, 22 January 1931, Jean Galbraith Papers, 3462.4.

Chapter 7. Writing the Garden

1. JG to John Lothian, 10 January 1932, Jean Galbraith Papers, 3462.6.

2. Ralph Boardman to JG, 15 January 1932, Jean Galbraith Papers, 3463.7.

3. 'Gathering Flowers', *Australian Garden Lover*, October 1928, pp. 220–1.

4. EE Pescott to JG, 19 April 1931, Jean Galbraith Papers, 3463.7.

5. 'Protected Plants', *Australian Garden Lover*, October 1931, p. 235.

6. 'Wild Nature Exhibition', *Victorian Naturalist*, 1931, p. 168.

7. JG to John Lothian, 25 July 1935, Jean Galbraith Papers, 3462.2.

8. 'The River's Tragedy', *Australian Garden Lover*, July 1935, pp. 41–42.

9. 'A Wider Path', *Australian Garden Lover*, October 1935, p. 23.

10. *My Garden*, Editorial, July 1934.

11. Donald Macdonald to JG, 14 January 1932, Jean Galbraith Papers, 3463.1.

12. 'A Garden in a Valley, Always Growing – Always Changing', *Australian Garden Lover*, November 1935, pp. 41–43.

13. 'The First Era of the Roses', *Australian Garden Lover*, March 1936, p. 27.

14. See Katie Holmes, 'A Literary Gardener', *Australian Garden History*, July/August 1997, p. 4.

15. See Deborah Kellaway (ed), *The Virago Book of Women Gardeners*, Virago, London 1995, pp. xii–xix.

16. 'The Garden Claims a Friend', *Australian Garden Lover*, May 1936.

17. Walter Thornby, Diary, 5 December 1932; 'Gregory and Gwendoline', *Australian Garden Lover*, February, March 1937; 'How to Make a Sundial', *Australian Garden Lover*, September 1939.

18. 'The Vegetable Garden', *Australian Garden Lover*, October 1936.

19. 'A Garden Seat', *Australian Garden Lover*, April 1937.

20. JG to John Lothian, 5 April 1936, Jean Galbraith Papers, 3462.2.

21. JG to John Lothian, 11 November 1934, Jean Galbraith Papers, 3462.2.

22. JG to John Lothian, 1 September 1936, Jean Galbraith Papers, 3462.2.

23. 'Garden Adventures', *Australian Garden Lover*, May 1937.

24. JG to John Lothian, 31 August 1937, Jean Galbraith Papers, 3462.2.

25. See 'The Daffodils Come', *Australian Garden Lover* August 1937 and 'The Increase of the Daffodils', September 1937.

26. JG to John Lothian, 7 October 1937, Jean Galbraith Papers, 3462.2.

27. 'The Golden Hours', *Australian Garden Lover*, January 1938.

28. John Lothian to JG, 9 June 1938, Jean Galbraith Papers, 3462.2.

29. JG to John Lothian, 17 April 1938, Jean Galbraith Papers, 3462.2.

30. A full account is included in Ian Hyndman, *Andrew and Sarah Galbraith and Family: Pioneers of Beechworth and Tyers*, Bethel Publications, 1997, pp. 153–160.

31. *Andrew Galbraith and Sarah Galbraith and Family*, p. 140.

32. Amy Galbraith, Diary, Jean Galbraith Papers, 3474.

33. JG to Amy and Matt Galbraith, [1938], Jean Galbraith Papers, PA93/55/folder 2.

34. Charles Ladson to JG, 18 May 1938, Jean Galbraith Papers, 3463.7.

35. Arthur Galbraith to JG, [1938] Jean Galbraith Papers, 3463.5.

36. 'The Paddock', *Australian Garden Lover*, October 1938.

37. John Lothian to JG, 29 December 1938, Jean Galbraith Papers, 3462.

38. Jean Galbraith, *Garden in a Valley*, Horticultural Press, 1939.

39. E.E. Pescott, Foreword, *Garden in a Valley*, 1939.

40. John Lothian to JG, 2 February 1940 and March 1940, Jean Galbraith Papers, 3462.4.

41. *Wild Life* August 1940, p. 41.

42. Ralph Boardman to JG, 10 February 1943, Jean Galbraith Papers, 3464.2.

Chapter 8. From Three to One in the Garden

1. Jean Galbraith, *A Garden Lover's Journal 1943–1946*, Five Mile Press, Melbourne, 1989, p. 21.

2. *A Garden Lover's Journal*, p. 85.

3. Interview with Bon Thompson, Traralgon, 2011.

4. Mabel Elijah to JG, 10 October 1937, Jean Galbraith Papers, 3463.1.

5. Mabel Elijah to JG, 14 May 1939, Ian Hyndman Collection.

6. John Lothian to JG , 7 December 1939, Jean Galbraith Papers, 3462.6.

7. *A Garden Lover's Journal*, p. 117.

8. *A Garden Lover's Journal*, p. 59.

9. See *A Garden Lover's Journal*.

10. Interview with Elizabeth Dexter, Anne Burnet's niece, 21 July 2010.

11. *A Garden Lover's Journal*, p. 93.

12. Les Morgan to JG, 6 December 1940, Jean Galbraith Papers, 3464.1.

13. Edith Ladson to JG, 28 October 1940, Jean Galbraith Papers, 3464.1.

14. 'From Day to Day in the Garden', *Australian Garden Lover*, August 1944.

15. 'On Cradle Plateau', Jean Galbraith Papers, 3469.1.

16. 'Bird Calls in a Gippsland Garden', *Wild Life*, June 1939, p. 15.

17. 'Flowers of the Wayside', *Wild Life*, September 1940, pp. 12–14.

18. Marjory Burgess, Notes on Jean Galbraith, 2008.

19. '"Little Chap" – the Story of a Sugar Squirrel', *Wild Life*, October 1941, pp. 395–7.

20. 'In the Wimmera –Now', *Walkabout*, November 1942, p. 32.

21. 'Epacris Impressa: Who Grows it Now?', *My Garden*, June 1941, pp. 55–57.

22. 'Red Correa', Jean Galbraith Papers, 3471.

23. 'The Bark and the Trees', *My Garden*, October 1944, pp. 357–8.

24. 'Onions for England', *My Garden*, June 1942, pp. 432–4.

25. 'A Garden and a Child', *My Garden*, November 1944, pp. 315–17.

26. 'Autumn Trees', *My Garden*, November 1942, p. 387.

27. 'Autumn Trees', p. 387.

28. See for example, Edna Walling, *A Gardener's Log*, 1948, pp. 63–4, p.142.

29. 'A Letter to Dad', *New South Wales School Magazine*, October 1943, pp. 130–3.

30. J.W. Hayes to JG, 17 August 1943, Jean Galbraith Papers, 3464.2.

31. *A Garden Lover's Journal*, p. 100.

32. *A Garden Lover's Journal*, p. 106.

33. Ian Hyndman, *Andrew and Sarah Galbraith and Family*, p. 141.

34. *A Garden Lover's Journal*, p. 109.

35. Peter Galbraith, 'Remembering Jean and Dunedin', 2012.

36. Compiled from the 'Dunedin' memories of Peter Galbraith, David Galbraith and Dena Galbraith, 2012.

37. 'Dunedin' memories of Joanna Galbraith, April 2012.

38. Marjory Burgess, 'Notes on Jean Galbraith'.

39. Poem written by Geoffrey Galbraith for his aunt's 90th birthday in 1996, Jean Galbraith Papers, 4108.1.

40. *Your Garden*, December, 1948; March 1949.

41. Nancie and Ralph to JG, 11 February 1960; Dorothy Hartshorn to JG, 20 July 1955, Jean Galbraith Papers, 3465.2.

42. 'From Day to Day in the Garden', August 1947.

43. 'From Day to Day in the Garden', February 1948.

44. 'From Day to Day in the Garden', November 1948.

Chapter 9. *Wildflowers of Victoria*

1. 'Miss Winifred Waddell', *Victorian Naturalist*, December 1972, p. 356.

2. Robin Marks, 'From Head's Nook to the High Plains: Winifred Waddell and the Native Plants Preservation Society of Victoria', *Australian Garden History*, vol. 22 no. 4, 2011.

3. 'From Day to Day in the Garden', January 1949.

4. 'Miss Winifred Waddell', *Victorian Naturalist*, p. 356.

5. JG to Overton, Nelson's, 11 December 1961, Jean Galbraith Papers, 4091.

6. See J.H. Willis, *Handbook to Plants in Victoria*, Melbourne University Press, 1962, 1973, and Helen Aston, 'Obituary Dr James Hamlyn Willis', *Muelleria*, vol. 9, 1996, pp. 1–4.

7. Interview with Helen Aston, botanist at the National Herbarium of Victoria, 3 November 2011.

8. Jim Willis to JG, 11 July 1949, Jean Galbraith Papers, 4102.6.

9. JG to Jim Willis, 12 January 1949, Records of James Hamlyn Willis, series 2 box 2, WILL00023, State Botanical Collection, Royal Botanic Gardens, Melbourne.

10. JG to Jim Willis, 12 January 1949; 29 January 1949, Records of James Hamlyn Willis, series 2 box 2, WILL00023.

11. Jim Willis to JG, 12 January 1950, Jean Galbraith Papers, 4102.6.

12. Interview with Helen Aston.

13. JG to Commonwealth Literary Fund, 28 May 1965, Jean Galbraith Papers, 3466.2.

14. 'From Day to Day in the Garden', July 1949.

15. Jean Galbraith, *Wildflowers of Victoria*, Colorgravure Publications, 1950, pp. 13–14.

16. *Wildflowers of Victoria*, p. 15.

17. Jim Willis to Colorgravure, 7 August 1950, Jean Galbraith Papers, 4102.6.

18. JG to Jim Willis, 11 August 1950, Records of James Hamlyn Willis, series 2 box 2, WILL00023.

19. JG to Nelsons, 11 December 1961, Jean Galbraith Papers, 4091.

20. Mollie Elder to JG, 19 November 1950; C. Currie to JG, 13 October 1950, Jean Galbraith Papers, 4091.

21. See Patricia Sinclair to JG, 7 September 1986, Jean Galbraith Papers, 4109.2; comments from naturalists Alan and Eunice Harding.

22. Eric Webb Ware, 14 August 1970, Jean Galbraith Papers, 4091.

23. Betty Conabere to Esther Wettenhall, 14 February 1990.

24. JG to Jim Willis, 6 May 1951; 13 November 1951, Records of James Hamlyn Willis , series 2 box 2, WILL00023.

25. Ian Hyndman, *Andrew and Sarah Galbraith*, pp. 173–4.

26. JG to Arthur Swaby, 15 May 1958, Jean Galbraith Papers, 4091.

27. Vera Francis to JG, 5 May 1955, Jean Galbraith Papers, 4091.

28. JG to Jim Willis, 13 May 1955; JG to Jim Willis, 7 June 1955, Records of James Hamlyn Willis, series 2 box 2, WILL00023.

29. JG to Arthur Swaby, 15 May 1958, Jean Galbraith Papers, 4091.

30. Edna Walling to JG, 19 July 1958, Jean Galbraith Papers, PA 97 38.

31. E. Coghill to JG, 15 May 1958, Jean Galbraith Papers, 4091.

32. Arthur Swaby to JG, 16 July 1958, Jean Galbraith Papers, 3465.1.

33. Arthur Swaby to JG, 29 July 1958, Jean Galbraith Papers, 3465.1.

34. Hooke to JG, 8 June 1962, Jean Galbraith Papers, 4091.

35. Reviewer's Report, Nelsons to JG, 7 December 1961, Jean Galbraith Papers, 4091.

36. JG to Overton, Nelsons, 11 December 1961, Jean Galbraith Papers, 4091.

37. JG to Overton, Nelsons, 11 December 1961, Jean Galbraith Papers, 4091.

38. Ethel McLennan to JG, 1 March 1962, Jean Galbraith Papers, 4091.

39. JG to Jim Willis, 10 May 1962, Records of James Hamlyn Willis, series 2 box 2, WILL00023.

40. JG to Jim Willis, 10 May 1962, Records of James Hamlyn Willis, series 2 box 2, WILL00023.

41. JG to Jim Willis, 26 May 1962, Records of James Hamlyn Willis, series 2 box 2, WILL00023.

42. Interview with Helen Aston.

43. Diary of Trip to Queensland, 1962, Jean Galbraith Papers, 4095.2.

44. JG to Jim Willis, 21 August 1962, Records of James Hamlyn Willis, series 2 box 2, WILL00023.

45. 'From Day to Day in the Garden', October 1962.

46. Diary of Trip to Queensland, 1962, Jean Galbraith Papers, 4095.2.

47. Diary of Trip to Queensland, 1962.

48. Diary of Trip to Queensland, 1962.

49. Diary of Trip to Queensland, 1962.

50. JG to Norman Wakefield, 31 May 1963, Jean Galbraith Papers, 4091.

51. JG to Jim Willis, 11 August 1963, Records of James Hamlyn Willis, series 2 box 2, WILL00023.

52. JG to L. Godfrey, Longmans, 23 May 1964, Jean Galbraith Papers, 4091.

53. Reviews in Jean Galbraith Papers, 4091.

Chapter 10. Freelancing

1. JG to Jim Willis, 10 October 1956, Records of James Hamlyn Willis, series 2 box 2, WILL00023.

2. Crosbie Morrison to JG, n.d., Jean Galbraith Papers, 4110.7.

3. 'Know Your Trees', *Educational Magazine*, April 1949, p.138.

4. G. Charlton (ABC) to JG, 21 June 1949; Frank Watts (ABC) to JG 5 August 1949, Jean Galbraith Papers, PA 97 38.

5. See Jean Galbraith Papers, PA 97 38.

6. Janet Mitchell to JG, 27 May 1952, Jean Galbraith Papers, PA 97 38.

7. Ann Roberts to JG, 22 March 1955, Jean Galbraith Papers, 3465.3.

8. Ann Roberts to JG, n.d., Jean Galbraith Papers, 3465.3.

9. Judith Parker to editor, *New South Wales School Magazine*, 23 June 1956, Jean Galbraith Papers, 4105.1.

10. Noela Young to JG, 18 June 1963, Jean Galbraith Papers, 4110.7.

11. Noela Young to JG, 18 June 1963, Jean Galbraith Papers, 4110.7.

12. Joan Webb, *Thistle Y. Harris: A Biography of Thistle Yolette Stead*, Surrey Beatty and Sons, 1998.

13. Thistle Stead to JG, 25 February 1963 Jean Galbraith Papers, PA 96 38.

14. JG to Thistle Stead, 27 May 1963, Jean Galbraith Papers, PA 97 38.

15. See Moira Pye, *Kiwi and Koala Readers* series, Reed, 1968.

16. JG to L. Godfrey, 6 July 1965, Jean Galbraith Papers, 4091.1.

17. Barbara Ker Wilson to JG, 15 July 1965, Jean Galbraith Papers, 4097.5.

18. See Jean Galbraith Papers, 4097.5.

19. *New South Wales School Magazine*, September 1970.

20. See 'The Sea, the Shore and the Pool', in Patricia Wrightson (ed), *Beneath the Sun: A Collection for Children*, Collins, Sydney, 1972.

21. 'Acacias', Jean Galbraith Papers, 4102.8.

22. See J.H. Willis and A. Swaby, 'Award of the Australian Natural History Medallion', *Victorian Naturalist*, October 1970, p. 298; Helen Aston, *Victorian Naturalist*, April 1999, p. 74.

23. John Turner to JG, 14 March 1963, Jean Galbraith Papers, 4103.7.

24. Leon Costermans to JG, 22 October 1981, Jean Galbraith Papers, 4089.2.

25. Anne Latreille, *Kindred Spirits: A Botanical Correspondence, Letters by Jean Galbraith, Drawings by Joan Law-Smith*, Australian Garden History Society, 1999.

26. 'Natural History School at Mount Beauty', 1969, Jean Galbraith Papers, 3465.4.

27. 'From Day to Day in the Garden', January 1966.

28. Betty Conabere to Esther Wettenhall, 14 February 1990.

29. 'From Day to Day in the Garden', December 1965.

30. 'From Day to Day in the Garden', November 1970.

31. Dorothy Hartshorn to JG, 31 October 1954, Jean Galbraith Papers, 3465.2.

32. J. Armitage to JG, 8 February 1959, Jean Galbraith Papers, 3465.1.

33. See Jean Galbraith's camping equipment in the Jean Galbraith Collection, National Museum of Australia, 1993.0013.0007.

34. 'From Day to Day in the Garden', February 1952.

35. 'From Day to Day in the Garden', January 1954.

36. Anne Latreille, *Kindred Spirits*, p. 165.

37. 'From Day to Day in the Garden', November 1961.

38. See Anne Latreille, Jean Galbraith Obituary, *The Australian*, 14 January, 1999.

Chapter 11. Changes

1. See Meredith Fletcher, *Digging People Up For Coal: A History of Yallourn*, Melbourne University Press, 2002.

2. See Jean Galbraith Papers, 4102.1 for correspondence relating to conservation campaigns.

3. Notes for talk to Yarram Apex, 1967, Jean Galbraith Papers, PA 93/55.

4. JG to P. Atherstone, 24 November 1960, Jean Galbraith Papers, 4102.1.

5. Notes for talk to Business and Professional Women's Club, no date, Jean Galbraith Papers, PA 92/10/1.

6. JG to Henry Bolte, 22 June 1955, Jean Galbraith Papers, 4102.5.

7. Draft of undated talk, Jean Galbraith Papers, 4093.6.

8. JG to Mr Mitchell, Draft of letter, 28 April 1949, Jean Galbraith Papers, 4102.1.

9. See Jean Galbraith Papers, 4102, for negotiations with the SEC.

10. Notes for Professor John Turner, May 1963, Jean Galbraith Papers, 4103.2.

11. 'From Day to Day in the Garden', October 1955.

12. 'From Day to Day in the Garden', November 1954.

13. 'From Day to Day in the Garden', October 1959.

14. L.H. Smith, 'The Morwell National Park', *Latrobe Valley Naturalist*, no. 42, June 1967.

15. Interview with Bon Thompson, Traralgon, October 2011.

16. 'Ferns', *Educational Magazine*, May 1965, p. 182.

17. ' Heath', *Educational Magazine*, June, 1964, p.100.

18. 'Story of a Schoolground', *Educational Magazine*, December 1965, pp. 521–2.

19. 'From Day to Day in the Garden', November 1968.

20. 'From Day to Day in the Garden', December 1965.

21. Jean Galbraith, 'The Northern Strzelecki Heathlands', *Victorian Naturalist*, March 1971, pp. 71–73.

22. See Richard Aitken, *Garden of Ideas: Four Centuries of Australian Design*, Miegunyah, 2010, and Gordon Ford with Betty Ford, *Gordon Ford: The Natural Australian Garden*, Bloomings Books, 1999.

23. 'From Day to Day in the Garden', February, 1955.

24. JG, obituary for Bill Cane in Jean Galbraith Papers, 4090.8.

25. John Nicholls, 'Two Gippsland Naturalists', *Gippsland Heritage Journal*, no. 1, 1987, p. 36.

26. 'Two Gippsland Naturalists', p. 36; Duncan Fraser, 'Bill Cane: a Short History of a Pioneering Australian Plant Enthusiast', 2003.

27. Bill Cane to JG, 21 May 1958, Jean Galbraith Papers, 4090.8.

28. 'From Day to Day in the Garden', February 1962.

29. See Bill Cane correspondence, Jean Galbraith Papers, 4090.8.

30. John Walter, *The Story of Arthur Swaby and the Society for Growing Australian Plants*, Australian Plants Society, 2007, pp. 51–56.

31. JG to May Galbraith, fragment, Jean Galbraith Papers, PA 93/55.

32. See John Walter, *The Story of Arthur Swaby and the Society for Growing Australian Plants*, for a comprehensive history of the society, now known as the Australian Plants Society.

33. See *Australian Plants*, September 1960.

34. 'From Day to Day in the Garden', October, 1959.

35. Brian Mackenzie, Interview with Jean Galbraith, broadcast on ABC's Radio National, 20 October 2013; Edna Walling to JG, 19 July 1958, Jean Galbraith Papers, PA 97 38.

36. Sara Hardy, *The Unusual Life of Edna Walling*, Allen and Unwin, 2005, pp. 207–8.

37. Edna Walling to JG, n.d., Jean Galbraith Papers, 3465.1.

38. Edna Walling to JG, 3 May 1963; 15 May 1963, Jean Galbraith Papers, 3465.1.

39. Edna Walling to JG, 22 May 1963, Jean Galbraith Papers, 3465.1.

40. Notes for 'The Harvest', Jean Galbraith Papers, 3471.4; Edna Walling photographs, Jean Galbraith Papers, 4099. *Helipterum anthemoides* is now *Rhodanthe anthemoides*.

41. Edna Walling to JG, n.d., Jean Galbraith Papers, 3465.1.

42. Edna Walling to JG,17 October 1963, Jean Galbraith Papers, PA 97 38.

43. See Sara Hardy, *The Unusual Life of Edna Walling*, p. 232.

44. Edna Walling to JG, n.d., Jean Galbraith Papers, 3465.1.

45. Edna Walling to JG, 13 October 1963, Jean Galbraith Papers, PA 97 38.

46. Edna Walling to JG, 11 October 1972, Jean Galbraith Papers, 3465.1.

47. Edgar to JG, 19 December 1979, Jean Galbraith Papers, 4103.5.

48. Josephine Piggin to Marjory Burgess, 3 March 1999.

49. Interview with Evan Chesterfield, September 2011.

50. JG to Jim Willis, 23 July 1973, Records of James Hamlyn Willis, series 2 box 2,WILL00023.

51. Interview with Evan Chesterfield.

52. See Libby Robin, *Defending the Little Desert: The Rise of Ecological Consciousness in Australia*, Melbourne University Press, 1998.

53. See Danielle Clode, *As for a Thousand Years: A History of Victoria's Land Conservation and Environment Conservation Councils*, Victorian Environmental Assessment Council, 2006.

54. JG to Daphne Pearson, 19 August 1977, Records of James Hamlyn Willis, WILL 004.

55. Interview with Bon Thompson, October 2011. The park is sited on part of the original Holey Plain squatting run.

56. See Parks Victoria, *Holey Plains State Park Management Plan*, 2009, p. 1. Also included is a list of significant species.

57. John Turner, 22 August 1984, TURN 00804, University of Melbourne Archives.

58. David Langmore, *Planning Power: The Uses and Abuses of Power in the Planning of the Latrobe Valley*, Australian Scholarly Publishing, 2013, p. 280.

59. *The Age*, 17 June 1980.

60. Langmore, *Planning Power*, pp. 270–1, 287.

61. Langmore, *Planning Power*, p. 286.

Chapter 12. A Commission from Collins

1. JG to Jim Willis, 22 June 1964, Records of James Hamlyn Willis, series 2 box 2,WILL00023.

2. Diary of Trip to Western Australia, Jean Galbraith Papers, 4095.3.

3. Diary of Trip to Western Australia, Jean Galbraith Papers, 4095.3.

4. Newspaper clipping in Diary of Trip to Western Australia, Jean Galbraith Papers, 4095.3.

5. Diary of Trip to Western Australia, Jean Galbraith Papers, 4095.3.

6. 'From Day to Day in the Garden', September 1964.

7. 'From Day to Day in the Garden', November 1964.

8. Draft talk, Jean Galbraith Papers, 4106.4.

9. 'From Day to Day in the Garden', September 1964.

10. 'From Day to Day in the Garden', November, 1964.

11. Diary of Trip to Western Australia, Jean Galbraith Papers, 4095.3.

12. Greg Kieghery and Neil Wilson, 'The Influence of Robert Brown on Western Australian Botany', *Australian Garden History*, vol. 14, no. 3, 2002, pp. 5–8.

13. Diary of Trip to Western Australia, Jean Galbraith Papers, 4095.3.

14. 'From Day to Day in the Garden', January 1965.

15. Diary of Trip to Western Australia, Jean Galbraith Papers, 4095.3.

16. 'From Day to Day in the Garden', January 1965.

17. John Cody to JG, 10 March 1965, Jean Galbraith Papers, 3466.2.

18. JG to John Cody, 11 March 1965, Jean Galbraith Papers, 3466.2.

19. JG to Commonwealth Literary Fund, 11 May 1965, 28 May 1965; A.L. Moore to JG, 24 May 1965, Jean Galbraith Papers, 3466.2.

20. JG to Jim Willis, 15 July 1965, Records of James Hamlyn Willis, series 2 box 2, WILL00023.

21. Cheque sent from Collins, 2 November 1965, Jean Galbraith Papers, 3466.2.

22. Stephen Dearnley to JG, 24 February 1966, Jean Galbraith Papers, 3466.2.

23. Michael Walter to JG, 16 May 1966; JG's response noted on this letter, Jean Galbraith Papers, 3466.2; see also Dominic Redfern, 'Art, Science and the Botanical Image', *Australian Garden History*, vol. 23, no. 3, 2012, pp. 12–13.

24. JG to Stephen Dearnley, 29 July 1966, Jean Galbraith Papers, 3466.1

25. JG to Jim Willis, 3 June 1967, Records of James Hamlyn Willis, series 2 box 2, WILL00023.

26. 'From Day to Day in the Garden, October, 1967.

27. 'From Day to Day in the Garden, November 1967.

28. See 'From Day to Day in the Garden, December 1967, January 1968.

29. JG to Stephen Dearnley, 9 October 1967, Jean Galbraith Papers, 3466.2.

30. JG to Michael Walter, 11 April 1968, Jean Galbraith Papers, 3466.2.

31. 'From Day to Day in the Garden', December 1969.

32. Patricia Wrightson to JG, 14 August 1972, Jean Galbraith Papers, 4104.19.

33. 'From Day to Day in the Garden', July 1970.

34. Australian Native Plants Society (Australia), www.anpsa.org.au.

35. Helen Aston, 'Jean Galbraith: a Tribute', *Victorian Naturalist*, April 1999 pp. 73–75.

36. JG to Jim Willis, 6 September 1970, Records of James Hamlyn Willis, series 2 box 2, WILL00023; J.H. Willis and A. Swaby, 'Award of the Australian Natural History Medallion', *Victorian Naturalist*, October 1970, pp. 297–8.

37. Lottie Banfield to JG, 6 August 1970, Jean Galbraith Papers, 4104.9.

38. Madge to JG, 4 August 1970, Jean Galbraith Papers, 4104.9.

39. Draft acceptance speech, Australian Natural History Medallion, Jean Galbraith Papers, 4106.4.

40. Betty Conabere to Esther Wettenhall, 14 February 1990.

41. 'From Day to Day in the Garden', February 1971.

42. Michael Walter to JG, 19 January 1971, Jean Galbraith Papers, 3466.4.

43. JG to Michael Walter, 28 January 1971, 3466.4.

44. Dr Winifred Mary Curtis, www.utas.edu.au/library/exhibitions.

45. Stephen Dearnley to JG, Jean Galbraith Papers, 9 February 1971, 3466.4.

46. Elizabeth Hoseason to JG, 21 May 1973, Jean Galbraith Papers, 3466.5.

47. JG to Jim Willis, 14 June 1975, Records of James Hamlyn Willis, series 2 box 2, WILL00023; Winifred Waddell, *A Wildflower Diary*, Native Plants Preservation Society, 1976.

48. JG to Jim and Mavis Willis, 13 July 1973, Records of James Hamlyn Willis, series 2 box 2, WILL00023.

49. Jean Galbraith, *A Field Guide to the Wild Flowers of South-East Australia*, Collins 1977.

50. JG to Jim Willis, 26 August 1975, Records of James Hamlyn Willis, series 2 box 2, WILL00023.

51. *The Herald*, 11 October 1977.

52. Sheila Ridland to JG, 10 July 1977, Jean Galbraith Papers, 4092.12.

53. *Canberra Times*, 3 September 1977.

54. Patricia Wrightson to JG, 1 July 1977, Jean Galbraith Papers, 4092.12.

55. Keith Rogers to JG, 19 July 1977, Jean Galbraith Papers, 4092.12.

56. Betty Conabere to JG, 24 July 1977, Jean Galbraith Papers, 4092.12.

57. *Victorian Naturalist*, July/August 1977, pp. 171–2.

Chapter 13. Fame

1. 'From Day to Day in the Garden', December 1975.

2. JG to Jim Willis, 15 September 1970, Records of James Hamlyn Willis, series 2 box 2, WILL00023.

3. 'From Day to Day in the Garden', December 1975.

4. JG to Jim Willis, 15 January 1976, Records of James Hamlyn Willis, series 2 box 2, WILL00023.

5. See letters in the Jean Galbraith Papers, 4093.6.

6. John Nicholls, Interview with Jean Galbraith.

7. Alfred Nicks to JG, 20 March 1974, Jean Galbraith Papers, 4104.9.

8. *The Age SEC Victorian Wildflower Portfolio*, artist Terry Nolan, text Jean Galbraith, 1977.

9. JG to Ellen Lyndon,12 August 1985, Ian Hyndman Collection.

10. JG to Ellen Lyndon, I2 August 1985, Ian Hyndman Collection.

11. JG to John Turner, 5 February 1985, University of Melbourne Archives, TURN00804.

12. Richard Aitken, *Gardenesque: A Celebration of Australian Gardening*, Miegunyah Press, 2005, pp. 185–6.

13. 'From Day to Day in the Garden', September 1965.

14. Stephen Dearnley to JG, June 1983, Jean Galbraith Papers, 3466.5.

15. Jean Galbraith, *A Gardener's Year*, Collins 1987, p. vii, p. 3.

16. Peter Cuffley, 'Garden Reminiscences', *Australian Garden History*, vol. 9, no. 1, 1997, pp. 8–9.

17. Peter Cuffley, 'Our First Visit to Jean Galbraith at Dunedin', Peter Cuffley Collection.

18. Peter Cuffley, *Cottage Gardens in Australia*, Five Mile Press, 1983. See John Turner's foreword to *Garden in a Valley*, p. 7.

19. JG to John Turner, 7 December 1983, University of Melbourne Archives, TURN00805.

20. JG to John Turner, 23 January 1984 University of Melbourne Archives,TURN00805.

21. Flora Thompson, abridged by Julian Schuckburgh, *The Illustrated Lark Rise to Candleford*, Century Publishing Co., 1983.

22. Peter Cuffley to John Turner, 16 April 1984, University of Melbourne Archives, TURN00805.

23. Letter from John Turner, 17 August 1984, University of Melbourne Archives, TURN00804.

24. Peter Cuffley, 'History in the Making: Garden in a Valley', p. 34 and 'Garden Reminiscences', pp. 8–9, *Australian Garden History*, vol. 9, no.1, 1997.

25. John Turner to JG, 8 January 1985, Jean Galbraith Papers, 4089.2.

26. Jean Galbraith, *Garden in a Valley*, Five Mile Press, 1985, p. 12.

27. JG to John Turner, 8 August 1984, University of Melbourne Archives, TURN00805.

28. See Victor Crittenden, 'How I Became an Edna Walling Publisher', *Australian Garden History*, no. 1, vol. 12, 2000, pp. 16–18.

29. See Glen Wilson, 'Guest Editorial', *Australian Garden History*, vol. 10, no. 3, 1998, p. 2.

30. JG's 'Foreword' in Edna Walling, *Country Roads: The Australian Roadside*, Pioneer Design, 1985.

31. JG to Daphne Pearson and Mervyn Davis, 20 July 1984, Records of James Hamlyn Willis, Biographical Information on Australian Botanists, WILLS 004. The documentary appeared in July 1985.

32. Jenny Herbert, Five Mile Press, to JG, 23 January 1986, Jean Galbraith Papers, PA 95/146.

33. See letters of appreciation for *Garden in a Valley* in Jean Galbraith Papers, 3468; 4109; 4089.

34. Marjory Fenton to JG, 5 March 1986, Jean Galbraith Papers, 3468.1.

35. Margaret Rogers to JG, 8 January 1986, Jean Galbraith Papers, 4109.2.

36. Meryl Hunter to JG, n.d., Jean Galbraith Papers, 4089.2.

37. See letter 8 May 1985, Jean Galbraith Papers, 4109.2.

38. Russell Page, *The Education of a Gardener*, Harville Press, 1995, p. 45.

39. Lin Bullen to JG, 21 May 1988, Jean Galbraith Papers, 4089.2.

40. Barbara Kell to JG, 22 February 1990; 9 March 1990, Jean Galbraith Papers, 3468.6.

41. See *Landscape Australia*, no. 4, 1986, p. 319.

42. JG to John Turner, 21 August 1986, Melbourne University Archives, TURN 00804.

43. JG to Anne Latreille, 19 February 1986, Jean Galbraith Papers, 4088.6.

44. Isobel Tipping, *The Age*, 3 July 1993.

45. Elisabeth Murdoch to Jean Galbraith, 17 August 1989, Jean Galbraith Papers, 3467.7.

46. Julie Langford, 'To Jean Galbraith', reproduced with permission.

47. Anne Latreille, *Kindred Spirits*, pp. 205–6.

48. JG to Anne Latreille, 10 February 1986, Jean Galbraith Papers, 4088.6.

49. Anne Latreille, *Kindred Spirits*, p. 206.

50. See article in John Turner Papers, Melbourne University Archives, TURN 00985.

51. JG to John Turner, 21 August 1986, Melbourne University Archives, TURN 00804.

52. *Daily Advertiser*, 6 June 1987.

53. *The Age*, 9 June 1987.

54. Manuscript, Letters to My Friends, Jean Galbraith Papers, 3464.

55. JG to John Turner, 28 May 1989, Melbourne University Archives, TURN 00806.

56. Betty Conabere to JG, 4 February 1990, Jean Galbraith Papers, 3468.7.

57. See Jean Galbraith Papers, 3468.6.

58. To Jean Galbraith, 15 June 1993, 4109.4; see scrap books in my possession.

59. JG to Esther Wettenhall, 30 March 1990.

60. To Jean Galbraith, 6 October 1991, Jean Galbraith Papers, 4107.1.

61. June Hedditch to JG, n.d. Jean Galbraith Papers, 3468.1.

Chapter 14. Old Age

1. JG to John Turner, 25 August 1989, University of Melbourne Archives, TURN00806.

2. JG to John Turner, undated, University of Melbourne Archives, TURN 00805.

3. Draft introduction, Jean Galbraith Papers, 3470.7.

4. Joanna Galbraith, 15 April 2012.

5. JG to Esther Wettenhall, 30 March 1990.

6. JG to Esther Wettenhall, 1 December 1989.

7. JG, *A Gardener's Year*, p. 239.

8. Poem by Nancy Byrd Turner, see also *A Gardener's Year*.

9. Compiled from Jean's description of Christmas in *A Gardener's Year*.

10. Sheila Carew to JG, November 1991, Jean Galbraith Papers, 4107.1.

11. JG to International Biographical Centre, Cambridge, Jean Galbraith Papers, 4106.5.

12. Ethel Temby to JG, 31 March 1991, Jean Galbraith Papers, 4107.1.

13. Janice Cayzer to JG, 8 September 1992, and other letters in Jean Galbraith Papers, 4109.3.

14. JG to Jim Willis, 21 August 1988, Records of James Hamlyn Willis, WILL00023, series 2 box 2, National Herbarium of Victoria.

15. D. Albrecht, *Muelleria*, vol. 8 no. 24, 1993, p. 21; see also Sue Forrester, 'Modest Lady, Dainty Flower', *The Age* 26 August 1994 and JG to David Albrecht, 15 June 1992, Jean Galbraith Papers, 4109.3.

16. *The Age*, 26 August 1994.

17. JG to John Turner, 7 October 1987, University of Melbourne Archives, TURN 00806.

18. JG to John Turner, 4 July 1988, University of Melbourne Archives, TURN 00806.

19. Discussion with Joan Good, Traralgon, 2008.

20. *The Age*, 3 July 1993.

21. Ian Hyndman, Eulogy, January 1999.

22. Fragment, Jean Galbraith Papers, 4106.5.

23. Elizabeth Dexter to Anne Latreille, 8 February 1994, Elizabeth Dexter Collection.

24. Ian Hyndman, Eulogy, January 1999.

25. JG to Verna Clarke, 2 June 1994, Ian Hyndman Collection.

26. Edith Ladson to JG, 14 October 1993, Jean Galbraith Papers, 4109.4.

27. JG to Anne Latreille, undated, 4088.6.

28. *The Age*, 22 April 1995.

29. JG to Peter Galbraith, 10 December 1995, Jean Galbraith Papers, 4109.5.

30. Ellen Lyndon to JG, 23 March 1997, 4109.

31. See Jean Galbraith Papers, 4108.2.

32. May Galbraith to JG, 13 June 1997, Jean Galbraith Papers, 4108.2.

33. May Galbraith to JG, 13 June 1997, Jean Galbraith Papers, 4108.2.

34. Marjory Burgess, Notes on Jean Galbraith.

35. 'Dampiera galbraithiana', *Telopea*, vol. 7 no. 4, 1998, pp. 321–4.

36. Jean Galbraith, *Poems for Peter*, Printland Press, 1998.

37. Ian Hyndman, Eulogy.

38. Ian Hyndman, Eulogy.

39. Interview with Evan Chesterfield.

40. *The Australian*, 14 January 1999.

41. Helen Aston, 'Jean Galbraith, 28 March 1906 – 2 January 1999, a Tribute', *Victorian Naturalist*, April 1999.

42. Josephine Piggin to Marjory Burgess, 3 March 1999.

SELECT BIBLIOGRAPHY

Unpublished Sources

Archival Collections

Field Naturalists' Club of Victoria
Monash University Centre for Gippsland Studies
National Museum of Australia: Jean Galbraith Collection
Public Record Office of Victoria: Tyers School Correspondence Records, VPRS 640, Unit 2182
State Botanical Collection, Royal Botanic Gardens, Melbourne: Records of James Hamlyn
    Willis
State Library of Victoria: Jean Galbraith Papers, ms 12637, Australian Manuscripts
    Collection; Edna Walling Collection, ms 13048, Australian Manuscripts Collection
Traralgon and District Historical Society
University of Melbourne Archives: John Stewart Turner, Post Retirement Files

Private Collections

Marjory Burgess
Peter Cuffley
Elizabeth Dexter
Ian Hyndman
Esther Wettenhall

Interviews and Discussions

Helen Aston
Marjorie Burgess
Evan Chesterfield
Peter Cuffley
Elizabeth Dexter
Joan Good
Ian Hyndman
Bon and Ollie Thompson

Other

Burgess, Marjory, Notes on Jean Galbraith, 2008
Cuffley, Peter, Our First Visit to Jean Galbraith at Dunedin, 1983
Dow, Coral, 'Tatungalung Country: an Environmental History of the Gippsland Lakes',
    PhD Thesis, Monash University, 2004
Galbraith, Peter, Memories of Jean and Dunedin, 2012
Nicholls, John, Interview with Jean Galbraith, 1986
Wettenhall, Esther, Interview with Jean Galbraith, 1992

Published Sources

Journals, magazines and newspapers to which Jean Galbraith made substantial contributions

Age
Argus
Australian Garden Lover
Australian Plants
The Christadelphian
Educational Magazine
Gardeners' Chronicle of America
Latrobe Valley Naturalist
Leader
My Garden
New South Wales School Magazine
Victorian Naturalist
Victorian School Paper
Walkabout
Wild Life
Your Garden

Books and Articles

Abbot, Rosemary, 'A Chance Encounter with Jean Galbraith', *Wellspring*, vol. 3, 2000.
Age SEC Victorian Alpine Flowers Portfolio, Artist Terry Nolan, Botanical Descriptions Jean Galbraith, [1977].
Aitken, Richard and Looker, Michael (eds), *The Oxford Companion to Australian Gardens*, Oxford University Press in association with the Australian Garden History Society, 2002.
Aitken, Richard, *Gardenesque: A Celebration of Australian Gardening*, Miegunyah Press, 2004.
——— *The Garden of Ideas: Four Centuries of Australian Design*, Miegunyah Press, 2010.
Albrecht, D.E. and Walsh, N.G. 'Two Species of Boronia (Rutaceae) Endemic in Victoria', *Muelleria*, vol. 8 no. 1 1993, pp 21–25.
Allen, Terri Gitsham, *Gippsland Lady Botanists*, South Gippsland Conservation Society Inc, 2007.
Anderson, Hugh, 'Macdonald, Donald Alaster (1859–1932)', *Australian Dictionary of Biography*, Melbourne University Press, vol. 12, 1986.
Archbold, Ollie, 'Living in a Garden in a Valley', *Australian Garden History*, vol. 11, no. 3, 1999, pp. 10–13.
Aston, Helen, 'Obituary Dr James Hamlyn Willis', *Muelleria*, vol. 9 1996, pp. 1–4.
——— 'Jean Galbraith: a Tribute', *Victorian Naturalist*, April 1999, pp. 73–5.
Barrett, Charles, *In Australian Wilds: The Gleanings of a Naturalist*, Melbourne Publishing Company, 1919.
Bernhardt, Peter, *Wily Violets and Underground Orchids: The Revelations of a Botanist*, University of Chicago Press, 2003.
Blake, L.J. (ed), *Vision and Realisation: A Centenary History of State Education in Victoria*, Education Department of Victoria, 1973.
Bonta, Marcia, *Women in the Field: America's Pioneering Women Naturalists*, Texas A&M University Press, 1991.

Brinsmead, Greg, 'The Development of Butter Factories in Gippsland', *Gippsland Heritage Journal* no. 3, 1987, pp. 3–11.

Burk, Ian, 'Establishing Vocal Lineage: AE Floyd and the Voice Production', *Context Journal of Musical Research*, no. 24, 2002.

Chisholm, A.H., 'Barrett, Charles Leslie (1879–1959)', *Australian Dictionary of Biography*, Melbourne University Press, vol. 7, 1979.

Close, Cecily, 'Lothian, Elizabeth Inglis (1881–1973)', *Australian Dictionary of Biography*, vol. 15, 2000.

Coles, Gladys, *The Flower of Light: A Biography of Mary Webb*, Duckworth, 1978.

Conn, Barry, '*Prostanthera Galbraithiae*', *Telopea*, vol. 7, no. 4, 1998.

Cran, Marion, *The Garden of Ignorance: The Experience of a Woman in a Garden*, Jenkins, 1924.

Crittenden, Victor, 'How I Became an Edna Walling Publisher', *Australian Garden History*, vol. 12 no. 1, 2000, pp. 16–18.

Cuffley, Peter, *Cottage Gardens in Australia*, Five Mile Press, 1983.

———'Garden Reminiscences', *Australian Garden History*, vol. 9 no. 1, 1997, pp. 8–9.

———'History in the Making: Garden in a Valley', *Australian Garden History*, vol. 9 no. 1, 1997, p. 34.

'Dr Winifred Mary Curtis', www.utas.edu.au/library/exhibitions.

Dunscombe, Kordula, 'In the Service of Infinite and Glorious Creation: the Nature Writing of Louisa Anne Meredith', *Papers*, Victoria Park Western Australia, vol. 8 no. 2, 1998, pp. 16–30.

Elijah, J.W., *Principles and Methods of Teaching*, 1924.

Ellis, Mary, *People and Plants: A History of Gardening in Victoria*, M. Ellis, 2003.

'Exhibition of Wild-Flowers', *Victorian Naturalist*, November 1922, pp. 80–84.

'Exhibition of Wild-Flowers', *Victorian Naturalist*, November 1925, pp. 147–149.

Farrer, Reginald, *Alpines and Bog Plants*, Edward Arnold, 1908.

Fish, Margery, *We Made a Garden*, Collingridge, 1956.

Fletcher, Meredith, *Digging People Up for Coal: A History of Yallourn*, Melbourne University Press, 2002.

———'"Exotic" Natives: The Field Naturalists' Club of Victoria Wildflower Shows', *Victorian Historical Journal*, May 2008, pp. 93–106.

———'Becoming Correa: Jean Galbraith and 'Australian Native Flowers', *La Trobe Journal*, no. 84, December 2009.

Ford, Gordon with Ford, Gwen, *Gordon Ford: The Natural Australian Garden*, Bloomings Books, 1999.

Foster, John, 'Natives in the Nineteenth Century Garden', *Australian Garden History*, vol. 2 no. 4, 1991.

Fraser, Duncan , *Bill Cane: A Short History of an Australian Plant Enthusiast*, 2003.

Galbraith, Jean, *Garden in a Valley*, Horticultural Press, 1939.

———*Wildflowers of Victoria*, Colorgravure, 1950, 1955.

———*Grandma Honeypot*, Angus & Robertson, 1962, 1964.

———*From Flower to Fruit*, Longmans, 1965, 1975.

———*Fruits*, Longmans, 1966.

———*Wildflowers of Victoria*, Longmans, 1967.

———*The Wonderful Butterfly*, Angus & Robertson, 1968.

———*A Field Guide to the Wild Flowers of South-East Australia*, Collins, 1977.

———*Garden in a Valley*, Five Mile Press, 1985.

———*A Gardener's Year*, Collins, 1987.

———*A Garden Lover's Journal*, Five Mile Press, 1989.

———*Doongalla Restored: The Story of a Garden*, Mulini Press, 1990.

———*A Poet's Spring*, Printland Publications, 1990.

———*Poems for Peter*, Printland Publications, 1998.

Garnet, J. Ros (text), Conabere, Betty (paintings) *Wildflowers of South-eastern Australia*, Nelson, 1974.

Gates, Barbara, *Kindred Nature: Victorian and Edwardian Women Embrace the Living World*, University of Chicago Press, 1998.

———*In Nature's Name: An Anthology of Women's Writing and Illustration 1780–1930*, University of Chicago Press, 2002.

Gibbs, May, *Snugglepot and Cuddlepie*, Angus & Robertson, 1918.

Gillbank, Linden, *From System Garden to Scientific Research: The University of Melbourne's School of Botany under its First Two Professors 1906–1973*, University of Melbourne, 2010.

Griffiths, Tom, *Hunters and Collectors: The Antiquarian Imagination in Australia*, Cambridge University Press, 1996.

Hammett, Jenny, 'Eva West: Leading the Way in Local Government', *Gippsland Heritage Journal* no. 10, 1991.

Hardy, Sara, *The Unusual Life of Edna Walling*, Allen and Unwin, 2005.

Harris, Thistle, *Wildflowers of Australia*, Angus & Robertson, 1971.

Holmes, Katie, 'A Literary Gardener', *Australian Garden History*, July/August 1997.

———*Between the Leaves: Stories of Australian Women, Writing and Gardening*, UWA Publishing, 2011.

Holmes, Katie, Martin, Susan K. and Mirmohamadi, Kylie (eds), *Green Pens: A Collection of Garden Writing*, Miegunyah, 2004.

———*Reading the Garden: The Settlement of Australia*, Melbourne University Press, 2008.

Houghton, Sheila, Presland, Gary, *Leaves From Our History: The Field Naturalists' Club of Victoria*, Field Naturalists' Club of Victoria, 2005.

Hyndman, Ian, *History of Beechworth*, Bethel Publications, 1995.

———*Andrew and Sarah Galbraith and Family*, Bethel Publications, 1997.

———*Alfred and Jane Ladson and Family*, Bethel Publications, 2006.

Jekyll, Gertrude, *Home and Garden: Notes and Thoughts, Practical and Critical, of a Worker in Both*, Longmans, 1900.

———*Colour Schemes for the Flower Garden*, Country Life, 1919.

Kellaway, Deborah (ed), *The Virago Book Of Women Gardeners*, Virago Press, 1996.

Kieghery, Greg and Neil Wilson, 'The Influence of Robert Brown on Western Australian Botany', *Australian Garden History*, vol. 14 no. 3, 2002, pp. 5–8.

Keeney, Elizabeth, *The Botanizers: Amateur Scientists in Nineteenth Century America*, University of North Carolina Press, 1992.

Klickmann, Flora, *Flower Patch Among the Hills*, Jepson Press, 2010.

Langmore, David, *Planning Power: The Uses and Abuses of Power in the Planning of the Latrobe Valley*, Australian Scholarly Publishing, 2013.

Latreille, Anne, *The Natural Garden: Ellis Stones, His Life and Work*, Viking O'Neill, Ringwood, 1990.

———'Jean Galbraith: Adieu Correa', *Australian Garden History*, vol. 10 no. 6, 1999, pp. 4–5.

———*Kindred Spirits, a Botanical Correspondence, Letters by Jean Galbraith, Drawings by Joan Law-Smith*, Australian Garden History, 1999.

Lear, Linda, *Rachel Carson, a Witness for Nature*, H. Holt, 1997.

———*Beatrix Potter: A Life in Nature*, Allen Lane, 2007.

Littlejohns, R.T. and Lawrence, S.J., *Birds of Our Bush or Photography for Nature Lovers*, Whitcomb and Tombs, 1920.

Leopold, Aldo, *A Sand Country Almanac With Other Essays on Conservation From Round River*, Oxford University Press, 1966.

Lyndon, Ellen, *Door to the Forest: Collected Stories From One of Nature's Lifelong Friends*, South Gippsland Conservation Society, 1993.

Macdonald, Donald, *Gum Boughs and Wattle Bloom, Gathered on Australian Hills and Plains*, Cassell, 1887.

————'At the End of the Moonpath', in Joshua Lake (ed), *Childhood in Bud and Blossom: A Souvenir Booklet of the Children's Hospital Bazaar*, Atlas, 1900.

McLaren, Ian, 'Pescott, Edward Edgar (1872–1954)', *Australian Dictionary of Biography*, vol. 11, Melbourne University Press, 1988.

Mabey, Richard, *Gilbert White: A Biography of the Author of The Natural History of Selborne*, Hutchinson, 1986.

————*The Oxford Book of Nature Writing*, Oxford University Press, 1995.

Mack, Amy E., *A Bush Calendar*, Angus & Robertson, 1909.

Marks, Robin, 'From Head's Nook to the High Plains: Winifred Waddell and the Native Plants Preservation Society of Victoria', *Australian Garden History*, vol. 22 no. 4, 2011.

Maloney, Betty, Walker, Jean, *Designing Australian Bush Gardens*, Horwitz, 1966.

Nicholls, John, 'Two Gippsland Naturalists: Jean Galbraith and Bill Cane', *Gippsland Heritage Journal*, no. 1, 1986.

Nicholson, Phillippa (ed), *V. Sackville-West's Garden Book*, Athenaeum, 1983.

'Obituary on H.B. Williamson, 1860–1931', *Victorian Naturalist*, vol. 47, March 1931, pp. 172–5.

Page, Russell, *The Education of a Gardener*, Harville Press, 1995.

Parks Victoria, *Holey Plains State Park Management Plan*, 2009.

Pescott, Edward Edgar, *The Native Flowers of Victoria*, George Robertson & Co, 1914.

Rajput, M.T.H. and Carolin, R.C., 'Dampiera Galbraithiana', *Telopia*, vol. 3 no. 2, 1988, p. 204.

Rayment, Philip, *To Protect and Enjoy: The First Fifty Years of the Latrobe Valley Field Naturalists' Club, 1960–2010*, Latrobe Valley Field Naturalists' Club, 2010.

Redfern, Dominic, 'Art, Science and the Botanical Image', *Australian Garden History*, vol. 23 no. 3, 2012, pp. 12–13.

Robin, Libby, *Defending the Little Desert: The Rise of Ecological Consciousness in Australia*, Melbourne University Press, 1998.

————'Nationalising Nature: Wattle Days in Australia', *Journal of Australian Studies*, vol. 73, 2002, pp. 13–26.

Shulman, Nicola, *A Rage for Rock Gardening: The Story of Reginald Farrer, Gardener, Writer & Plant Collector*, David R. Godine. Boston, 2004.

Spaull, Andrew, 'McRae, James (1871–1939)', *Australian Dictionary of Biography*, vol. 10, Melbourne University Press, 1986.

Stones, Margaret, Curtis, Winifred, *The Endemic Flora of Tasmania, Part 1, Painted by Margaret Stones, Botanical and Ecological Text by Winifred Curtis*, Ariel Press, 1967.

Stratton Porter, Gene, *Music of the Wild: With Reproductions of Performers, Their Instruments and Festival Halls*, Hodder and Stoughton, 1910.

Thomas, John, *Elpis Israel*, the author, 1867.

Thompson, Ian, *The English Lakes: A History*, Bloomsbury Publishing, 2010.

Thompson, Flora, abridged by Julian Schuckburgh, *The Illustrated Lark Rise to Candleford*, Century Publishing Co., 1983.

Thoreau, Henry David, *Walden* [1854], J.M. Dent and Sons, 1908.

Tredinnick, Mark, *Place on Earth, an Anthology of Nature Writing from Australia and North America*, University of New South Wales Press, 2003.

———*The Land's Wild Music: Encounters with Barry Lopez, Peter Mathiessen, Terry Tempest Williams and James Galvin*, Trinity University Press, 2005.

Victorian Naturalist, 1911–1999.

Waddell, Winifred, *A Wildflower Diary*, Native Plants Preservation Society, 1976.

Walling, Edna, *A Gardener's Log*, Oxford University Press, 1948.

———*On the Trail of Australian Wildflowers*, Mulini Press, 1984.

———*Country Roads: The Australian Roadside*, Pioneer Design Studio, 1985.

Walter, John, *The Story of Arthur Swaby and the Society for Growing Australian Plants*, Australian Plants Society, 2007.

Watts, Peter, 'Walling, Edna Margaret (1895–1973)', *Australian Dictionary of Biography*, vol. 16, Melbourne University Press, 2002.

Webb, Joan, *Thistle Y. Harris: A Biography of Thistle Yolette Stead*, Surrey Beatty and Sons, 1998.

Webb, Mary, *Precious Bane*, J. Cape, 1924.

———*Poems; and the Spring of Joy*, Cape, 1978.

Wheeler, David (ed), *The Penguin Book of Garden Writing*, Penguin, 1993.

———*Hortus Revisited: A Twenty-first Birthday Anthology*, Francis Lincoln Limited, 2008.

White, Gilbert, *The Illustrated Natural History of Selborne*, Thames and Hudson, 2004.

'Who Are the Christadelphians? And What Do They Believe?' *Herald of the Coming Age*, December 1971.

Willis, J.H., *Handbook to Plants in Victoria*, Melbourne University Press, 1962.

Willis, J.H. and Swaby, A., 'Award of the Australian Natural History Medallion', *Victorian Naturalist*, October 1970, pp. 297–8.

Wilson, Emily Herring, *No One Gardens Alone: A Life of Elizabeth Lawrence*, Beacon Press, 2004.

Wilson, Glen, 'Guest Editorial', *Australian Garden History*, vol. 10, no. 3, 1998, p. 2.

Wollaston, T.C., *Our Wattles*, Lothian Book Publishing, 1916.

Woods, Carole, *Beechworth: A Titan's Field*, Hargreen Publishing Company, 1985.

Worster, Donald, *A Passion For Nature: The Life of John Muir*, Oxford University Press, 2008.

Wrightson, Patricia (ed), *Beneath the Sun: A Collection for Children*, Collins, Sydney, 1972.

INDEX

INDEX